RED ROSE
BLUES

Joe Ashton was born in the Sheffield slums in 1933. He started work on the shop floor at fifteen and climbed the union and Sheffield City Council ladder, with Roy Hattersley, to win a famous by-election in coal-mining Bassetlaw in 1968. He is a playwright and a novelist and for nine years wrote a twice-weekly column for the *Daily Star*. He won Granada TV's *What the Papers Say* 'Columnist of the Year' award for his features on the miners' strike.

RED ROSE
BLUES

The Story of a Good Labour Man

JOE ASHTON

PAN BOOKS

First published 2000 by Macmillan

This edition published 2002 by Pan Books
an imprint of Pan Macmillan Ltd
Pan Macmillan, 20 New Wharf Road, London N1 9RR
Basingstoke and Oxford
Associated companies throughout the world
www.panmacmillan.com

ISBN 0 330 39148 8

1 3 5 7 9 8 6 4 2

A CIP catalogue record for this book is available from
the British Library.

Typeset by SetSystems Ltd, Saffron Walden, Essex
Printed and bound in Great Britain by
Mackays of Chatham plc, Chatham, Kent

To Maggie and Lucy;
and the seed and the soil

Contents

ACKNOWLEDGEMENTS

Joe Ashton would like to acknowledge all the loyal support, votes, encouragement, and even friendly abuse given to him over the years by the lovely people of Bassetlaw, and most of all by the Bassetlaw Labour Party.

List of Illustrations

1   a) Uncle Joe, my mother and Aunt Delia.
    b) Joe aged eight, 1941–2.
    c) First election, Sheffield City Council, 1961.

2   a) By-election 1968, on the stump with Maggie.
    b) Me and Maggie arriving at the House.

3   a) Labour headquarters, 1970.
    b) 'You can't vote for a better man!'

4   a) The canal, Attercliffe, 1971 (*Stuart Hastings/Sheffield Star*).
    b) Attercliffe prior to demolition (*Stuart Hastings/Sheffield Star*).

5   a) Harold Wilson opening Bassetlaw Headquarters, 1971 (*Worksop Guardian*).
    b) Me and Maggie.
    c) Pit visit, Manton Colliery, Worksop (*Worksop Guardian*).

6   a) Can't beat cats and kids on a 1974 election address.
    b) The Prime Minister meets Lucy Ashton (*Retford Times*).
    c) A rare day off, 1976.

7   a) On the cover of *The House Magazine*, 1980 (*Clan Williams/The House Magazine*).
    b) Highly secret three-line whip.
    c) It's the clock that's leaning. Not me. (*Kenneth Saunders/Guardian*).

8   a) Diana Dors, 1984.
    b) Me, Prescott and Skinner – Clegg, Foggy and Compo.

Foreword by

ROY HATTERSLEY

MOST of the human race tiptoe through life barely noticed and rarely heard. A minority make their entrances and exits with a bang. The difference is not a question of class, status or position. It is a matter of personality. Some of us are born with an extrovert gene and others are destined by fate to be self-effacing. Joe Ashton comes very definitely into the first category. It is, therefore, not in the slightest degree surprising that I recall exactly the time and place where I first met him – even though it was more than forty years ago.

On the day that Joe Ashton took his seat on the Sheffield City Council we were introduced to each other in the Town Hall library. A reporter from the local newspaper announced – much to my relief – that I was no longer the council's youngest member and went on to ask if, when I was elected three years earlier, I was younger than Ashton on the day of his election. Quite rightly Joe believed the enquiry to be a total waste of time and typical of trivia-obsessed journalists. He said so in the most direct language. He has been expressing similarly forthright and controversial opinions ever since.

Many – some people would say most – of his views are gloriously politically incorrect. But under the sharp suit and fashionable haircut there is a man of firm principle. Joe Ashton remembers where he came from and which side he was on.

Talking with him about our earlier days in politics, I asked, perhaps a little cynically, 'Did we really believe that we were going to change the world?' He assured me that he did and reminded me 'what a rotten world it was'. He quoted the number of South Yorkshire slums which, back in 1960, had no bathroom or indoor lavatory. 'At least,' he said, 'they've all gone.' Joe Ashton may not be Old Labour. But he is certainly Old Sheffield, and none the worst for that, although neither of us was able to find a Sheffield seat to send us to Parliament.

Somewhere in the cardboard boxes in which I keep my memories and mementoes there is a Labour Party leaflet that has a photograph of Joe Ashton and me on the front. At the time it was printed my mother complained how untidy I looked in comparison. Side by side with Ashton I always do. But I regard the caption beneath the picture as more important than the sartorial comparison. Joe and I were chairman and vice-chairman, respectively, of the Sheffield City Council Public Works Committee and therefore the titular heads of one of the biggest building organizations in the country. There were many complaints about the Public Works Department's failure to complete council house repairs on time if at all. But almost everyone marvelled – and private builders complained – that it was able to beat the great contractors (Wimpey, Gleeson and Laing) at their own game and win competitive contracts for the massive housing developments in which Sheffield specialized during the sixties.

Parkhill Flats, which was ours, is now a listed building. By building high, inexpensively and at an extraordinary speed we managed to clear the slums which Ashton still remembers. Thanks to the work of those years, the slum tenants' hopes having been fulfilled, they are living in flats with bathrooms and indoor lavatories.

Life on the City Council was not always solemn or even serious. Ashton and I sat side by side in two desks, directly in the line of sight of the Lord Mayor. Immediately behind us was the Labour Chief Whip. Ron Ironmonger was a man of extraordinary ability, remarkable perception and considerable piety. But nevertheless, throughout one council meeting, Ashton managed – without being detected from the desk behind him – to read an unexpurgated edition of *Fanny Hill* from cover to cover. I suppose that at one moment he must have abandoned his reading to second the proposal 'That the minutes of the Public Works Committee be accepted.' I have always liked to think that Cleland's less than masterpiece was what inspired Joe's highly successful literary career. Joe's writing has never been inhibited by the thought that it might be read in vicarage studies.

Too many people – thinking of Joe Ashton as a Sheffield Wednesday supporter and plain-speaking member of Parliament – forget that Granada's *What the Papers Say* made him its 'Columnist of the Year' in 1985 following the miners' strike. When, almost ten years ago, I toyed with the idea of editing a weekly magazine I told him that I would want an Ashton article inside the back page. Because the great thing about Joe Ashton is that he has ideas and is not afraid to express them in the language in which he feels most at home.

Reading these memoirs I am astonished, and slightly jealous, to realize what a thoroughgoing Member of Parliament he is and always has been. During my thirty-three years in the House of Commons I never went on a parliamentary delegation to anywhere, spent little (perhaps too little) time in the tea-room and rarely if ever, attended a meeting of an 'All-Party Committee'. As a result, I do not possess one tenth of the political anecdotes and parliamentary memories which Joe Ashton is able to record. He could, of course, have spent far longer on the Front Bench, both in Government and in Opposition. But by opting to return to the ranks and write about politics instead, he managed to acquire a fund of stories which would much improve the average biographies of Home Secretaries and Chancellors of the Exchequer. As a result, *Red Rose Blues* reveals a little-known fact about the House of Commons. Membership can be tremendous fun.

Joe Ashton and I share a joint misfortune. We are both supporters of Sheffield Wednesday Football Club and for more than half a century we have followed the team. In that time 'The Wednesday' have been relegated from the First or Premier Division five times, sunk into the Third and have been beaten in four Cup Finals. To add to our grief we have to face the scorn of taxi drivers, ticket collectors and barmen who regard our devotion as less than heroic. Despite the possession of a lively sense of humour, Joe Ashton never finds their jokes funny. Ten years ago I expressed a thought which I know Ashton would endorse. 'Any fool can support Manchester United. It takes a real man to support Sheffield Wednesday.'

On the way home from one match – trying to take my mind off the latest defeat – I considered what it was that I most admired about him. I decided that his supreme quality was an absolute lack of discretion. If Ashton is for something – or for that matter against – there is no holding him back. He is incapable of moderating either his support or his antagonism.

For that reason he has become a figure of continual controversy. In the House of Commons in 1974 he antagonized other members by exposing what he described as 'MPs for hire' long before the attacks on sleaze became fashionable. He spoke at the Labour Party's 1980 Conference with terrifying frankness about the consequences of expecting Labour MPs to face reselection by their party activists in the middle of every Parliament every five years and received, as a result, the most unjustified insult in a week when insults were flying thick and fast. Ashton warned that MPs who feared that they might not be nominated to stand at the next election would feel an irresistible temptation to join David Owen and the SDP. What he forecast proved tragically correct. A foolish constitutional change that was anti-MP in feeling cost the Labour Party dozens of seats in the 1983 election. Sometimes

Ashton's truth is too painful for others to bear. So he was told that if he proposed to defect with the Gang of Four (along with twenty other MPs) nobody would mind.

There was, of course, no question of that happening. Ashton – perhaps more than any other member of the 1997 Parliament – is a 'Labour Man'.

In the late eighties in his Bassetlaw Notts constituency he was constantly assailed by Scargill miners. He fought them off, with the combination of energy and certainty which characterizes all he does. A member of his local Labour Party management committee told me that not once, during those difficult years, had anybody persuaded him to change his mind about anything.

Because of his highly developed and unshakeable opinions he has written what the critics will describe as an unusual autobiography. It is full of humour of the sort which made him, albeit too briefly, a star of tabloid journalism, and also deeply offended the pompous and the politically correct. No doubt, like Joe Ashton himself, it will annoy almost as many people as it attracts. And it is all the better for that. There are too many politicians and too many biographers who always choose the uncontroversial and the anodyne. Joe Ashton, in life and in literature, has always taken a different route. Bravo for him and bravo for his story.

PREFACE

HALF the world has seen the award-winning film *The Full Monty*. It starts with a famous scene where unemployed steelworkers stand on a derelict car in the canal to steal scrap metal.

It was shot at Bacon Lane Bridge, in Attercliffe, Sheffield, about 200 yards from where I was born, and about 300 yards from where I started work at fifteen.

Back in 1933 the giant steel mills were silent. There were no jobs anywhere.

My grandma insisted I should be called Joe, in memory of one of her sons who had been run over by a steamroller. Don't laugh, it is perfectly true. Little Joe, aged six, was playing football in Savile Street, when the back wheel of a Corporation steamroller came off. It ran down the hill and into the wall of Firth Brown's steelworks, taking Joe Maloney with it.

Grandad Paddy Maloney agreed entirely with the choice of name, because at that time he genuinely believed Joe Stalin would not only lead the Soviet Republic to the promised land of socialism, but would then come over here from Russia to sort out the British Government too.

Grandma refused to marry old Maloney until she was twenty-eight, because that was the only form of birth control Catholic women were allowed, but she still finished up with six daughters and three sons. All three lads died as children.

One daughter, the lovely Josie, lost her life at the hands of a back-street abortionist. She was single, in her early twenties, and fell in love with the only bloke in Attercliffe who had a motor-bike, and who promptly went off on it when Josie found she was pregnant. The Catholic priest from St Charles' Church refused to give her the Catholic last rites funeral and burial, which was when Grandad Maloney threw him bodily out of the house, and every single one of us, including me aged four, left the Church.

'We are all the products of our seed and our soil,' the philosopher said. From Sheffield's seed and soil grew Old Labour politicians.

One

ATTERCLIFFE

ATTERCLIFFE must have been pretty at one time, because there were places called Broad Oaks, Salmon Pastures and Oaks Green. Even Attercliffe was originally two words, Otter Cliffe. What a laugh.

Sheffield has twice as many hills as Rome and only one strip of flat land where the River Don (from which school kids could fill their inkwells) eventually winds down from the Pennines to Rotherham and Doncaster. The Don Valley when I was growing up was the most polluted place in Europe. Seven miles of stinking, belching chimneys, and 20,000 houses packed together with furnaces, drop forges, steam-hammers, strip mills, bar mills and machine shops.

The statue of Vulcan, god of fire and power, stood proudly above Sheffield Town Hall to show where the weapons of war were forged and machined into gun-barrels and iron sides for battleships, or wheels and turrets for tanks.

Thirty miles north, in Leeds, the huge textile factories of Montague Burton made the uniforms for the forces, and also the free demob suits, shirts and ties the troops were given when they were discharged.

The squaddies always swore that the first thing they would do when they got back to their wives and girlfriends would be to strip off the Full Monty ensemble from Burton's, ready for action

1

as soon as they walked through the door. And that is how the phrase came to be.

It was Sheffield's proud boast that it made the weapons of war for the troops while Leeds made the WAAF's knickers. Which was why Goering never bothered bombing Leeds.

The canal was intended to get the cannon balls and swords across to France for the Napoleonic wars. Unfortunately, with typical upper-class arrogance, the Duke of Norfolk, who owned half of Sheffield, blocked the bill in Parliament because the 'Cut' was straight. He refused to allow the bill until the canal was bent in curves to pass all his collieries, and it was not passed until June 1815; by the time the navigation had been dug by the 'navvies', the war was over and the army did not need the cannon balls. The workers never forgave him and rioted in the streets. Twenty years later, the railways put the canal out of business anyway.

In 1860 when Prime Minister Lord Palmerston sent his gun-boats up the Limpopo to sort out the natives of the British Empire, the boats would be made of Sheffield armour-plate, tough enough to stand up to any cannon. Whether he knew of the conditions the steel was made in was doubtful.

Our house in Harriet Street, off Birch Road, stood across the street from Jonas and Colver's steelworks and literally twenty yards from a drop-hammer which went crash, bang, wallop twenty-four hours a day. The row of outside lavs in the yard had not worked since 1899 and all of us walked round to the next street to use Grandma's. There were at least a thousand cockroaches and maybe a hundred crickets (we never counted the bugs) infecting every house, breeding in the heat, soot, sparks and smoke from the forge.

Those nostalgic stories about the olden days, with a tin bath in front of the open coal fire, look good on Catherine Cookson television. In reality it was a cruel, hard life for any steelworks family. Not necessarily grinding poverty, because when work was plentiful steelworkers were well paid for their hard slog and round-the-clock shifts, but an awful, often miserable existence.

In fact, the best favour anybody did our family, including two grandmas, three aunties and umpteen other extended members of the clan living within a stone's throw, was when Adolf Hitler's Luftwaffe bombed the lot of us and flattened the neighbourhood.

Hitler was aiming to wipe out the centre of Britain's armour-plate steel industry, just as our boys later demolished the Krupps' factories in the Ruhr Valley. Except that his navigators missed. On Thursday night, just before Christmas of 1940, they bombed Sheffield city centre and killed 600 people in the pubs and pictures. Then they came back on Sunday and bombed us. Another mile east and they would have obliterated the whole Don Valley, and maybe won the war.

Instead, they demolished our lav and took the roof off our house and all the others in the street. Plus they destroyed several streets, schools, shops, pubs, canal bridges, tramlines, sewers, water-pipes and gas and electricity supplies.

For kids it was wonderful. A lot better than Bonfire Night.

A hundred yards from the steelworks was the Foundry Working Men's Club, nicknamed the 'Moulders'. As the bombs fell, the committee quickly passed a resolution that there was no point in all the ale going to waste, especially when everybody might be dead by morning, so they let any member brave enough to stay out of the shelter take what he wanted. And the whole street did.

Fiction writers everywhere have fantasized about what folks would get up to if the end of the world was nigh. I actually saw it. My only regret is that at six years old, I was too young to enjoy it. I certainly do not recall anybody saying any prayers. Or starting off singing 'Abide with Me', like they did in the war pictures. Most of the street seemed determined to go right through every single one of the seven deadly sins before the roof fell in.

Including some very respectable neighbours.

By some miracle, the 'Moulders', survived while all the slum houses around it were set on fire by incendiary bombs. But not before the free booze had encouraged enough brave souls to run through the flames and loot the wireless from every house. No one cared. They were all on hire purchase anyway.

We kids couldn't wait to get to the pictures next day to see if we would be on Pathé News doing our bit for Britain. Perhaps the King and Queen would pay us a visit like they always did to the cheering Cockneys in London's East End. Perhaps old Churchill would turn up with his Homburg hat and his two fingers up giving the V sign.

He daren't, said my grandad Maloney, he barely escaped in one piece the last time he got off the train in the Sheffield depression. Attercliffe must have been one of the very few places in Dad's Army Britain where Mr Churchill got booed every time he appeared on the screen.

Actually we kids should not have been involved in the bombing. When the war broke out our school was evacuated to the green fields of rural Leicestershire, with joyous mothers waving us off at Sheffield station. My mam and dad weren't half disappointed when two weeks later they heard a kicking on the door at ten o'clock at night and found little Joe standing on the step after hitch-hiking home with his pal Georgie aged ten. We just couldn't stand the silence, the bath every night and bedtime at half past seven.

The Jerries even bombed the chip shop. Now that was a blow. With food on ration, fish and chips were one of the few pleasures available without having to produce coupons in the queue to get served. The chippies were little goldmines.

The street families escaped by hiding in their cellars then running to a brick-built air raid shelter near the canal. But the terraced house with the chippy in the front room was badly damaged.

There is a legend I heard years later (it had travelled to every town) that the two women running the chippy had been fading good-time girls, who bought it so that they wouldn't be compelled to work in a munitions factory.

The day after the blitz, some wag wrote on the wall in chalk, 'Thanks to Hitler, chips will be littler'. The next day another mystery message appeared, 'Thanks to Himmler, fish will be similar'.

Only to be followed the day after with, 'Thanks to Goering – gone back to whoring'.

I asked Grandad lots of times what old Goering had been up to, but he never would tell me. He'd show me another picture of Joe Stalin in the *Daily Worker* instead, pour out some of his beer into a small glass for me, and have a competition to see who could spit into the fire without hitting the bars.

It was marvellous, the blitz. We never went to school for three months. Our gang kept busy trying to pull down the walls which had been left standing. Until two kids got buried, and then the Council did it for us. All we had to do then was turn up at Mrs Johnson's, one of the few houses still intact, to chant the times tables for half an hour.

We lived and slept anywhere. Any relative who had a space on the floor, or under a sideboard where a kid could fit in, would do.

The whole neighbourhood became an adventure playground. The Council were too busy trying to run a city with no food, beer, water, street-lights or transport to bother about kids. The Government told them to look after the war machine first, so we just sneaked into the pictures every afternoon. We clubbed together for one kid to pay, then in the dark he would quietly open the emergency exit for the others to creep in.

We saw Boris Karloff in *Frankenstein* twelve times. The film was classed as 'H' for horror and restricted to over-sixteens, but why bother about kids being scared in a city where 630 people were killed and buried in two nights of bombing?

Streetwise Artful Dodgers didn't worry about Frankenstein monsters. We told each other real ghost stories in bombed-out cellars where dead bodies had been dug up not ten feet away.

To pass the time, my pal Georgie promised to take me horse-riding. There were no horses within ten miles of Attercliffe, except the one which pulled the Co-op milkman's cart, so he simply borrowed that. And the milk tokens too.

Georgie kept the horse for a week on the canal bank, and only got found out when he took it to his auntie's to show her how he could ride bareback better than Geronimo. The only problem was that he didn't notice the clothes-line across the yard, and when the horse went under it Georgie got garrotted.

Fortunately for Georgie, the magistrate was a kindly Old Labour JP, who was known locally as a good Labour man. He was nicknamed as 'The Judge', because he always carried an unrolled umbrella when he went round collecting insurance in his starched 'Sick and Divide' wing-collar.

The Judge said it was obvious that the lad loved horses, and the animal had been well fed and had no doubt enjoyed the rest. What's more, as the Co-op had got all its milk tokens back, he would simply report the matter to the boy's headmaster so that he could take the necessary steps.

Georgie said nowt about the school being bombed and the teachers all away, but just touched his forelock and said, 'Thank you, Mester Judge,' and as counselling, or social worker's reports, hadn't even been invented, that was that.

It had to end sooner or later. My mother Nellie actually managed to find another terraced house to rent a few hundred yards down Attercliffe Road, on another street, Bodmin Street, ending at the canal.

This time the rolling mills of Brown Bayley's were a hundred yards away, and if it wasn't frosty the outside lav would work. If it was, we had to take a red-hot poker with us to melt the ice.

Both grandmas found houses in the same neighbourhood, but theirs only had electric lights in two rooms.

Between the wars in 1933, when I was born, there was no demand for Sheffield's weapons and armour-plate, but the cutlery trade was staggering along. Cutlery workers, especially the women, worked in appalling Dickensian conditions. They stood all day in old attics and garrets in tenement warrens in the centre of Sheffield and came home as black as chimney sweeps.

Especially if they were buffer girls, like my mam.

The 'girls' polished the nickel-plated silver knives, forks, tea services and coffee pots with pumice, because the buffing wheel made the metal hot, and using water to cool it would spoil the finish. In no time, the pumice looked like soot and flew everywhere, into the women's hair, eyes, ears, mouths and noses. It ground into their skin, despite the brown paper leggings they wore. Their fingers were skinned and burned and cut where they caught the wheel, but it paid good money.

The only perk was that cutlery workers were paid by the gross of 144 pieces and manufacturers usually delivered two or three extra to allow for scrappers, or waste. These two or three eventually finished up in half the kitchens in Sheffield.

We regularly used a nickel-silver plated cake server with 'Savoy Hotel' stamped on it to scrape off wallpaper, and it was said that the River Don had more silver in it than the Spanish Main with the scrappers which had been thrown in out of tenement windows. Including two top-level racing and football cups.

With my dad out of work and no money coming in, Nellie had no option but to go back to work three weeks after I was born. My dad, Ike (nicknamed after an early eye injury), had his nineteenth birthday three days before mine.

My mother put me with a childminder down the yard. She was an old woman who liked a drink and I bear the scars to this day from when she turned the washtub mangle while little Joe's finger was in the cogs. Plus a split head and ten stitches trying to ride a big dog like a bucking bronco and a broken arm playing acrobats on the 'Moulders' railings.

Where was Dad? On the market at the pit. Since leaving school, Ike had worked at Nunnery Colliery, belonging to the Duke of Norfolk, about a mile down the canal. The Board of Guardians ruled that he was not eligible for the £1.35 a week dole money unless he actually reported to work every day and lined up ready to start, should any of the regular men not turn up. Ike had to walk to the pit every night, hang around for several hours to have his card signed, and get back home about two in the morning.

The week I was born he did not get any dole at all. The pit was shut because all the pit ponies had gone down sick with colic. A few years later, he was carried out of the colliery on a stretcher, and when Mr Chamberlain decided Britain had better start making tanks again, Ike went into the melting shop as a furnace man.

He worked on a three-shift system in front of a furnace full of ninety tons of molten steel, shovelling chemicals into it, then stirring and puddling out the gases before teeming the steel into a ladle the size of a house. The melting shop was dark, airless and hotter than the Sahara desert.

Ike, and the other men, had to sweat, tug and lift the long, heavy puddling irons, wearing a long-sleeved thick woollen shirt, cap, apron, dark glasses and heavy clogs to keep off the fierce heat of the molten steel. If he did not hold a sweat-towel clenched between his teeth, the glare roasted his neck and face. The iron on the clogs was there to stop him slipping and stop the heat from rotting his boots and feet.

Once, when the metal splashed him, I went to see him in hospital. Ike was lucky. When the ladle tipped over a man the week after, all they found was his belt buckle.

Next door to the melting shop was the rolling mill. Here the ingots were heated up again and rolled out like a stick of

Blackpool rock 200 feet long. Bar men had to grab the red-hot rods with tongs as they flashed past, twist them over and under like hot toffee, and steer them back through the rolls. It was not uncommon for a length to spear a man straight through his stomach like a long, red-hot bullet. It took about five or six hours for him to die after the rod had been cut off with a flame-cutter on both sides of his body.

These guys earned big money on the anvils of war whenever the generals demanded their arsenals be filled.

But we still did not have a bathroom, running hot water, or a lav which worked all year round.

There were probably 20,000 families living in the cobbled streets of Attercliffe, and hardly a single one had a bathroom, or inside toilet, or running hot water, never mind a garden.

Every Friday morning, the teacher would come round the class and sniff at the lads. Then she would line up the smelliest for one of the senior boys to march them half a mile to Maltby Street School, which actually had showers. They were all ordered to strip off, and then were frightened to death by an enormous dragon wielding a long cane, who slashed out indiscriminately until they dived under the scalding spray to scrub themselves with carbolic soap. I tried it once out of curiosity. Once was enough.

Maybe the Sheffield Education Committee thought it was in the lads' own interest. Most of the boys had already lost all their hair to the nit barber. To make it worse, a lot of them had their shaven skulls painted with gentian violet in an attempt to get rid of ringworm. They caught it from playing marbles in the gutter among the dog dirt, then scratching the nits on their heads. Whenever I see old war pictures of refugees and bombed houses, it reminds me of wartime Attercliffe. No wonder Old Labour grew up wanting to change the world.

Attercliffe was three miles from the nearest hospital, and all the kids suffered from infected tonsils because of the pollution.

At the age of eight, we were taken down to the wooden-hut school clinic, next to the Adelphi Cinema, and had a cylinder of gas clamped to our mouth. Our tonsils were cut out, we were laid on a mattress to wake up, and then we were half carried home and allowed two days off school to recover.

There's a war on, was the usual excuse.

I read *Treasure Island* in the queue of kids to take my mind off it. Six months later, for our routine wisdom teeth extraction, I read *Robinson Crusoe*. My pal Harold chickened out and went inside the Adelphi pictures instead to see Abbott and Costello meet the Wolfman, then he went back to school two days later and nobody said a word to him.

He was smart, was Harold. I wish I had thought of it. Although I bet he gets toothache now.

Believe it or not, the school had the wonderful name of Huntsman's Gardens. There was not a garden within two miles of it (although it was only a hundred yards from the canal) but it was on the site where Benjamin Huntsman was supposed to have discovered crucible steel back in the eighteenth century.

If the kids stank, it was not always the fault of their mothers. It was impossible to hang out washing in Attercliffe. The sheets were polka-dotted with soot in ten minutes. Instead, the enlightened Labour Council provided a public wash-house on Oaks Green. It had the first indoor parking lot in Sheffield – for prams and barrows to wheel the washing there and back.

The wash-house, where the melters' woolly shirts were washed on stalls, was the social equivalent of women kneeling by the River Nile in ancient Egypt. In exactly the same way, it was the hub where gossip was king, scandals were aired, and shotgun weddings were sorted out by the mothers before the dads and brothers resorted to violence. If any young couple went for a walk on the canal bank after dark on Sunday, then their mothers and the whole wash-house would know by Tuesday.

Yet, astonishingly, few folk in Attercliffe ever complained. The steelworkers' wages were good and the 'Cliffe, like Chicago, was a toddlin' town. The families were big earners and big spenders too. In the mile-long tramtrack of Attercliffe Road were at least six working men's clubs, twenty pubs, another twenty places to buy a suit (including two Montague Burtons' shops with billiard halls on top), department stores, pawnshops, swap shops, chip shops and hot pie shops, all doing a roaring trade whenever the Government chose to spend money on war.

Steelworkers, after their shifts in a black, airless hole, demanded beer, music, bright lights, entertainment, belly laughs, back-street bookies, football, fairgrounds, with punch-ups and fist-fights thrown in.

Every pub had a piano and a sing-song. Every working man's club (there were over sixty in the city of Sheffield) was a training ground for budding singers, comics, jugglers, acrobats and music-hall turns.

Stars like Tom Jones, Shirley Bassey, Engelbert Humperdinck (who was once paid off after his third song in Dial House working men's club with three pound notes shoved in his hand, and told to 'Gerrof, tha'rt rubbish') and hundreds more, cut their teeth in northern wheeltappers' and shunters' Labour clubs.

Totally ruthless audiences would not even bother to lower the Saturday night *Green 'Un* football paper unless the turn was top class. And all under the supervision and control of a chairman at the side of the stage shouting 'Order! Order!' – like the Speaker of the House of Commons. It was often said back then that there were only four ways out of sweat and muck for working-class kids. Show business, sport, crime or politics.

That working-class show business scene in Sheffield forged stars like Marti Caine, Joe Cocker, the best white blues singer in the world, Human League, Def Leppard and Jarvis Cocker of Pulp. Michael Palin grew up in Sheffield, as did Sean Bean, the TV star Sharpe and James Bond (his dad and mam, Brian and

Rita, were in my class at school, and lived next door to the canal) and Peter Stringfellow, who went on to own trendy night-clubs in New York and Miami as well as London. Peter String-fellow started off by booking the Beatles into St Aidan's church hall for £60 just before they soared to fame. Then he cleverly switched the gig to a larger hall and took £600 (worth about £10,000 today). He then rented an old building in Pitsmoor, called it the Mojo Club, and signed up fading stars like Ike and Tina Turner, and newcomers like Billy Fury and Freddie and the Dreamers before angry neighbours and drug-pushers forced him to take a gamble on a plush night-club called Cinderfellas in Leeds.

Cabinet ministers such as Roy Hattersley and David Blunkett grew up in the city, and within a hundred square yards of the canal and Huntsman's Gardens School a Sir, a Dame and two MPs emerged. Sir Ron Ironmonger and Dame Grace Tebbut were both Leaders of Sheffield City Council; Jim Marshall, MP for Leicester South, and myself both managed it to Westminster.

As for sport, the best fighter in the world right now, pound for pound, is Prince Naseem Hamed, born to a Yemeni family next to the steelworks of Brightside. How Roger Taylor ever managed to become a world-famous tennis star on the hills of Sheffield, nobody ever knew. And Seb Coe's tireless training in Sheffield won him Olympic medals.

Other famous names within a twenty-mile radius who took the same paths were Michael Parkinson, Freddie Truman, Kevin Keegan, Arthur Scargill, Dickie Bird the umpire, William Hague, now Leader of the Opposition, Dennis Skinner and Labour Lords like Roy Mason and Eric Varley.

The canal had its share of strippers in those days too, even though the still water not only looked like urine, but smelled like it. That never stopped Full Monty teenage lads from swimming in it totally naked where the aqueduct passes over Worksop Road arches, and waving to the office girls in the factory windows.

There was a municipal swimming baths a few hundred yards away, but on hot days it was standing room only in the blue chlorined water. Around the upstairs gallery of the pool there was always a two-hour queue for a slipper bath. These had real hot water in a tub, in its own cubicle, carefully measured out by elderly women from the turnkey taps outside.

The clever Council even sited the baths next to the Attercliffe Library. That way lads like me could pass away the two-hour wait reading books by Upton Sinclair, Jack London, Charles Dickens, Émile Zola and any other writer who knew what hard conditions the poor sods of this world had to live and work in, and which we were fighting a world war to preserve.

The real Full Monty strippers, though, were at the Attercliffe Palace. Attercliffe Road and its tramlines ran parallel with the canal, and the streets and steelworks ran across it.

One of them was called Titterton Street.

Everybody has heard of The Street of a Thousand Armholes. Titterton Street was the street of a thousand jokes, all trundled out at the small, cosy, tatty Attercliffe Palace. Outside, stretching across the building, was a poster claiming 'This is the Show!', with the capital letters spelling 'TITS' standing out like chapel hatpegs, as they say in Yorkshire.

The Palace put on girlie-show revues titled 'Naughty Nudes of 1947' or 'Bareskins and Busbies', modelled on the Windmill Theatre in London. It had a different touring show every week guaranteeing visits to Gay Paree, an authentic cancan from Montmartre, Living Statues at the Louvre Museum, fan dancing, stand-up comics, Apache dancers, hypnotists, strong men, Irish tenors, footballing dogs, flaming knife-throwers and the worst pit band in the world.

When old-time entertainers like Spike Milligan, Jimmy

Edwards, Hylda Baker, Jimmy Jewel and Ben Warris (from Sheffield), and dozens of others came to write their memoirs of early days, every single one would say that the Attercliffe Palace was the toughest booking on the circuit.

The ambition of every kid in our street was to have two whole shillings (10p) to sit in the front row, literally eight or ten feet from the shaven naked girls. But all we could ever afford was a shilling for the back stalls, or one and sixpence in the balcony.

Amazingly, although cinema censorship was strictly controlled in allowing kids to attend adult films, the censors were either unaware of, or did not care about, young lads of ten or under staring dry-mouthed at Peaches Page balancing on one leg and one high heel to slip her G-string off the other. Or Forces Favourite Jane of *Daily Mirror* fame posing as the statue of Daphne at the Well. Or Rhoda Rogers lying on her back across the lid of the white Dulux-painted grand piano. We kids could never work out how the pianist managed to keep on playing with the view he had.

Astonishingly, in a society where no newspaper dared show a nipple or print a mild swear word, and with a tough Hollywood code of morals clamping down and setting the standards on all entertainers, the theatre licences allowed nudity – provided the nudes, all women, did not move.

Even in the freezing cold Christmas fairgrounds, local amateur strippers would parade in front of kids in a tent next to the boxing booth, where daft lads tried to win a quid by going three rounds with an ex-pro. The law may have ruled the girls could not move when naked. But the young Paul Raymond soon solved that on his touring shows. He put them on a conveyor belt with a straining stage-hand turning a crank to judder and wobble the girls down to the front stalls.

The kids in Attercliffe had a better idea. They simply chucked a white mouse on to the stage. It was even funnier one night when a stray dog found its way in front of the footlights and put its cold nose against the back of Venus de Milo's leg, then ran amok knocking the scenery over.

Another night, the fifty-year-old curtains got stuck and the stripper had to stand there for a full five minutes while the manager tried to fix them. Until finally she yelled 'Sod this!' and marched off, waving to us all, shaking her hips with her hands in the air.

But the real artists, and probably the finest trade union in Sheffield, were the pit band. They had their job off to a fine arpeggio. They regularly downed tools if the turns upset them.

The pit band ran the show. If the singer did not give them a good drink at the beginning of the week, the lads would blast off too soon in the wrong key.

When the comic was doing his seven-and-a-half minute slot, they ducked under the stage and into the pub next door before he got to the first titter, and were back picking up their instruments exactly ten seconds before he got to the last.

The 'musicians' had a closed shop tighter than Grimethorpe Pit. When they traded in their two complimentary tickets for two suppers at the chip shop on Mondays, the queue would want to know if it was hot stuff that week. One wrong word that the comic was Brahms and Liszt or the singers were Novak 'n' Good and the strippers should be modelling for Toby jugs, and the box office might as well shut until the following Monday.

The strippers and chorus girls stayed in lodgings on Titterton Street at Mrs Beggs'. She had a schoolboy son about fourteen who had the best job in the world. He worked the floodlights at the Palace from the front row of the balcony. We often tried to bribe him to put them on full beam, instead of the soft blue haze, but he reckoned it would get the place banned by the City Fathers and the Watch Committee, whoever they were. And anyway, we would not enjoy it because, he said, when it was rehearsals with the lights on, you could see all the varicose veins.

Still, it was better than my job. All kids had jobs then, there was nobody to say we couldn't. The school bobbies were all fighting Hitler.

I became a worker at the age of eleven. From six-thirty in the morning until school started at a quarter to nine, I delivered morning newspapers over a square-mile area. In the school dinner hour, it was back to run errands and fetch stock for the old dragon who owned the shop, then back again at four to deliver the *Sheffield Star* until five-thirty.

Fortunately, on Sunday there was no evening paper. So it was only from six-thirty to noon because I had to collect the cash from the customers as well. Almost thirty hours a week – and the wages? Six shillings. About 30p. Which was lousy money even for those days.

Often the tips would be as high as 10p per week (which Ike let me keep). They came mainly from the old souls who could hardly read and would be grateful if I spent a minute telling them what the words said under the pictures, or who had scored for Sheffield Wednesday.

Lovely, lovely Attercliffe. Its seed and its soil taught me and thousands of others how to hate the bosses, the ruling classes, those who had made the world such a mess, and those who had made our lives so hard.

Even better, it lit the Old Labour fire in the belly to change it.

Two

ECCE, ECCO, BEHOLD THE HORSEMUCK LUMPS

THE war in Europe ended in May 1945 and Mr Attlee's Labour Government swept home in a landslide to rebuild the world. Mine in particular.

As the war was ending, all children aged eleven had to take the eleven-plus exam to grade us into clever know-alls and the rest. Including me. For the first time, scruffy urchins from Attercliffe would be given the chance to go to top grammar schools and these could not refuse to let us in. Socialism was here at last.

Kids who had never worn underpants in their life (and never would until the army issued them when we were called up for national service) would from henceforth stop wiping their snotty noses on their sleeves, and use a bit of old flour bag instead. They might not know what toilet paper was except for the pages of the *Sheffield Star*, or have ever seen hot water running from a tap, but soon they would learn to love the pleasures of Shakespeare and Latin verbs.

Their previous classes might have been full of kids who slept six to a bed, when if one rolled over, another one rolled out. They might never have used anything but salt for toothpaste, but in this great new world, there would be no more nit nurses, no more school barbers with mechanical shears to crop their heads bare, and soon these kids would discard their working-class accents and be taught and trained to become lawyers, doctors, classical

scholars, language teachers and rocket scientists, undistinguish-
able at Oxford and Cambridge from the other undergraduates
sent there by Eton and Harrow.

Old Maloney was very enthusiastic. He bought me a second-
hand set of Arthur Mee's *Children's Encyclopaedia* and we would
read it every night. Our headteacher at Huntsman's Gardens, Mr
Cattel, had once even been to the Lyceum to see George Bernard
Shaw's *Pygmalion*. So had Mrs Ramsden, our class teacher, but
not together.

He was very big then, was George Bernard Shaw. All the
architects of the Labour Government's policy on education
thought he was magic. These well-meaning early socialist Cabinet
ministers who had been educated at Winchester, or Haileybury,
like Mr Attlee, had said that if Professor Higgins could do it, why
couldn't they? The fact that Professor Higgins didn't try to whack
'The Rain in Spain Falls Mainly on the Plain' into Eliza Doolittle's
brain with a leather strap, slipper or even a rubber tube from a
bunsen burner, and that she was not sent out to do her homework
in a hovel in Covent Garden, never seems to have entered their
heads.

Neverthless, my encyclopaedia reading paid off and I was into
grammar school. The grammar schools were obviously at the
poshest end of the cities, well away from the factories' grime and
slums. It meant a six-mile journey (no bus pass) on a tram, and
then bus from East End Attercliffe to High Storrs Grammar in
the West End, where the moors began. It took an hour each way.
Afterwards, I had to try to do my homework with all the family
in one room huddled round one coal fire, rationed to one bag of
coal per house per week, with wet washing hung round it, the
wireless blaring out Glen Miller, Dad on shifts, parents who
couldn't help with the homework in any way, shape or form,
simply because they had never had any education, and all the
other kids in the street still enjoying life at the pictures, billiard
halls, youth clubs and the Palace.

Homework? I'd take a whacking instead.

Here was a brand-new grammar school, the proud flagship of the Labour Council, with all its masters in long, flowing black gowns, expected to put aside their class prejudice, centuries-deep in Britain, and welcome 'Dee-daas' as the Sheffield underclass is called, because these ragamuffins don't even say the traditional 'thee' and 'tha' of Yorkshire, but corrupt it to 'dee-daa' instead. Half a dozen of us at High Storrs wore no school uniform except the traditional Attercliffe hobnail boots, corduroy trousers, woollen shirt and jersey and ex-army jerkin, every day until we grew out of them. We stood out like the bombed refugees in Pathé News bulletins.

I never even knew there was a school uniform until the first day I got off the bus. Nobody bothered telling my family, and Ike was on nights when the school had the parents' meeting, so we couldn't get twelve miles there and back in time for him to go to work.

I was glad. Rebels should not belong to the mass ranks of deferential forelock-touching lumpenproletariat, as Old Maloney called them, but be defiant and bolshie heroes like Che Guevara twenty years later. Grandad consulted a barrack-room lawyer in the local Labour Party, who told him there was no way the school could force kids to wear school uniforms while clothing was on ration. His advice was, 'Just tell the school your mother has used up all the coupons in the ration book' (or say she had sold them, as most of Bodmin Street did, because they could never afford new clothes anyway), and they 'can't touch you for it', as the wartime saying went in those days.

So I never did wear one. I was a dee-daa and suffered the consequences. The Latin master would have a bit of fun by pulling Eastenders to the front of the class, taking us by the ear, and telling the blazers, 'Here is a word – "ecce ecco". It is a command. A demand for attention. It means "Behold". But for the benefit of Ashton from Attercliffe, we can translate it as "sithee".' Which was a regular dee-daa word, and still is in Sheffield, except they pronounce it 'siddy'.

We learned Latin like the eleven-times table. *Amo. Amas. Amat. Amamus. Amatis. Amant.* I can chant it still. However, it always seemed as if the favourite word was *voluptas*, meaning voluptuous, or pleasureful in English, but pronounced 'wallop t'arse', easily understandable in Yorkshire, and which the teachers certainly seemed to enjoy at High Storrs.

The eleven-plus Eliza Doolittle theory was a disaster. George Bernard Shaw? He made it all up and the early-century *Manchester Guardian*-reading Hampstead theatregoers fell for it, iambic pentameter, warts and all. Dee-daas were a different race, just like the Jamaicans and the Pakistanis who came fifteen years later.

I have a very grateful and high regard for that Latin master. He was one of those teachers who put a chip on my shoulder for the next thirty years. Without him and High Storrs Grammar School, I would never have become a Labour MP.

Not only the working-class winners hated the grammar school eleven-plus system, the middle-class losers hated it even more. Here were valuable places in a top-class school being taken by kids who didn't want them, and their own middle-class sons and daughters, desperate for education and qualifications, couldn't pass the entrance exam.

What a stigma! What a humiliation! Teachers' kids were failing and steelworkers' kids were passing. Those with white collars and mortgages were losing out to the terraced houses and weekly pay packets. The newspapers protested loud and long. So did the teachers. So did a lot of Labour MPs on behalf of their own kids.

The plain and simple fact was that the eleven-plus was a doddle for streetwise smart arses, for those who lived by their wits and natural nous, and not by their educational training and skills. It was money in the bank for wide boys, barrow boys and Sergeant Bilkos. Dedicated study is a marathon for the professional classes. Others need no coaching to become natural spielers, tabloid newspaper headline-writers, bookmakers, traders in futures on the London Stock Exchange, crime reporters, sports correspondents and commentators. Even politicians, who have to think on their feet and invent plausible answers.

The eleven-plus exam was laid down and set solely to test IQ, a very popular word at that time. It meant intelligence quota. Something the armed forces used to decide whether to stick Private Jones in the Pioneer Corps to build latrines, or give him a chance to train as a fighter pilot and use his brains and balls to fire Spitfire machine-guns flying at 300 miles an hour upside down. It worked marvellously well for the armed forces, but disastrously badly for university recruits from the underclass.

The eleven-plus was the equivalent of planting champagne vines on the polluted banks of the canal. The seed was good but the soil was crap.

There was one ray of sunshine, a lifeline in fact. The system was due to be changed in 1949 when I was fifteen, the minimum school-leaving age. Grammar school kids then were supposed to stay on until sixteen and take School Certificates in all nine subjects. In 1950 these were to be changed to equivalent 'O' levels. But for one year only it would be possible, but only for the top two classes, to take all nine subjects at fifteen and leave a year early.

What a sigh of relief! Time off for good behaviour. The parole board couldn't stop me walking out if I managed to scrape through and stay inside the top two forms. If I lived in the local library every evening where it was quiet, or stayed at Maloney's where he never put the wireless on, it could be done. I passed and got credits in all nine subjects. And I never went back to High Storrs for forty years, by when it had gone comprehensive and scruffy Joe was its most famous pupil.

Eat your heart out, George Bernard Shaw!

*

In 1949 grammar schools taught every subject but airily refused to give any careers advice to pupils except to go to university. Getting jobs then was, and maybe still is, based on who you know, rather than what you know.

The Ashtons and the Maloneys knew nobody outside the underclass. Not a single member of the two tribes had ever been a skilled man, never mind a white-collar worker. And in a world where dads 'asked for their lads', that's how most sons got a job.

'I want to be a journalist, Dad, and then a Labour MP,' I said to Ike.

He laughed and like all Attercliffe dads replied, 'I'll ask if tha can start at our place on Monday.' 'Our place' was the gigantic English Steel Corporation, a huge conglomerate which melted steel, forged it, rolled it, machined it, and sent it away to be assembled into battleships, tanks, anti-aircraft guns and Vulcan's other weapons of war. It was one of three or four giant firms which dominated Sheffield.

Just down the road was Firth Brown's with its Glasgow shipyard connections. It was where Richard Caborn MP served his apprenticeship and rose to the rank of chief shop steward. His dad, George Caborn, was the most feared, but respected, Communist union leader in Sheffield, who would have been proud to see his son rise to Minister of State at the Department of Environment, and become number two to John Prescott.

The English Steel machine shops were enormous and awesome. They had to be to machine the propeller shaft for the *Queen Mary*. The south machine shop could house two *Queen Marys* side by side. The west machine shop was literally a quarter of a mile long. The north planer, where I was sent to work, after two years' skill training of a very high standard, was the smallest.

After a couple of years' training and night school, the paternalistic company put their young apprentices out into the jungle to get some of their money back. We started work on the magnificent sum of £1.24 a week (apprentices were expected to starve like Oliver Twist), but later the firm gave us the chance to earn up to £4 a week on piecework. The fact that eighteen-year-old lads were expected to turn out as many highly skilled products as the fully time-served men, who were earning £10 a week, seemed to the bosses to be a fair return on what they had laid out to teach us our skills.

A shop-floor apprenticeship was where Old Labour lads began to learn economics.

My tutor was a guy called Fred Bear, known to one and all as Professor Threadbare, because he had mastered the art of existing on the bare necessities of life. As he drilled holes in tank wheels at 2s 9d (13p) each he would say: 'Monday I work for the rent. Tuesday and Wednesday for the missus' housekeeping. All day Thursday for the hire purchase, and most of Friday for the taxman. But when it gets to two o'clock on a Friday afternoon, I'm going like the Grand National favourite because from then on, I'm working for Fred.' Then he would look upwards and say, 'Please God, send some overtime because Christmas is coming and the geese are getting thin.'

Professor Fred had another economic theory too, this time on psephology. One which the opinion pollsters who study voting trends, and forecast how the punters will move the graphs on *Newsnight*, have never once taken into consideration.

'I am careful how I vote,' said Fred. 'I vote Communist for the union ballots because I reckon they do best for the pay rises and fight hardest for the workers. I vote Labour for the local council because they are best at keeping the council house rents down, and I vote Conservative for Parliament because they cut the income tax.'

If any civil servant economic expert in the Treasury had bothered to ask Fred, he would have soon found out why Britain had about forty years of stop-go booms and slumps, as the voting pendulum swung, and Chancellors despaired of the voters' fickle stupidity.

Fred, like all the blokes on the shop-floor then, feared and would bend the knee to no man. These were blokes who had spent years on the dole, then more years in the British Army Desert Rats, or sailing the Arctic waters with the Royal Navy, and for the first time in their life were getting a full wage packet.

On the top of his tool cupboard, he had two jars full of water floating with frog-spawn. The label on one jar said, 'Workers' Brains £5', on the other jar, 'Bosses' Brains £25'.

When the rate-fixer came round and congratulated him on getting the price right, Fred would nod and say, 'Yeah, well, the boss's brain has never been used.'

Fifteen years later, television companies hit on the idea of making working-class sit-coms such as *The Rag Trade*, *On the Buses*, *Steptoe and Son*, *Till Death Do Us Part*, *Are You Being Served?*, *Porridge*, *It Ain't Half Hot Mum*, *Hi De Hi*, and many others, using British working-class salty humour, wit and sheer cheek, showing that there was a wider world of fun beyond Jeeves and Wooster. Now, apart from Rab C. Nesbitt, it has vanished. Yet the repeats delight our kids.

The humour sprang, as it did in the trenches, and probably even in gaol, from true-life situations where conditions are grim and rewards minimal. At English Steel, work stopped for exactly forty-two minutes for lunch. No tea breaks. No time to nip out to the shops or the pub, and barely long enough to run across to the canteen and join the lengthy queue.

Like prisoners in Alcatraz being let out into the exercise yard, some of the blokes would take their sandwiches and enamel tea-mashing cans outside, just to have a look at daylight in winter. A worker on the track at the Ford and British Leyland car factories had to hold his hand up to go to the lavatory, knowing the foreman would tell him to wait his turn because there were six other guys in front of him.

Car firms were notorious at speeding up the conveyor belt when there was a high demand and a waiting list for a new model. If the wheels fell off it was always the unions and the lazy British workers who were to blame.

Equally, if the demand for cars fell away and sales were down, what would be simpler to get rid of surplus stock than manufacturing a convenient strike? Simply take away a valuable tea break, or put the lads on a four-day week, without notice, and let the hotheads call a walkout. It reduced stock and saved wages too.

Tea-break strikes and clocking-in strikes were common. It was the mind-bending, numbskulling monotony and grind that turned intelligent men and women into raving Trots with Militant Loony Tendencies. Especially when some time and motion expert, slaving over a hot slide-rule in an office, would decide to abolish the hand-washing time. That's when three whole minutes, twice a day, adding up to half an hour a week, became the last straw, and the lads walked out.

That's when every Fleet Street pundit, politician and television commentator, all of whom could smoke when they felt like it, go to the bog for a read if they were bored, and phone home when it suited them, made the strike worse by shrieking and abusing the factory workers and hardening their attitude.

How many of those journalists and writers of letters to *The Times* had ever stood with aching feet and back, one eye on a clock which never moved, keeping sane only by means of the oasis of the tea break getting close, and the colour picture of the Page Three tits on the tool cupboard door? If Mrs Thatcher or Norman Tebbit or the Chairman of the CBI had ever had to do jobs like that they would have been more bolshie than Arthur Scargill.

At that time, manual workers were maligned daily in every media outlet, with their side of the dispute never getting a fair hearing. No wonder, as with any other beleaguered minority, they took revenge in being awkward.

At the cinema, films such as *I'm All Right Jack*, with Peter

Sellers, cruelly lampooned shop-floor trades unions in ways which went far beyond satire and into propaganda as bad as anything produced by Goebbels denigrating the Jews in Nazi Germany. The British class system of the Fifies and Sixties was at its most vicious towards unions and manual workers.

In the Fifties and Sixties, the Cold War wasn't just with Moscow, it was with the bosses too. Unemployment was negligible. Profits were high, and for the first time in their lives, the workers found themselves in a seller's market.

My first job in the north planer was milling 'horsemuck lumps' as they were called. Every piece of the tanks made for the Korean War had a nickname, such as handbags or waggon wheels, to save having to use long Ministry of Defence part numbers.

Horsemuck lumps were actually part of the hinge on the lid of the tank. It was very important that they were cut to a thousandth of an inch, the boss told me seriously, because when all the tanks were lined up for Field Marshal Montgomery to drive past taking the salute, the lids had to open and lean at exactly the same angle, or he would be furious and send them back to be done again.

No doubt this piece of nonsense had been decided by some Ministry of Defence bowler hat in Whitehall, irrespective of what it was costing the tax payer and the balance of payments. When Nye Bevan and Harold Wilson resigned from the Cabinet in 1951 to protest about defence expenditure getting preference over Health Service spending, they were perhaps unaware that it might have been due to me.

The rate for the horsemuck lumps had been agreed with the rate-fixer at fourpence ha'penny a pair. Agreements between rate-fixers and the men were hard-fought battles. Working out a price was like negotiating a Middle East Peace settlement. The lads would want the oldest and slowest man in the shop to be put on the job and timed, while the rate-fixer would insist on the youngest and fastest, until eventually both sides would spit on a handshake and do a deal.

At fourpence ha'penny a pair I might earn enough to buy a barrel-backed drape suit on hire purchase, with a pair of blue suede brothel-creeper shoes and a string tie, and look just like Frankie Laine, Frank Sinatra or Dean Martin.

The old josser on the next miller, tired of toil, tapped me on the shoulder and said, 'Take it easy, son. There's all day tomorrow not yet started on. You get nowt by rushing at your age, except bastard kids, so slow down. Otherwise there will be no overtime, and we will all be skint for Christmas.'

I was too sassy and too smart. An hour later it dawned on me that if I could put four in the machine together, instead of two, I could mill horsemuck lumps twice as fast and double the money. It might even add up to a week's holiday in Blackpool.

The gaffer and the rate-fixer came round and beamed. 'Well done, lad,' they said. 'You'll go far at this firm with ideas like that.' The next day, as a reward, they sent me a new workcard. This time the price was – guess what – fourpence ha'penny for four, not two!

What an own goal! To make it worse, I had let the lads down. I was mortified. I'd ignored the first defence of the workers united and the first commandment of all shop-floor bibles: 'Thou shall not help the bastards to do the grinding down'.

After that, promotion soon followed. Success came thick and fast. Chairman of the Sheffield AEU Junior Workers Committee one year. Strike leader of the apprentices the next. Then we linked up with the apprentices in Glasgow (including a lad who is now Lord Macdonald of Tradeston, Minister for Transport and former boss of Scottish TV), London, Newcastle, Bristol and big cities everywhere, to call an all-out strike for decent wages to end a cheap labour rip-off.

We won, too. And gained a fifty per cent pay rise.

While the Ministry of Defence were paying for full-page

newspaper adverts stating that an army officer career was excellent training for a managerial post in industry, three years as a shop steward would have taught a recruit how to avoid strikes for ever.

He would have learned all about the perks we enjoyed. No sick pay of course, but in 1950 one full week's paid holiday every year. No firm's pension, but there might be a chicken at Christmas for each pensioner from the social club, paid for out of our wages.

Not only did we get free gas to boil hot water for the tea, but later we got free hand cream to prevent dermatitis compensation payouts, and even a free cover for the cyanide bath (which hardened tools) after the cat fell in. It didn't matter about the fumes spoiling our sandwiches. It's just that the boss was more scared of the RSPCA than he was of the factory inspector.

In later years my very good friend Roy Hattersley could never understand my resentment as a teenager at having to pay tax towards his student grant at university, while I was freezing cold and wet in winter from the splashing coolants of the machines, and thinking how nice it would be to have a student's two-month holiday in summer and hitch-hike across Europe instead of spending the time in a glass-roofed, clattering, sweating machine shop.

I used to say to Roy, 'It's not your mam and dad who fuck you up, as your mate the poet Larkin used to tell you at Hull University – it's the Capitalist system.' That's because he was studying literature at Hull, while I was skiving off to the river caves as we called the bogs, for a ten-minute breather to read Keith Waterhouse in *Titbits*. At dinner-time it was forty-two minutes of *The Ragged Trousered Philanthropist*, Upton Sinclair's *Flivver King*, and *The Jungle*, Émile Zola's *Germinal*, or the *History of the Labour Party* by Sidney and Beatrice Webb.

It may have been that all bosses originally fixed wages at a level just high enough to pay the masses enough money on a Friday to ensure that they had to come back again on Monday, but it was amazing how many labourers whose education was absolutely nil could immediately work out how much nine and a half hours' overtime at six shillings and two pence an hour, plus one third, less a forty-two-minute meal break, all at an extra ten per cent minimum rate, with 7 per cent bonus, came to. They would have the answer in one minute using a piece of chalk, even faster if it was an each-way Derby Day bet on a Yankee accumulator with another four horses in three cross doubles.

We called each other 'brother' at the meetings, we had funny accents, we dressed in oily overalls, we learned our trade in huge factories as Hughie Scanlon did in Trafford Park, Manchester, or Jack Jones did on Merseyside, or in a Lancashire pit like Joe Gormley. Uncouth, ill-mannered, tactless, abrasive and hostile we may have been. But we were not daft, and the union's members knew it.

Yet in any oppressed group where a few have control over many, there is always the safety valve of sabotage, ridicule and the underdog's revenge. No wonder those old films where Norman Wisdom would put one over the Noël Coward top hat and his cigarette-holder lady, when they stepped out of the taxi and into the puddle, were immensely popular. Now we look at them on kids' TV and wonder what the hell we used to laugh at. The fact is, we laughed in revenge, like kids laughed at every *Beano* and *Dandy* comic where the rich got their come-uppance, and the crusty colonel in a bathchair with his gout-wrapped leg went arse over tip into a duckpond.

It was the same on the shop-floor.

If there was a separate lav for the foreman he had better take his trousers off when he used it, and hang them on the nail. Otherwise, a bucket of muddy water would come swooshing under the door round his ankles. Or a shovelful of snow would come over the top. That would teach him not to be too tight on the seven minutes' toilet time, or the forty-two-minute lunch break.

If the rate-fixer became too unreasonable with his prices, then a card from Blackpool to his house, signed 'Phyllis', saying how much she missed their dinner-time sessions on the canal bank, would guarantee at least a week's misery at home from his wife. Even worse, when he dug his fingers into a tin of brown soft soap to wash the oil off, he might not realise he was washing his hands in another soft brown substance until he noticed the smell instead of the lather.

The gaffers had a rule that anybody late the morning after a Bank Holiday would lose their holiday pay. We worked New Year's Day, which was only a holiday in Scotland then, so it was a desperate struggle having to clock in following the New Year's Eve booze-up. And a waste of time as the bosses realized many years later, because half the lads were hungover and working on dangerous machinery, to say nothing of feeling mutinous at having to stand waiting for a non-existent New Year's Day tram, breathing on their hands like Ivan Denisovich in Siberia.

We had a foreman there and the lads swore that Winston Churchill awarded him the MBE in the New Year Honours List for being the most rotten bastard in the country, in the same year as the Governor of Dartmoor Prison only got mentioned in despatches.

The underground resistance soon softened him up. The first time he tried to cut the prices, he found an old pair of false teeth at the bottom of the mug when he drank his pint of tea. The next time a dead mouse. As well as the bucket of water under the lav door, he would get a smoking rag over the top, while a mysterious hand reached across from the next cubicle and pulled the chain as he sat there. When he cut the lavatory time to five minutes (well, who could pick out a decent horse in five minutes?), the lads all took short at the same time and lined up outside the lavs in a long queue, with legs crossed.

We called it a bog-in, not a sit-in.

He finally asked for a transfer when his wife made a lovely steak and kidney pie to take to work for his dinner. He handed it to the old lad who made his tea, saying, 'Heat it up for me, Ernest.' Ernest did. He took it in earnest and ate the lot. With Yorkshire relish.

That gaffer was a lucky man. The week after, the lads were planning to fasten a live ferret inside his raincoat pocket. In fact I only once ever heard of a bunch of workers who failed to beat the boss at that time. It happened at Blackpool.

It was one disastrously wet June when the punters were staying away in droves, and a Blackpool rock manufacturer found he had enough already made to last until the illuminations. Without any remorse at all, he simply told the lasses making it they would all be sacked on Friday. Which made them a bit miffed so early in the season.

So to make matters even and to let him know what they thought of the firm's economic policy and budgetary forecasting, the women altered 'BLACKPOOL' to 'BOLLOCKS', and ran it through about 500 yards of rock. Funnily enough, when the boss didn't notice and it went on sale on the Golden Mile, the rock made a fortune. It was just what the wage slaves on holiday had been wanting to send back to their own boss for years. Alas, once again it was the working-class shop-floor designer who got nowt and the capitalist who got the profit. Even worse, the bosses have made a profit ever since. Now they roll 'UP YOURS' down the rock and it sells by the mile.

Which is why through horsemuck lumps and Blackpool rock, British industry began to die.

Three

US VERSUS THEM

Piecework, where you get paid on what you turn out, was a tough life on the shop-floor, but at the age of nineteen or twenty, lads can stay awake forever. I would regularly start work at six in the morning and go on until five, doing the overtime at dawn. On three nights a week, I'd make a perfunctory but compulsory appearance at night school to 'study' engineering and try to keep awake until half past eight, when miraculously the adrenaline and energy would reappear, to go dancing and pick up a 'bird' as we called young women then. At eleven o'clock, if the smooth talk had worked (all the smooth talk and long hours into the night were perfect training for a politician), we'd be catching the last tram to her street, and then, depending on how the spiel had gone, I had a long lonely trek home through a deserted city where taxis just didn't exist, to fall into bed by one o'clock and up again at five to catch the first tram to work. We played football on Saturdays, then literally slept round the clock on Sundays.

I had the best chat-up line of any young blood in Sheffield. The two dance halls in the city centre were at the Council-owned City Hall, and the Cutlers' Hall, which belonged to the employers and the Freemasons. As we waited for the tram I'd point up at the Town Hall clock and the statue of Vulcan and say, 'See that place there, love? Well, one day I am going to be Lord Mayor of this city. I'm going to ride in that Rolls Royce [which was probably the only one in Sheffield then because the steel barons were too mean to buy their own] and I'm going to take you round the town, to wave to all your friends as they come out of work.'

Most of the birds had been brought up on Hollywood films of bold, brash Al Jolson pointing down Broadway and saying, 'Honey, that's the Great White Way, it belongs to me and from now on it's all yours,' so they were quite used to daft lads making bragging promises. Although nobody was crackers enough to promise a Rolls Royce, or even a six-seater Armstrong Siddeley, unless they worked for the Co-op funeral depot.

Mind you, it was hard work for likely lads then. Every so often, one of them would come up to his mates in the pub and say, with a white face, 'Gordon's copped it,' as though he had disappeared into enemy territory, instead of a forced shotgun wedding. Although how Gordon had ever found a time and place to 'cop it' kept us wondering for weeks.

Teenagers didn't have cars then, even their dads didn't have cars. And cinema seats squeaked so loudly that usherettes would come chasing up the aisle with a shining torch checking whether raincoats were still buttoned up, or daringly folded across.

The only other courting places were entries. Sheffield had 40,000 slum houses and another 40,000 in endless streets of terraces. Most of these had an entry, or covered gennel into the backyards, between about every eight or ten houses. Some of these had their kitchen fire backing on to the entry wall. It warmed up the tunnel and the entries were in great demand by courting couples.

By about Tuesday none of us had any money for the pictures or pub, and no option but to walk the streets, or the canal bank, waiting for it to go dark, and the kids to be called in for bed. When young lovers finally found an entry which wasn't full up, they would have half an hour of stepping sideways to let the night shift get past to go to work, followed by another half-hour to let the afternoon shift come home.

All the birds I knew earned about £3.50 a week and had to make a new outfit last four years at least. It was one continual moan of 'Mind my best coat on these mucky bricks', and singing, 'Don't Step on My Blue Suede Shoes' out loud, to let the pub customers know there was somebody else in their urinal.

Entries were all pitch-black and if you didn't keep a fag going in the dark, and she didn't cough every thirty seconds, her dad would come out to see why everything had gone quiet. All mothers had ears like fox terriers and could sense a zip being lowered, through two brick walls and a front door. And if there were ever three uninterrupted minutes to get her breathing heavy, some daft dog with a cold dripping wet nose could be guaranteed to touch the back of her leg and spoil everything.

What with balancing the lighted fag behind the ear, holding her off the wall, whistling 'Blue Suede Shoes', reminding her to cough, and standing on one leg to kick the dog away, it was a miracle anybody ever got to a shotgun wedding. Funnily enough, about 80 per cent of these marriages survived, even though later on upwardly mobile eldest daughters were highly embarrassed at Mother's Silver Wedding when they realized their own birthday was a lot closer than nine months away.

Those families were very lucky. The real bonus of growing up in a working-class neighbourhood and living all your life in a three-mile radius, is that it contains 127 baby-sitting relatives, and 200 friends from an army of mates who served their time as plasterers, electricians, plumbers, car mechanics, bricklayers and other kindred trades as the unions call them, and who will come round tomorrow if the wife's Mini is coughing better, and do the job if you will buy a £40 pedigree pup.

Meanwhile, apart from making tanks, and being part of the barmy army on the shop-floor, the dreaded finger of conscription was pointing at me and all my mates too. At eighteen we were supposed to sign on for two years' national service ready for the next war, which Attlee and Churchill were convinced could start at any minute, this time against Joe Stalin, not Adolf Hitler. Apprentices like us, however, could choose not to join up until we were twenty-one and had finished our training.

With fingers crossed (which had never worked for pregnancies anyway and didn't work for wars either), the war might never happen because Joe Stalin and President Eisenhower might suddenly become pals and make friends with each other. They never did. Once again, working-class proletarians like us had to suffer in order to swell the coffers and profits of international capitalists and defeat the struggle of the Russian peasants. Well, at least that's what they used to tell us at all the weekend jazz concerts sponsored by the Communist Party, who would regularly lay on coaches to take shop-floor lads for free weekends in London to be brainwashed. We didn't mind. It was a seven-hour overnight journey on a dark bus, full of middle-class birds from Sheffield University, who were a bit dowdy but hospitable comrades, and it was a damn sight warmer than the entry. Once we got there we would go to the rally for about half an hour, then bunk off round Soho, or to watch the Arsenal, and then on to the world-famous Hammersmith Palais to bop to Joe Loss. The comrades would have fixed us up with lodgings for the night, often in surprisingly posh houses of intellectuals in Holland Park or Hampstead, who were entranced and amused at actually meeting real live young specimens of the oppressed Northern working class.

The sad thing then was that Old Grandad Maloney was at death's door. He had toiled and sweated working regular night shifts in front of a furnace full of ninety tons of molten steel until he was sixty-seven. He once showed me a wage packet he had saved, for £6 dated 1918, when nobody in the street had ever earned more than two quid. Yet he died penniless in a rented slum house with no hot water, inside lav or bathroom, about a hundred yards away from the one we lived in on Bodmin Street, and about fifty yards from the canal.

At least ours had full electricity. His had none in the bed-rooms, or the front room, where he lay with throat cancer for three long solitary years, dwindling down to a skeleton. The five-year-old National Health Service of the day simply cut a hole in the bottom of his neck to let the fluid dribble out, and left Grandma to change the dressings.

He couldn't eat, speak, sleep, read, listen to a radio (no electricity and no transistors yet invented). It taught aspiring young politicians like me more about the need for socialist medicine and a Health Service than any lectures from Hampstead professors.

At the age of sixteen I joined the Labour Party and knew I was going to be a Labour MP. The training for the real future was at the union meetings, the Labour Party wards, the shop-floor disputes and the combat of political warfare of 'Us' versus 'Them'.

It came out of the two world wars, and the working class should be eternally grateful to those public school officers and drill sergeants for the education they gave us. They taught us discipline. Taught us how to organize. How to march in step. How to parade and show bags of swank strutting along the streets behind a stirring brass band. How to show our strength in numbers waving to the crowds and shouting, 'Come and join us, brothers, we are in this fight for you.'

Until the First World War in 1914 the workers had been a ragtag and bobtail bunch of protesters, badly organized and easily scattered by working-class troops well trained to quell native riots in India, Africa and all points of the British Empire. Now the protests would be organized on military lines. The idle warriors quickly laid down the foundations of another army with the same regimental bonding and loyalty – the Labour Party and Trade Union Army. They had been taught how to picket. How to mount guard duty to stop lorries and blockade supplies. How to accept discipline in the field. And if that discipline was administered by leaders selected by ballot and not by birth it was readily acceptable.

For years the code of regiment had been drummed into them. All for one and one for all. United we stand, divided we fall. Just as the army punished malingerers, draft dodgers and deserters, so the unions' members fiercely ostracized or sent to Coventry scabs and traitors who broke rank by crossing picket lines.

Those who wanted to enjoy all the benefits of pay rises, holidays, shorter working weeks, pensions and better conditions, also had to pay the union subs and suffer the hardship or the strike battle to win ground. If they didn't, they were classed as the same cowards as those who refused to fight or ran from gunfire in the war. A white feather was not enough. There was no no man's land for blacklegs.

It was total war. A man was either on his mate's side or on the bosses'. Only rock-solid unity could create the mass ranks which would not buckle under shot and shell. Even the suffragettes had shown the men how to do it.

From now on the Attercliffes of this world had nothing to lose but their chains.

The Armistice was announced after November 1918, Labour Party branches were quickly formed right across Britain. Dozens and dozens of constituencies bought cheap second-hand army surplus barrack-rooms and assembled them on any spare land with the know-how of ex-sappers from the Royal Engineers, then put up a sign saying 'Labour Hall' and went into the political business of winning elections.

And still found time for a good laugh too.

Just after the First World War, a combination of steel barons, Conservative city fathers, Freemasons, charity benefactors, churches and the professional gentry from the western heights was still in control of Sheffield City Council. Every February, their big event of the year was the annual Master Cutlers' Feast in their own Cutlers' Hall. In the nineteen twenties this wasn't just a black-tie do, it was white tie and tails. So important that the Chancellor of the Exchequer, or at least a Cabinet minister like the President of the Board of Trade, would attend to make a speech to the nation. Their ladies, of course, were allowed to accompany them, but not to dine at the sumptuous banquet, merely to sit in the gallery and listen and delicately sip tea and nibble iced cakes.

The nobs with starched dickies and long gloves would roll up in posh carriages to alight at the pillars and front steps of the magnificent 300-year-old hall to be told how the poor were getting too much parish relief. Unfortunately, the entrance of the Cutlers' Hall was directly opposite the Sheffield Cathedral grave-yard. As the carriages halted, the unemployed ex-Fusiliers would hide in the dark behind the tombstones and set the ambush they had been well taught by their company sergeant majors. Only, instead of using hand grenades, they used real horsemuck lumps.

Horsemuck droppings do have a peculiar shape, rather like a flat, cobbled pyramid with rough sides and a shiny, polished curved top. Absolutely top-hole for lobbing, and better than any snowball because they splatter. In February, horsemuck was thick on the ground and too early to use for rhubarb, my Old Grandad Maloney told me, and lay three inches deep between the tramlines outside the Cutlers' Hall.

As the gentry alighted on the red carpet, the veterans of the York and Lancs would fire salvo after salvo to the command of 'Load! Aim! Fire!' And then sound the retreat and run down the surrounding alleyways, scattering in the dark.

It was no good the Keystone cops chasing them. The cobbles and tramlines were too slippery. Only the unemployed in their clog irons could remain standing.

The lads would then rendezvous under the railway Wicker Arches and march down the Attercliffe Road to Darnall Labour Hall. They swaggered in perfect step to the tune of 'It's a long way to Tipperary', but what they actually sang was,

It's a long way to the pawnshop,
It's a long way to go,
It's a long way to the pawnshop
Where my mother has to go.
Goodbye, shirt and weskit,
Farewell, watch and chain,
Oh, I'd better keep an eye on me trousers
Or they'll go again.

In the Labour Hall the women's section of the Barmy Army would have cooked a pea and pie supper with, for a treat, mint sauce on the mushy peas. To be eaten wearing gloves.

But the best demos and parades in later years were undoubtedly the Miners' Galas. On successive Saturdays in May, June and July, the big meetings were held in Durham, Doncaster or Barnsley, Mansfield, Cardiff, Wigan, Edinburgh, or anywhere else where coal was ripped out of nature's bowels.

The miners supped ale by the barrel. Rabbits, dogs, caged birds, retired pit ponies and beauty queen contestants (restricted to colliers' relatives) were all exhibited, often in the open air, whether it rained or not. Which was a shame for the old miners because their bit of pleasure looking at the bikinis on the catwalk was ruined if their specs got wet.

There were at least ten pit bands, a dozen juvenile bazooka marching teams, a score of floats, with the prize usually won by the best lampoon of a Tory Prime Minister or an unpopular wage-restricting Labour Chancellor, and before the IRA bomb scares, a Cabinet minister to lead the way through the cheering streets. All of which would get five seconds' coverage on the TV news because it gave a very good image of the workers and their organizations and because there had been no violence.

The bands played 'The Thin Red Line', 'Kenilworth', 'Slaidburn' and 'The National Emblem'. You would know all the tunes if only I could whistle the tiddly-om-pom-pom bits on paper. And anybody who saw the magnificent film *Brassed Off*, about pit closures and its effects on the men and women whose life revolved around their work, their mates and their music, will have misty eyes at the memories.

We wore red ties and red carnations, and those who had suffered a soaking on previous parades carried rolled-up red umbrellas to the huge marquee, where it all ended with a hymn. The miners would bellow out 'The Lord is my Shepherd' on a day when the pubs opened at ten, because anybody who worked down a pit never knew if it would be his turn next week to be buried alive in a coal grave. Although naturally at the end we would sing 'The Red Flag', just to keep things in proportion.

The big meetings were a spirit-enhancing experience which put faith and fire into bellies, and made the men and their women proud to be part of a huge, united workforce. Invariably, some famous trade union leader or TUC General Secretary had the great honour of addressing the packed marquee, the press and the TV cameras. Nothing of what he said would be reported unless he attacked the Labour leaders. The TUC's job was to make the Henry V Agincourt speech to rally the ranks.

Union leaders like Vic Feather and Norman Willis were experts. Vic liked boxing and would tell the story of how one night in New York at an international union conference the American unions took him to Madison Square Gardens to watch the Friday night fights, and he found himself sitting next to a Rabbi and a Catholic priest. They had been invited because the bout was a welterweight qualifier between a Jewish boy from the lower East Side and an Irish lad from Brooklyn who crossed himself and mumbled a few words.

So the Rabbi cheekily leaned over and said to the priest, 'What does that mean, Father?'

The priest looked back at him and said, 'If the kid can't fight, it don't mean a thing.'

So, lectured Vic, all the parades are wonderful. All the music and the banners and the flying colours are marvellous – but you've got to fight too, and fight to the last man and the last vote.

Norman Willis had his own parody of the Golden Rules. He reckoned it went back to the days of Long John Silver and the Pirates of the Spanish Main. Long John took the chest of doubloons and buried it on a lonely island at a spot which only he and his trusted rowing-boat crew knew. Then he promptly shot the diggers and pushed the dead men on to the chest as well. When the pirate chief rowed alone back to the ship, the crew mutinied and grabbed him by the throat to make him walk the plank. Long John calmly cried out, 'Remember the Golden Rules.'

'What are they, Long John?', the crew demanded.

'Them what's got the gold make the rules,' said John, 'and only I knows where it's buried.'

But it is only the crew who can drive the trains, dig the coal, switch on the lights, fill the food shops, man the hospitals and create the wealth of this great nation, said Norman, and we have as much right to make the rules as anybody. And the gold is buried in the ballot box.

We had. So we copied what the big companies did.

After the First World War the unions bought shares in the Labour Party. Just as the Stock Exchange was set up for investors to buy shares and receive dividends from companies, Beatrice and Sidney Webb, the Labour Party architects and rule-writers, allowed unions to pay a hard cash affiliation fee to register millions of their members as affiliated voters at the Labour Party Conference.

The big battalions controlled at least four million votes which could decide the policy of the Party when it was in opposition, and the manifesto which they would pay for and fight elections on. The unions even chose a very large number of the Party's MPs at Westminster.

Of course, newspaper proprietors screamed that this was undemocratic. They furiously complained that the 2 or 3 per cent of the membership who bothered to attend meetings in closed rooms should not have the power to decide these issues. Yet we never read a single editorial which complained that two or three directors of a company, or even a newspaper, employing thousands of workers, could make decisions affecting their wages, mortgages, job locations, kids' education, or anything else without once consulting them. Or that what the directors were doing was wrong in any way.

None of them ever complained about the closed shop of the Old Bailey lawyers where barristers compel clients to pay for an assistant at two-thirds of the barrister's hourly rate, often out of legal aid and taxpayers' money, or that this was overmanning in any way at all. None of the newspapers complained of the stranglehold that solicitors then had on the conveyancing of houses, which was an automatic percentage of rocketing house prices.

Pay rises for union leaders? How many savers with the massive building societies could manage to attend the annual general meetings held mid-week in London when directors would award themselves large sums of cash for turning up for one meeting, one afternoon, every month? Which newspapers screamed about the block vote then?

Was our Labour Conference where the unions had such huge votes worse than a Tory Party Conference where their members were not even allowed a vote at all? And were given nothing except the privilege of standing to sing 'Land of Hope and Glory' when the Tory leader deigned to turn up at the end of the week to tell them what their policy would be. Then to touch their forelock and shout hip, hip hooray, just like the survivors of the Bridge on the River Kwai did to their officers.

The simple fact is that the unions were superbly organized, financially sound and very well-run outfits, which in twenty years after the Second World War had brought immense benefits and protection for their members. Their tactics might not always have been convenient for the Government or the public, but they were undoubtedly doing the job they were set up for.

What the unions had going for them was Word of Mouth. No matter what newspapers or television say, no matter how much advertisers spend, nothing beats word of mouth. There is an old working-class saying – 'Always eat where it is full'. The best chip shop is always the one with the longest queue, because everybody passes on the recommendation. It needs no advertising. And the punters trust their neighbours, or family and friends, more than they trust newspaper press barons or advertisers.

Working-class people trusted each other and believed in the unions. To achieve the same sort of power which the bosses, the banks and the City of London had, the unions set up their own political fund with a voluntary penny per member, per week, levy to put their own kind in Parliament. They said, quite rightly, that Barnsley had every right to be represented by a member of the Miners' Union who knew about pit safety, pneumoconiosis, emphysema, the problems of paraplegics who would never walk again, and the true price of coal.

There is no substitute for the practical experience of knowing exactly what it feels like to come off night shift totally exhausted and try to sleep in a terraced bedroom on a street full of noisy kids. A nomination for a Parliamentary seat in a town like Barnsley was a job for life where the majority vote could be weighed instead of counted. The unions probably controlled 150 seats in the House of Commons and in similar workshop towns, no matter which party was in. Some were dominated by the railways, in others it was coal, steel, dock, textiles, shipyards, car factories – anywhere where massive numbers of working men and women lived to do a job.

Unions never did anything corrupt and were scrupulous about observing the law, but if there was a loophole, they were as astute in finding it as any highly paid barrister in the High Court. When secret ballots were held at branch meetings to elect officers or delegates to the Conference, there was no need to fiddle the ballot papers as was often alleged by the media.

I learned ballot tricks at the age of fifteen at the old AEU meetings every Friday night above the Co-op funeral parlour on Attercliffe Road. At the Attercliffe Branch a guy nicknamed Charlie Wag, who was uglier and bigger than Mike Tyson, would stand at the door to give out ballot papers to every member who walked through it, all of whom knew that Charlie was well to the left of Joe Stalin, Lenin and Trotsky put together.

As he gave them the paper, Charlie would whisper threateningly, 'The lads and stewards are supporting number one candidate,' whereupon every single member would promptly vote for number two. Which was just what the lads and stewards wanted them to do.

Crucial votes could be delayed by inane, boring arguments until the branch emptied as the pub closing time approached and the attendance dwindled. Then the real decisions would be quickly taken and voted through with only the diehards left.

Once, a lunch-time meeting was called to discuss strike action, and hundreds stood outside in the cold before realizing it was 1 April, All Fools' Day. Furiously, they went back to work. Then, when the real meeting was called the day after to take the strike decision, very few bothered to turn up.

For years the bosses and the Conservatives and the newspapers howled for postal ballots whereby the ballot papers had to be sent to the union members' home address, which would then allow the bosses to bombard the wives of the men with scare stories about how a strike or a pay rise would put their husbands out of a job.

It was strange, however, that Tory MPs still insisted that their own votes to elect them to Parliament had to be cast in a ballot box, just like the unions did. Twenty years later Norman Tebbit and Mrs Thatcher brought in legislation to force all unions to ballot their members whether or not they wanted to pay the voluntary penny a week political levy.

Every single union was compelled to take a postal vote and lo and behold, every single union ballot resulted in an 80 per cent victory to keep its union political funds. Even Conservative trade union members (and there were some) resented the Government telling them what to do.

No rules were broken, in exactly the same way that no rules are broken when Mrs Thatcher or John Major decided to hold a General Election vote at any time they chose, when they thought they would have the best chance of winning, whether Parliament liked it or not.

The simple fact is that British trade unions never did anything which they hadn't learned before from the army, big business, the Conservative Party, the bosses, the churches, and all the rest of the British establishment who made the Golden Rules.

What's more, we knew how to fight too.

In 1954, when I was twenty-one, it was back to grinding poverty again – this time thanks to the RAF who paid national servicemen exactly one-third of what a regular airman or soldier got, to 'persuade' us to sign on for extra years. The Ministry of Defence had moved on from press gang days when they simply kidnapped lads in Portsmouth to sail with Nelson and Captain Bligh, but at least the pressed men got the same share of the loot and treasure.

We got nowt in national service. And no union either. It was supposed to be £1.40 a week all found. The food was ten times worse than in any gaol I've visited as an MP (including Strangeways the day after the riots) and not much of it either.

There was no way I was signing on for extra years in any non-union place. There were some rewards, however. Nowadays I wear my medals (for being at Suez) on the Armistice Day parade, and it brings in a few old soldiers' votes. And if ever the unemployed shout, 'Do you fat cat politicians know what it's like to be out of work for two years?' I can shout back, 'Yes I do, mate. And it's even worse with a pack on your back and no home to go to.'

What I can never work out is why so many MPs of my age seemed to have dodged national service. Perhaps college taught them something we never learned. The whole two years were an absolute total waste of time. Poetic revenge by the gods in making me pay for all the horsemuck lumps, rows and defence spending fiddling on the shop-floor.

Two months before demob, on a weekend pass, I met a beautiful, eighteen-year-old, feisty five-foot three-inch blonde bird at the Cutlers' Hall and gave her the usual chat-up line on the way home. She didn't believe a word of it. She told me it was total rubbish.

Her name was Maggie Lee, but like my family, hers were also from Ireland. Her grandad, John Dempsey, had come over from Bandon near Cork and he too had quit the Church. Sheffield, at the turn of the century, was full of Irish families who had arrived to work in the booming steel and armaments factories and who didn't give a damn about their old religion. The Irish (all Ireland was part of the UK then) who still retained their faith seemed to settle in Lancashire around Liverpool, Manchester, Preston (Priest town), etc., and built cathedrals, but the rebels carried on moving over the Pennines to work in the pits and furnaces of Yorkshire. The Catholic Cathedral in Sheffield is a modest affair on a backstreet, and right throughout the rows about legalizing abortion in the Seventies, Lancashire MPs would be under severe pressure from their local parties and voters, yet it was never an issue on the east side of the Pennines.

Maggie's grandad was a handsome hell-raiser too. When he arrived, he got a job delivering coal with a horse and cart and was the best worker the firm had, except that every Friday at the end of the shift, he would get blind drunk. Then he'd stand up on the empty cart and drive the horses like Ben Hur clattering right

through the cobbled streets and tramlines of Sheffield. The bobbies would just throw him into the cells for the night, and tie the
horse and cart in the backyard to stop it from being pinched.

He caused uproar when, sore at not getting a tip from the
nuns, he delivered a load to the convent on Burngreave Road and
tipped it over with a loud crash. When he was admonished
because the Mother Superior was dying inside, and prayers were
being said for her, he shouted, 'The old bugger should have died
years ago after all the times she rapped my knuckles at school.'
And then refused to apologize. On another occasion, when a very
rich Church supporter only gave him tuppence as a tip for
carrying twenty bags through the snow and up the stairs, he
dropped the next load against the front door, and the family
couldn't get out of the house.

To get away from the fuss, he volunteered for Kitchener's
Army in the trenches of the First World War, even though he and
his wife had four kids still at home. The War Department sent a
telegram to him in the trenches when she died and told him he
had forty-eight hours' leave to come home, see to the funeral and
fix up for the four kids to stay with relatives. Otherwise they
would be herded into an orphanage.

Me and this other Irish firebrand have now been married
forty years, and we reckon we have fought more rounds than all
the professional boxers from heavyweight to flyweight in the
history of the world. She has gone on strike more days than all of
Arthur Scargill's miners put together. She claims that I only bother
to come home for an hour a week for Sunday lunch and some
clean shirts. But she doesn't mind, she says, because it soon
passes.

And where did she work then? Right next to the canal, in
the office of the Brightside and Carbrook Co-operative Society
coal depot, next to their dairy and coffin-making shop. We
would even meet up at dinner-time to walk on the canal bank
and then row about her dad or my mother. Her mother was a

paid-up member of the Labour Party, so we got on marvellously well together. A year later, on Christmas Eve, Maggie and me got married. It was so quick all my mates were convinced it was a shotgun wedding, but this time they were wrong. It wasn't a stylish marriage, because we couldn't afford a carriage. Knowing that my mates had to work Christmas Eve, we fixed the wedding for four o'clock, and forgot that it would be dark in the church. Nobody could read the hymn books, so the vicar sang the songs on his own, because he was the only one who knew the words. We couldn't afford a reception, so all the wedding photos were taken in the dark at the pub and looked like pictures of a wake.

We couldn't afford a caterer, so the family did it. Unfortunately we couldn't borrow a tea urn at Christmas either, so the boiled ham was washed down with Guinness. We couldn't afford a wedding car, so I asked a mate of mine to give me a lift (Maggie lived next door to the church) and his old banger broke down. It was me who was late for the wedding.

But for £4 we hired a little three-piece band who played for four hours non-stop, and then we had to carry all the old 'uns home drunk and literally legless. Some of them couldn't walk for a week, and spent the New Year in bed. It was better than any ceilidh I've ever been to. Then we went back to Maggie's mother's on Dover Street, Netherthorpe, to start life, as every young couple did, with the in-laws.

Ten months later, Maggie's mother's house was pulled down under the first Sheffield slum clearance programme. The Lees were transferred miles outside the city, so we moved into a tiny back bedroom of my Aunt Kathleen's, as you would know, on Beall Street, about a hundred yards from the canal. The bedroom was so small we had to walk over the bed to get to the other side. And a po was essential, because otherwise it was a trail through another bedroom which Aunt Kath's kids had, to go down the stairs and across the yard for a pee. And don't forget to put the old overcoat on as a dressing-gown and your shoes too because in winter you could pee your name in the snow or frost when the lav was frozen solid.

It was all part of the seed and the soil.

Four

WORD OF MOUTH

NATURALLY, Aunt Kathleen's didn't have a bathroom, like about 40,000 other houses in Sheffield. So one night, in the long, hot, stinking, sweaty summer of 1959, I was sitting on the kitchen steps of her house, washing my feet in a bowl of water boiled in a kettle, and trying to get a breath of fresh air, with the back door open. This haughty posh Edwardian guy comes on television for a party political broadcast. It was Prime Minister Harold Macmillan, pouring forth about how the British people had never had it so good.

Every MP knows the exact moment of truth when the incisive laser beam switched on and made him or her decide to go for broke. To devote their life and risk their job to put right the injustice, the unfairness, and the prejudice of poverty, apartheid, no votes for women, unemployment, bad housing and all the other tragedies of society.

Frank Cousins, leader of the mighty Transport and General Workers Union, told me it happened to him when he was a lorry driver and had stopped at a transport café near Newark. A young couple with a baby were pushing a broken pram, proud but not begging (nobody ever, ever, begged then). Frank offered them some chocolate, which they gratefully accepted, then they asked if he had any spare newspaper to fold up and use for the baby's nappy.

With me, it was sweaty feet and Harold Macmillan. No bathroom. No fridge. No house. No furniture. No hope. No phone. No TV, except my Aunt Kath's. Me and Maggie owned nothing.

By this time I was doing well as an engineer. I had a white-collar office job, working for the bosses on estimating planning and value analysis, and working out how to design rolling mills better and cheaper than the Germans and the Japs. It was at an international firm called Davy United in a brand-new, very posh office block, which wasn't even near the canal. We used all the latest technology and ideas, and it was one of the most modern and progressive (and strong trade union) firms in the country.

But at the age of twenty-five, it was home at night on my knees to pee in a po. And this arrogant, haughty Tory tells me I have never had it so good.

I had been a paid-up member of the Labour Party since I was sixteen and old enough to join. By sheer coincidence, the bloke on one of the other machines who taught me the job was a little guy called Jack Nuttall. He was also Secretary of the Attercliffe Labour Party, one of those wonderful old-timers who never wanted glory, who would never stand for the local council, but did all the dogsbody jobs collecting bobs and tanners and selling raffle tickets and Party newspapers and running the local branch of the Amalgamated Engineering Union as well.

The housing situation in the big cities was appalling. No new houses had been built for thirty years, practically all the new council houses and flats were being handed out to slum clearance, and young couples came nowhere. Many had been living for over ten years with their in-laws, even bringing up two or three kids there. Coronation Street cities were as grim, bleak and scruffy as anything in Poland or Russia.

The local Labour Party in Attercliffe was desperately short of new blood, so me and Maggie were made welcome, and were at least thirty years younger than anybody else in the headquarters.

Which was of course about 300 yards the other side of the canal (near where Sean Bean's Mum and Dad grew up) and called Darnall Labour Hall. Actually it was a very large wooden hut, designed as barracks in the First World War, bought as army surplus, and immortalized by the Home Guard of the *Dad's Army* TV series later. It had a platform at one end, a piano, a toilet key hung on a nail, a gas ring, oven and kitchen and a little office for Sid. Alderman Sid Dyson was one of Sheffield's giants. Literally. He stood six feet four inches tall, weighed at least twenty stone and looked like a good-humoured Charles Laughton playing Captain Bligh. Which he often did, if any of the Town Hall officials decided they were going to do things their own sweet way, instead of the Labour Party's.

Alderman Sid was a full-time paid agent who ran the Attercliffe party like a genial benign dictator. Most local political parties, even in the Tories, are always hard up and stony broke. Not Attercliffe. Sid ran bingo in the Labour Hall four nights a week, long before J. Arthur Rank and Odeon cinemas cottoned on to it. It not only paid his wages, but made the party rich too. He quickly fixed it for me to be made treasurer of the constituency party, because I was the only member in it who could use a slide-rule. Every Monday night, Sid would throw me a paper bag full of pound notes, sometimes even £100 (worth about £1,200 today), and tell me to bank it.

Sheffield magistrates (practically all recruited from teetotal Methodists) still kept an iron grip on boozing and dancing in a city full of fun-loving, highly paid working-class swingers. These City Fathers adamantly refused to allow night-clubs, or Sunday entertainment, or any other activity after eleven o'clock, because all God-fearing steelworkers were expected to be up by six next morning to clock in bright and early fit for work.

Sid foxed 'em. Although Christmas Day in Sheffield apart from the working men's clubs was usually as festive as a tomb, Sid found a loophole in the law which said there was no reason why dancing couldn't start one minute after midnight, which would actually be on Boxing Day, when dancing was allowed.

Nobody ever knew it was run by the puritan, fuddy-duddy Labour party, but the punters fought for tickets at 30p each and the cash poured in. Sometimes we'd make £500 profit (worth about £6,000 today). Local parties then were full of natural, fearless leaders and entrepreneurs, who if they had gone in for wealth and not politics would have become millionaires faster than Richard Branson.

Today, most of these Labour pioneers would be economics graduates and experts on balance sheets and business studies. Then, they were just street-wise.

In 1968 Harold Wilson's Government was doing disastrously badly at the polls and the Sheffield Labour party knew it would lose control for the first time since 1931, simply because all the seats were up for election due to boundary changes. Alderman Sid didn't hesitate to give free bus passes to every old age pensioner in Sheffield, a month before the election.

When the councillors asked him how Labour could pay for it, he said, 'We won't. The Tories will win and we'll let them find the money.' The Tories were then trapped because there would have been an uproar if they had taken it off. They had to put up the rates and make other cuts instead and Labour were back in power a year later. And held it for the next thirty years.

Even so, the party was strictly run. Nobody walked on to the Council unless they had passed three correspondence courses and sat exams from the National Council of Labour Colleges. Or attended evening classes at the Workers' Educational Association (who later employed a young Neil Kinnock as South Wales tutor).

An Attercliffe bloke called Ron Ironmonger, later Alderman Sir Ron Ironmonger, was the Leader of the Council. He took over from Dame Grace Tebbut, the first woman Council Leader any-where in Britain. Both of them were born on Chippingham Street, backing on to the canal.

Alderman Albert Smith was another elderly Attercliffe fire-brand. He had done time in Armley gaol, Leeds, for fighting a landlord's eviction squad who were turning a family out on to the winter street. Later, when Labour won the 1926 local elections to make Sheffield the first big city in Britain Labour-controlled, Albert won his seat by speaking in 500 different backyards, standing on 500 different dustbins, telling the poor and the unemployed what Labour would do for better housing and more jobs. Then he handed in his election expenses declaration as tuppence for a box of chalk for writing his own posters on the walls.

At the first Council meeting Labour swept the steel barons off the Aldermanic benches and made them publicly walk the plank, to almighty cheers and boos from the public gallery.

Sheffield was a flagship for Labour. It was 1945 before similar big cities like Birmingham got their first Labour majority.

The Party didn't give a damn what the local Conservative newspapers said. It prospered on word of mouth. It was the neighbourhood bush telegraph and the 'one for all – all for one' brotherhood of the huge factories and pits which brought in the automatic block vote stretching over nearly fifty years.

For most of his life, Ron Ironmonger worked on night shift at Metro Vickers doing the same sort of job as I had done as an apprentice. Then he would snatch six hours' sleep from 7.00 a.m. until 1.00 p.m., and go straight down to the Town Hall to sort out all the Council problems in about two hours flat.

What's more, it worked. Unlike today, when councillors spend countless hours discussing trivial nuts-and-bolt difficulties, and endlessly moaning about funding, resources and liaison committees, and producing non-stop reports and surveys, the Labour machines in the Town Halls of the cities ran like clockwork.

The Labour group of councillors met on Monday night for three hours and sorted out the policy with blood on the walls and even threats of fisticuffs. Don't start getting worried until they put their glasses on, one old-timer advised Roy Hattersley. On? Yeah, he said, that's so they don't hit the wrong bloke.

Once the policy was agreed, it was set in tablets of stone. Chief Officers were told what to do, no arguments, and lo and behold, it got done. Square miles of slums were cleared, and families enjoyed the magic of a bathroom for the first time. Bins were emptied. Kids were taught how to read and write. Crime was negligible. The buses ran on time. There were jobs all round and common sense ruled everywhere.

Nowadays, full-time councillors listen to every pie-in-the-sky scheme proposed by full-time officials (who will have moved on to another higher-ranking job, in another city, by the time the bill has to be paid) and vote for any daft grand scheme which they think will 'put the city on the map'.

At the age of twenty-seven, I became the youngest Sheffield councillor, taking over the mantle from my old mate Roy Hattersley. He became the Chairman of the Housing Management Committee the following year, and I was his Deputy Chairman.

Tory Governments and Tory councillors hated council tenants. They regarded them as a block vote for the Labour Party, and poured scorn and abuse on them in the time-honoured British class system.

Every single middle-class voter was totally convinced that council tenants all kept coal in their bath. They believed it implicitly. The very first council houses ever built actually had the bathroom by the side of the back door. It was next to the kitchen, to share the hot water supply system.

Because these new houses didn't have cellars, and only a very small coal bunker outside, colliers getting half a ton of free coal from the pit every month had nowhere else to stack it except up against the outside wall of the bathroom. Conservative councillors promptly spread the lie that all council tenants kept coal in the bath. It is amazing how many Tory newspapers actually believed it.

Housing then was the biggest social problem in Britain. Half the racial problems, exacerbated by Enoch Powell's 'rivers of blood' speech later on, were caused not by whites hating new black immigrants, but simply by the protest that here was one more new family arriving to swell the existing housing and hospital waiting lists, and put British working-class families further down the queue.

Roy Hattersley and I didn't hesitate to build huge blocks of flats. It was the only practical solution. We couldn't build houses with gardens because there was no spare land. If we had to clear existing slum houses crammed at seventy to the acre, the only way to put them all back with fresh air and bathrooms was to build upwards on the same amount of land.

Neighbouring local councils outside the cities refused to let the cities expand their boundaries and fought vigorously to keep their countryside for themselves. They didn't want ex-slum-dwellers devaluing their property. In any case, the slum city folk didn't want to live out there – steelworkers started at six and they didn't own cars. So how would they be able to get to work except by getting up at four-thirty to catch a long-distance bus?

Tower-block flats were very popular then. The heating and hot water costs were included in the rent. There was no snow to shift in winter and folk didn't have to break the ice in the outside khazi. The tenants could walk to work, shops were nearby, they still lived close by their mates and families, and the slum-dwellers had never had gardens, and didn't want one anyway.

What's more, Granny could take the kids to school and babysit. Whole streets were pulled down at the same time and rebuilt vertically to keep the neighbourhood together. For about ten years it worked, until the slum-dwellers died off and then there was nowhere for new tenants to put the car, and crime and vandalism spread everywhere.

For me and Roy Hattersley, and others who came later, like David Blunkett and Sheffield MPs such as Clive Betts, Bill Michie and Helen Jackson, Sheffield Labour Group was a better training ground for politics than Oxford and Cambridge put together.

It included characters such as Alderman Issy Lewis, Chairman of the Finance Committee, who took me under his wing (probably because I could understand statistics). Issy actually owned a cutlery factory which employed about a hundred workers, but like many Jews at that time, he was a staunch loyal socialist.

The Conservative Party then had hardly any Jewish MPs, simply because of their prejudice towards them. Jews were often blackballed when they applied to join golf clubs, the Freemasons and other middle-class organizations. There were at least ten or twenty times more Jewish MPs and members of the Labour Party than there were in the Conservatives.

I was Issy's bag-carrier and minder. If Sid Dyson and Ron Ironmonger were my mentors, then Issy was my tutor. He ran the multi-million-pound affairs of the big city with a quiet style, guile and chutzpah – or just plain cheek – plus a few Jewish proverbs going back to Moses.

Never forget the noble art of the tummler, my boy, he would say. The tummler is a decoy. A diversion. You create a distraction to pick their pockets. Where did most pockets ever get picked? When the pickpockets were hanged from the cart at Tyburn Hill. Just at the crucial moment when the body dropped and the crowd gasped, the hands of every pickpocket in the crowd would be dipping into their neighbour's pocket.

The tummler is a very useful political device. If Issy wanted to borrow a few more million for education and stick it on the rates, he would go into the meeting and first propose that the charges for the ladies' public lavatories be increased from one penny to one shilling. There would be instant fury and uproar. Issy would let it run for an hour, then withdraw the recommendation and smoothly get half a dozen other schemes passed on the nod.

I saw a Jewish Chancellor, Nigel Lawson, once do the same

thing. He made massive cuts in the social security payments to pensioners and the poor, rocketed gas and electricity charges, cut overseas aid, but craftily announced just beforehand that the pound note would be abolished and replaced by a brassy coin, which immediately became headline news! When I told him later it was a classic tummler, a clever three-card trick, and a Bismarck red herring, he laughed like a drain. There is nothing new at all about spin-doctoring and news management. Politicians have been practising it since the bread and circuses of Roman days.

It was Issy too who taught me that it is always better to employ a thief than a fool, especially if he robs you nicely. A thief will make a bit, take a bit, and leave a bit for you. A fool makes nothing. At that time there was a civic restaurant run by the Council which made a nice profit, until some clever accountant found out that the manager was claiming thirty-two wage pack-ets, while in actual fact there were only thirty cooks, waiters and bottle-washers working on the premises. The other two were totally fictitious. The Labour Group, despite Issy's pleadings, demanded instant dismissal for the fiddler, and that the manager be replaced by a new Executive Director in charge of Provisions and Catering Distribution. The following year the restaurant lost £10,000 and had to be closed, putting thirty people out of a job.

But the puritan creed of socialism survived. Capitalism was all very well in its place, but the profits must be used for the benefit of the proles.

Sheffield City Councillors argued for years that all funerals should be run by the Town Hall. The welfare state should extend from the cradle to the grave, they said, not just as far as the deathbed. The undertaking industry should be nationalized and taken into public ownership. And the Labour Party Conference would have done it too – but the Co-op wouldn't stand for it. They said if folk no longer had to pay their own fare to the cemetery, it would knock two bob off the Co-op annual divi and the Party would lose two million votes. The municipal crematorium is already losing thousands every year they said, so leave the remains to us. When the Co-op does an embalming, relatives come from miles away to say doesn't he look well. Of course there are always smart alecs who will say that's because he died of a heart attack when he found he'd got the Tote double-up in the club, but it's just not true. It's all down to Co-op technology. Folk do not get paupers' funerals from the Co-op, they said, with the hearse doing four coffins at once, and driving at sixty miles an hour to get done before knocking off time, so leave well alone.

The councils do it in France, the Sheffield Labour Group declared, and in Moscow too, they yelled. Council tenants there can even have the free loan of a council hearse and do it themselves. In Scotland they can even bury the old dears in the back garden, providing the neighbours don't object and it doesn't interfere with the drains.

It was then seriously suggested – and this is all true – that the Sheffield crematorium could recoup its losses by charging by weight and having a tonnage scale. The heavy ones took a lot more lifting and fuel to dispose of, so, it would be a good socialist principle to make the fat cats pay more, and the starving thin elderly poor pay less. What's more, there should be open days to let folks come round to see what happens and to prove that it is just not true that any gold teeth are pulled out by the attendants. They do not get salvage money like the bin men do. The proposal was only defeated when it was pointed out that the chapel of rest could not hold the crowds of visiting spectators.

The advantage back in the Sixties was that Labour councils adamantly refused to allow the press into council committee meetings. Which meant that any daft idea could be discussed and rejected without ridicule in the papers. Labour councils, all faced with ferociously hostile Conservative-supporting local and national newspapers, knew exactly what they were doing.

Years later, when Mrs Thatcher's Government legislated to compel councils to let the press in, any silly suggestion that binliners should be changed from black to green in the interests of racial harmony would be plastered over every newspaper and television programme to damage Labour. The good work which all councils did was never even recorded, never mind praised.

There was one perk on the Council in the Sixties, though. Some of us got to read the dirty books before anybody else, so that we could decide whether or not to ban them.

One of the local Attercliffe councillors, who was called Alf, was actually on the Library Committee which had this plum job. Those books in the library which were a bit risqué were put on the shelves as wooden blocks with just the title on the spine. To actually see the copy, fearless young lads, or shy maiden aunts, had to take the block up to the old dragon (specially chosen for the job) on the desk and ask for it to be brought out from under the counter. It was the equivalent of going into the local chemist and asking for a packet of Durex, knowing that the woman serving there was a second cousin to your mother.

In the summer of 1963, when the poet Larkin said sexual intercourse was actually invented (he was wrong), Christine Keeler was having it away with Tory Cabinet ministers and Russian officers, and sex became big news. It was then that some enterprising publisher decided it was time to reprint *Fanny Hill*, the 'memoirs of a woman of pleasure', an upper-class pornographic masterpiece in its original form.

Naturally the Library Committee (chaired by Roy Hattersley's mother Enid) had serious doubts that young councillors like Roy and me should be allowed to read such filth. So only councillors on the committee were loaned a copy for two weeks, with strict instructions that such inflammatory material, which might send young men wild and rampaging through the streets, must be kept safely under lock and key.

My mate Alf had a copy, but he couldn't read it because it made him badly. He had a dicky heart and the book made him tremble and sweat all over. And he daren't let his missus see it.

So he kept it inside a stiff-back copy of Dickens' *Hard Times* with the inside pages cut out, and he let me borrow it for two weeks.

Well, he had to, because by this time I was the only bloke in Attercliffe Labour party who was running an old banger, and I told him if he didn't, then he would be waiting for the Town Hall tram home in future.

I took the book to work and the lads and shop stewards reckoned that by using a strict bog shift rota, all thirty-seven of us could get through it by Alf's next meeting. Especially if we let the gaffer have a turn too. He had always played hell about me having time off work (one afternoon a week for Council business), but after that he was much more affable.

Having a copy of *Fanny Hill* in your possession then was the equivalent of carrying a kilo of cocaine today. So, after we had all carefully read it, the lads at work agreed on a democratic vote that it wasn't fit material to put in the library, because it might make old folks badly, just like it did to Alf.

Roy Hattersley and I sat next to each other at the Council meetings at desks which had lift-up lids, just as schoolkids do, and I swear he spent the whole of one Council meeting with his desk lid half open, finishing it off just before the deadline, terrified that his mother might see him.

Eventually all the copies of *Fanny Hill* were ceremoniously burned on the Cleansing Department's refuse tip, with pictures in the local paper warning the public how such trash could damage the health of the voters and make young lads go blind.

Funnily enough, ten years later the film was in the cinemas in full glorious colour, whipping scenes as well. Not that I went to see it. Well-known politicians have to be very careful with things like that. In no time at all, the voters are going to nudge-nudge-wink and mutter that the dirty devils ought to be locked up. We were there to protect the public from antique upper-class porn, not to enjoy it.

Five

IF THE KID CAN'T FIGHT,
IT DON'T MEAN A THING

POLITICS, like sport, show biz, the media, or any other limelight job which brings glory, fame and usually very small fortune, is a razor-sharp profession, where the competition is ruthless, often unfair, and totally unsympathetic to the losers.

The first commandment is that there is no such thing as gratitude, either from the crowd or the critics – and from very few colleagues either. Every single member of the Party would love to be an MP, plus about twenty million voters too.

Few know how to do it. Or even how to find the path to make a start. The odds on getting to be an MP are higher, much higher, than getting to play for England at any sport. Just work out how many international footballers there have been from any big city in the last thirty years, and how few MPs.

Most folks think it is like winning the Lottery. Some magic finger points and a laser beam lights up. It does not. Winning a seat, or even harder, a nomination for one, is a career strategy, business game plan, all-to-lose marathon, with usually nothing at the end to show for twenty years' hard work and dedication to the Party.

Occasionally, very, very occasionally, a world-class lawyer or financial expert will be steered into a safe seat and the word put out that the Prime Minister would be grateful if, etc., but not even he can deliver one on a plate. Local party workers have only one real power, which is to choose the man or woman they want to represent them.

In the Sixties, rank-and-file Labour Party members regularly put two fingers up to the advice from London, and as only a select band of members, usually about 80 to 100, had a vote on the management committee, any candidate who could persuade half of them plus one to support him, was home and dry in Westminster. It was not until 1993 that the Party introduced one member one vote to choose MPs, and before that, wheeling-dealing, arm-twisting, promising, threatening and even paying for votes was rife.

Aspiring, budding wannabes, like I was, learned the route of the path at an early age. Working-class safe Labour constituencies invariably preferred a candidate with the same sort of accent they had, from the same sort of background and lifestyle. Somebody they and their wives could easily communicate with, and who could tell them, in simple words, what was happening down in Westminster and why they couldn't have what they wanted.

This wasn't exactly what the Party leaders or any Prime Minister wanted. He wanted graduates who could absorb the legalities of legislation, take on the civil servants, and argue the case in public, without the ranting and raving of a soundbite, soap-box rabble-rouser.

So, the Labour Party in Parliament consisted of about 250 MPs representing the horny-handed sons and daughters of toil who provided the foot soldiers and infantry, and about fifty others, usually Oxford and Cambridge graduates (polytechnics had only just started in 1968) to provide the brains of the officers' mess and usually lead the troops into election slaughters, because they had no idea what policies would be acceptable to pit-face workers and po-carriers.

MPs were much older then. Many of the unions rewarded their elderly leaders with a seat in Parliament (especially if a younger plotter wanted their well-paid union job). And as MPs' pensions didn't exist until 1964, most of the old union lags stayed in their Parliamentary seats until they died coughing their lungs up from Woodbines and coal dust.

There were far more by-elections, too, than the lean, diet-conscious MPs provide now – at least seven or eight a year. Sometimes it was easier to get a nomination for a by-election than a General Election. So every wannabe studied *Whitaker's Almanack* assiduously. This massive annual not only gave the majority in every constituency, but also the age of the MP. Some aspiring young candidates actually went to live in a seat held by an ancient stalwart, to join the local party and gather support for a couple of years, before the MP retired or turned up his toes. At least one future Labour Party leader had actually done that.

Others networked. And the best network was a union. Some unions, like the Miners, or Dockers, or Railwaymen or engineers, could swamp a constituency where they had hundreds of members. Union branches could nominate their champion, turn up on the day, and the other candidates might just as well not bother. It would be a one-horse race. The Trade Union Group in Parliament dwarfed any similar group based on religion, teachers, lawyers, military service or even farmers. Its chairman, George Brown, could pick up a phone and be put through to the Prime Minister at any time. The unions networked right across the country fifty years before today's mobile phone-carrying, computer-operating, pager-monitoring Millbank Labour Party acolytes introduced theirs. The unions even set up and paid for their own Ruskin College at Oxford University to train future politicians such as Dennis Skinner and John Prescott to become future leaders. Not me. I never applied or went. I'd had enough of school at fifteen. Some unions even owned grand country houses and convalescent homes where they would hold seminars and training weeks for aspiring MPs and union leaders.

Unions could offer 80 per cent of the cost of a General Election campaign to a constituency party. They could pay for a full-time agent, an office with equipment, and an organized army of helpers and supportive Party members. But like all those who pay pipers, they reserved the right to call the tune.

It was the sort of networking which infuriated London intellectuals and the university graduates in the Party, who thought that only those with a degree in government had the education and necessary qualifications to run the country. These would-be politicians were regular contributors to the *New Statesman*, *Tribune* and *Guardian*, who would be happy to do the Labour Party a favour by representing it in Parliament, if only the workers would stand aside to give them their chance.

Some of them had the biggest culture shock of their life when they came North seeking a solid safe seat with an impregnable majority and ended up with about ten per cent of the selection conference vote on a secret ballot.

Other smaller unions were not heavily represented in any one area, but had small branches spread across every part of the country. These couldn't command huge blocks of votes, but they could guarantee a nomination.

Consequently, the unions held the key to 250 safe seats in Parliament. Competition to get on the unions' 'panel' of candidates was very, very keen. Rigorous interviews were held in London, some unions even took prospective candidates away to a conference centre (many unions even owned one), for a week's grilling, training, written examinations, public speaking practice, etc., before choosing the lucky half-dozen or dozen classed as 'officer material'.

Some unions hated and loathed each other, and would cheerfully 'nobble' a favourite runner for a seat. All of them traded votes in secret meetings, on the understanding that if our man goes out, then we will switch to yours – and vice versa. It even went on at Party Conference elections until Tony Blair became Prime Minister and brought in a new voting system.

To make the situation even more tricky, a lot of the candidates were liars and their promises were worthless. Consequently, for union candidates it was usually a case of 'have speech will travel'. Up and down the country every weekend to perform at the schools the unions ran to educate their activists (usually at a quite nice seaside hotel with a good sing-song and booze-up afterwards, wives too, if they wanted to come) to get known and make acquaintances and future contacts, especially if the sitting MP looked as if he was coughing better.

Panel members had better attend every rally, march, demo, protest, sit-in or branch and regional meeting, three or four nights a week, or they would soon be thrown off it and replaced by another candidate. Considering the hours they put in, usually in freezing upstairs pub rooms, the time spent in travelling, and the studying of complicated legislation, it might have been simpler to get a doctorate in brain surgery with a guaranteed good job at the end of five years' hard work.

Most civilized, educated, normal folk tremble at the thought of having to get up and spout, cajole, educate and argue in front of a tough audience. There is no better way to learn how to control shaky knees, dry mouth, loss of memory and nervous horror than by practising it for years at union meetings. Every union leader I knew, from Arthur Scargill to Frank Cousins to George Brown, was a master orator. So too were Hitler, Mussolini and Castro. None of them read their speeches, like Kennedy or Clinton. Most of what they said read like gibberish afterwards, but they could weave a magic spell and convince an army to fight.

Meanwhile, in 1968, the Labour Government was having a terrible time.

Elected in March 1966 with a massive majority of ninety-nine, the Oxford dons led by Harold Wilson, Roy Jenkins, Dick Crossman, Barbara Castle, Peter Shore, etc., etc., had handed out money like drunken teenagers, fulfilling every promise made to the Labour Party Conferences that pensioners and poor, and teachers, Health Service and local councils, etc., would all get jam today to be paid for tomorrow. The only problem was that the Tories had left the kitty empty, and the Labour Government hadn't got any money to pay for the handouts.

Inside eighteen months, Chancellor Jim Callaghan was in deep trouble and had to go cap in hand, with the begging bowl, to the world's banks, who forced him to devalue the pound.

The political roof fell in. Wages were frozen. No more pay rises. Council rents rocketed, sometimes even doubled, public spending was slashed everywhere. The lucky few who could afford a holiday abroad then (probably in a caravan in Spain or France) were restricted to £50 each of foreign currency stamped on their passport.

Immigration was blamed for most of Britain's inner-city problems and in 1967 Enoch Powell became the most popular politician in Britain when he made his racist 'rivers of blood' speech in Wolverhampton and said, 'As I look ahead, I am filled with foreboding. Like the Roman I seem to see the River Tiber foaming with much blood.' He was also alleged to have made some highly inflammatory remarks about 'excreta pushed through letterboxes'. Even though Ted Heath instantly sacked him from the Tory Shadow Cabinet, London dockers, who had a history of supporting Oswald Mosley, the Fascist leader, marched on Whitehall in support of Powell. Practically every single one of them was a traditional Labour voter. The most popular TV programme in Britain then was about a racist docker from Wapping called Alf Garnett, a sit-com full of jokes about niggers, coons, sambos, sunshines and darlin' Harold Wilson, yet with the deepest respect for the Union Jack and Her Royal Majesty, The Queen.

That year Bobby Kennedy and Martin Luther King, the American Civil rights leader, had been assassinated in America. Race riots took place involving British MPs at the Democratic convention in Chicago, and racial tension was a very serious problem in British cities. The Labour Government came out strongly in favour of racial equality and went on to introduce a Race Relations Act making racial harassment a criminal offence.

No wonder, then, that the Labour Government's standing in the opinion polls was the lowest on record. It was 27 per cent behind the Tories.

Earlier that year, 1968, Labour lost every council seat in Birmingham. In the slums of the Liverpool dockers, the Conservatives had a majority of fifty seats on the local council. In Leeds, it was sixty-three. In Manchester, thirty. Labour lost Islington and Lambeth in a landslide. In London, Labour councillors were almost obliterated.

Labour even lost Sheffield for the first time in forty-one years, although there was some small excuse in that boundary changes meant every councillor had to stand for election, instead of the usual one-third. It was very nearly a total local government wipeout for Labour. As regularly happens, the voters took revenge on the Westminster generals by slaughtering the poor bloody infantry in the Town Halls.

It was a personal tragedy for me too. By that time, I was Chief Whip on the Labour Council. A faithful, loyal, zealous lieutenant of Sid, Issy and Ron, my job was to whip the mutinous rebels in to vote to double the council house rents, which hit not only their own pockets hard because they too lived in council houses, but also the pockets of everybody on the huge council estates they represented. In those days, all councillors went to work at normal jobs for three days and two half-days a week, and took terrible daily abuse about the local bus service or rents. It was democracy at its best, but also at face to face, when it is most cruel.

For some time I had been 'nursing' the seat of the sixty-six-year-old John Hynd, MP for Attercliffe, where I lived. He was a typical Labour MP of those years. Totally anonymous in Parliament. His name never appeared in the papers, either locally or nationally, on any subject, and apart from his monthly Sunday morning visits for his surgery or advice bureau, he would turn up once a year to make a speech – usually in September on his way to the Party Conference. He never indicated when he was going to retire, but his union rule-book (the Railwaymen) said he would get no more financial assistance after sixty-five, or for the next election.

As often happens, the fickle finger of fate took a hand. Three opportunities came all at once. The neighbouring seat to Attercliffe, Brightside, came vacant when Dick Winterbottom, a much loved Co-op MP, died after a long illness. Normally a young thirty-four-year-old local bloke like me, Chief Whip on a big city council, would have been a front runner. Maybe even the favourite. Instead, when it came to the shortlisting, I was nobbled. Never even got to the starting line. The councillors and Party members in Brightside, who bitterly opposed the rent rises, took their revenge, even though Issy Lewis and I had no option but to impose the increases. Not even a good tummler can work if the books have to balance.

Zealous lieutenants who carry out officers' orders get shot down, whether it is the Charge of the Light Brigade, or a gaol sentence for loyally carrying out the commands and secrets of the Mafia Godfather, for the sole reward of a pat on the back. Yet the generals usually survive.

As it happened, the Sheffield union branches did such a good job at knocking out each other's champions that Brightside finished up with a Welsh white-collar steelworks clerk, Eddie Griffiths, who loved sanctimonious psalm-singing as much as he loved booze and free-loading, and who, after being kicked out of the Brightside seat some years later, finished up supporting Mrs Thatcher. Griffiths narrowly beat John Horam, who eventually went on to become a Labour MP in Gateshead, then years later actually joined the Conservative Party and became a Tory MP in Parliament, and still is.

It was many, many years later that the vindictive, bitter, often sour union delegates realized that it was much better for everybody if they simply let the best man win, and Brightside chose the first local MP and Cabinet minister to hold a city seat, a blind man called David Blunkett, who was Leader of the Council and has made a magnificent Secretary of State for Education in the face of unbelievable odds. For any person to hold that job is a major, major achievement, but for a blind man who has to concentrate on listening to every word of every news broadcast, and has to take it all in through his ears, and remember the details, it is incredible.

To make matters even worse, on the day the Brightside party was shortlisting, my union, the small Draughtsmen's and Allied Technicians' Association, had sent me to Oldham, where the sitting MP had died. I was in competition with Michael Meacher, John Roper, later MP for Farnsworth, and a few others, but I knew that Labour would never hold Oldham in a by-election (it didn't and Michael Meacher lost it, but held the seat in 1970), whereas Attercliffe and Brightside were much better plums. So I told a few jokes and came third. Only to phone home and find I'd been nobbled.

That's politics. The bird in the hand is often no better than a bird in the bush. To make it even worse, after the Conservatives had won Sheffield, they took control, turned us out, and the other Labour councillors promptly sacked me from the Chief Whip's job. I was going nowhere. Four years earlier, when Roy Hattersley had decided to look elsewhere than Sheffield for a seat, and become an MP for Sparkbrook, Birmingham, he was a wise man.

The brutal fact is that the old saying 'No man is a hero in his own town' is absolutely true. Everybody at school remembers the scruffy, snotty-nosed kid who was certainly no better at anything than they were, so why should he become an MP and not them? But while there is death there is hope, as every politician knows. Just fifteen miles east of Sheffield, another constituency called

Bassetlaw was holding two minutes' silence at the news that their MP, the Rt Hon. Captain Fred Bellenger, aged seventy-three, had died suddenly in his bath.

Captain Fred had been the MP for Bassetlaw for the past thirty-two years, and my union mate George Keenan, from the pit village of Langold, knew everybody in the local parties. George would have stood himself, if he hadn't been a bit too young and knew that he too would get nobbled by the miners' unions, but he reckoned I might do it. To hell with the bird in hand in Attercliffe, I thought, there were foxes to be shot in Bassetlaw.

There were just a few problems. Bassetlaw covers the whole of North Nottinghamshire. It was then an incredible 300 square miles in area, containing thirty-eight parish councils and over forty odd towns and villages. It looked solid Tory to me, with five different District, Urban and County Councils, fox-hunting and landed gentry, five different dukes and ancient coal owners owning most of the rolling shire. What the hell did it want with a city boy from the slums and backstreets like me? The Rt Hon. Captain Fred, a former Labour Cabinet minister, always absent, might not upset the local gentry too much . . . but me?

It was natural Tory territory. 'That's what everybody thinks,' said streetwise young George. 'Six thousand miners work under these sods of earth, plus the votes of their families, and live in a concentrated mile-wide stretch of the county. There are no slums. No tower-blocks. No ethnic votes, not many council houses. Most of the rented houses belong to the pits. It's good rural farmworker votes too. And more important, the miners are split down the middle between the Yorkshire Union and the Notts. They hate each other. They will both put up a candidate and the Yorkshire bunch will nobble the Notts. They always do. And you, a union lad with the same accent, having offended nobody, could slip through the middle.' Young George was a natural politician.

There was another ingredient too, one which I have never heard a TV expert on elections ever try to measure in his forecasts. Called 'volatility', it's a measure of whether the voters are set in their ways and will vote for the Party through storm or flood, and stick by it faithfully no matter what happens.

Northern Ireland is like that. So too are the Highlands of Scotland. Sometimes it is religions which provide the glue, sometimes generations of history.

Rural areas then were not the commuter dormitories they often became later. They were stable and reliable. Bassetlaw had a history of dissent. For centuries, local people in Bassetlaw had put two fingers up and shouted 'BUM!' to their bosses and local squires. The founder of the Methodists, John Wesley, came from Epworth, just north of the seat. The Pilgrim Fathers didn't originate in Plymouth, as everybody thinks. Their leaders, William Brewster and William Bradford, came from Scrooby and Babworth in Bassetlaw. As for the mythical Robin Hood, his Sherwood Forest was just down the road. Add to that several thousand Geordie and Scots and Welsh miners who had moved there to work in the modern pits in the Fifties and Sixties, and it was enough to outvote the rural landed gentry and their faithful followers.

It was a classic 'Us Versus Them' society, with no room in the middle for anybody else. The Liberals didn't even bother to stand. And never yet, even thirty years later, have the Liberals won a seat from Labour in Bassetlaw, and only one or two from the Conservatives.

The split between the two miners' unions (which was to have another disastrous repercussion sixteen years later in the miners' strike) was bitter and historical. In 1926, the year of the General Strike, the Notts Miners had formed a breakaway union, led by a Labour MP from Nottingham called George Spencer, and gone back to work, while the Yorkshire miners stayed out and starved for a year on strike. The Yorkshire miners regarded it as an act of the grossest treachery and had never forgiven them.

My mate, George Keenan, was absolutely right in his forecast. The Yorkshire miners nobbled the Notts miners' nominee, just as I had been nobbled in Brightside and just as all contenders for a throne have been nobbled since the days of Richard III. But rural or not, the working-class people there were my kind of people, bonny battlers who bowed the knee to no man.

Bassetlaw is where the three counties and coalfields of Yorkshire, Nottinghamshire and Derbyshire meet. And the old advice was that Yorkshire men shout, Nottinghamshire men sulk, and they are both as stubborn as mules. As for Derbyshire, they were noted for being strong in the arm and strong in the head. Just ask Dennis Skinner, who became the MP for Bolsover, next door, eighteen months later.

Whoever said stubborn should have added cocky, brash and over-confident, as I had been in Brightside and the miners in the Labour Party were at Bassetlaw. In most mining seats, the local colliers simply turned up and voted for their man, and it didn't matter who the other candidates were.

Every single other candidate was an automatic also-ran before they opened their mouth. Just a few years previously, in 1959, in nearby North-East Derbyshire, the mighty General Secretary of the Labour Party, Morgan Phillips, had been put forward for the seat by Hugh Gaitskell, Leader of the Labour Party.

On the Sunday chosen for the selection, Tom Swain, the Derbyshire miners' nominee, simply rolled up with a busload of miners who had been paid seven and sixpence (which would buy five pints) to the Miners' Welfare where the selection was held. The bus was an hour early and it didn't matter what the candidates said later on, because most of the lads slept right through every speech, as hard-working men always do on Sunday afternoon, then put their cross on the ballot paper for Tom.

Some of them were not even members of the Labour Party although they might have been one-time comrades of Stalin. Tom wasn't breaking the rules at the time. The union had paid its dues and was entitled to send the delegates.

One hundred and fourteen applicants, many of them highly experienced, offered themselves for the Bassetlaw seat. Fourteen actually got a nomination from a local party branch or their trade union. A shortlist of five, including me, was chosen by the local party executive (which of course included my mate George Keenan). All of which simply confirms emphatically that in all walks of life it is who you know, rather than what you know, which leads to the paths of glory.

The Yorkshire miners on the executive carried out their orders and dutifully nobbled the Notts miner Herbert Robinson, from Harworth, immediately, and put in their front runner, Jim Marsden from Darfield Colliery. The other candidates strongly recommended by the Labour Government leaders in London were Geoffrey Robinson, later to become MP for Coventry and the Paymaster General in Tony Blair's Government, and also a Director of Coventry City Premier League football club (just like I became a director of Sheffield Wednesday). At that time, at the age of thirty-two, he was the managing director of Jaguar and a star of Harold Wilson's white-hot heat of technology, which Harold had promised would make Britain rich.

Other runners were John Harris, the Chancellor Roy Jenkins' right-hand man, who later became his Chef de Cabinet at the EEC and then Lord Harris, boss of the Probation Service, plus another bright young man from the regional office.

Bassetlaw Labour party had had to put up with their absentee MP Fred Bellenger for thirty-two years. He lived in Arundel in Sussex and visited Bassetlaw twice a year, once for the AGM and once for the annual dinner. Nobody ever encouraged him to visit more often. So the party wasn't in any rush to make the mistake of choosing another absentee who might be more concerned with his career and Westminster job than he would be with them. Especially as Labour were being annihilated in every local election and by-election the length and width of Britain. In the General Election in 1966 Bassetlaw had a comfortable 10,000 majority in a Labour landslide. In 1968, however, it meant nothing.

At Dudley, in May, the sitting MP had died and Labour there had a 10,000 majority. In the subsequent by-election the Tories not only overturned it, they converted it into a Tory majority of 10,000. Nationally the Tory lead of 27 per cent in the opinion polls was meltdown time for Labour. But ambition springs hope in all politicians.

In the six-month run-up to the by-election George and I went through the list of delegates like a race card. Women in politics were getting more and more important and there had been a tremendous row in the papers because some local Conservative parties, looking for a future MP, had also insisted on interviewing prospective candidates' wives, just as many companies had always done when choosing a new executive. There was uproar from feminists when it was suggested that Labour might do the same.

George and I took no notice. Maggie, my missus, went everywhere with me. She has always been able to bring in more votes than I ever could, and is an expert at remembering grand-kids' names, who has been poorly, who is getting better, and that absolutely essential understanding of people's problems and fears, which brings in trust and respect for the candidate, which hot-headed tub-thumpers never learn, and which the Tony Blairs and Bill Clintons are born with.

We worked out that the miners had only 48 per cent of the votes but we expected their wives would add to that and take them over the top. So for nearly six months, we were networking. Nobody, but nobody, who was working-class in Bassetlaw owned a phone then. It was all legwork. We would often keep my car hidden too, because hardly anybody had one of those. They walked to work at the pit, or rode a pushbike to the farm or factory.

The advantages we had were that nobody wanted another Captain Fred Bellenger, who had actually been a Cabinet minister at the War Office but got the sack for cocking up the Japanese prisoners' of war compensation and pensions, which the poor old lads are still fighting for today. But the members certainly wanted a working-class trade unionist who could understand and feel for their problems because he had gone through them too, and they weren't too happy about the miners nobbling the race and stitching it up to force a miner on to them. Any selection conference is like an audition for a part in a top West End show. Those sitting in the stalls usually know a great deal about the performers. Nobblers know how to ask stiletto questions about which school the applicant went to (which in many cases reveals their religion). That then prompts a question on abortion one way or the other. Which way would he vote on nuclear weapons?, etc., etc. All carefully researched and asked to lower his chances of beating a left-winger, or right-winger, and alienate any floating voters.

Five candidates get half an hour each to make a speech and answer questions. That's a long time. By the end of it, when the vote comes, most of the audience have forgotten what the first one said two hours ago. There's a draw to decide who goes first and which likely person gets the prime position of last.

My name came out of the bag first! Devastating! No chance. But no chance of walking away either. The only thing a politician can do in that situation is gamble and rely on emotion from the heart, not statistics from the head.

Tear up the speech with the big words, leave all the analysis and economics and theories of how Mr Wilson could save the pound to the other well-educated challengers. Leave the pit to the miner and tell them the Vic Feather story of how if the kid can't fight, it don't mean a thing.

Use every stirring battle cry of now is the time for all good men and women to come to the aid of the Party. Bassetlaw was the Alamo. It was Custer's last stand. Dunkirk. If Labour couldn't hold Bassetlaw it was finished. The campaign needed a candidate with fire in his belly who could fight. Otherwise the Government was dead.

It was the good old 'Us Versus Them' speech. My dad had been carried on a stretcher out of a pit owned by the Duke of Norfolk, I told them. How many pits round here had been owned by the Duke of Portland, the Duke of Newcastle, the Duke of Kingston and the Duke of Leeds? No wonder the area was called the Dukeries. Do you want these fat cats in the House of Lords to win the seat? To bring in another Tory Government who would shut all the pits? Are we going to let the fox-hunters and landed gentry with their tied cottages take it away from us? You got to fight to keep it. Bassetlaw is where we stand and draw the line in the sand.

It worked a treat. The miners' candidate spoke about nothing but the output of coal, which wasn't very clever because he already had the miners' votes, and George carefully and innocuously asked the others a few questions about was it a very posh part of London where they lived? And did their kids go to a comprehensive school or a grammar?

All we had to do after that was win the by-election.

The hardest job in politics is to fight a by-election defending the sitting Government in mid-term. That's when all Governments are at their most unpopular. Even its own supporters feel like teaching it a lesson by giving it a kick up the bracket and staying at home. Those of my mates in Parliament who swept in with the tide from the classes of '70, or '74 or '79 etc., especially if they were standing in a seat they lived in, knowing every local problem and every voter, will never realize what a doddle they had. A by-election is a horrendous, gruelling eighteen-hours-a-day grinning torture for the candidate every day for several weeks before polling day.

Candidates in a crucial seat are whisked off to London into a mock TV studio and cross-examined by friendly, professional television interviewers, who give them the Jeremy Paxman treatment on today's headline in the *Financial Times*. And surely this means the loss of thousands of votes in Slagtown where he is standing? And surely this is all the fault of his Government? And why should Labour voters turn out and vote for that?

Later, they show the poor mug the video of how he wriggled, stuttered, rolled his eyes, couldn't answer, and nearly wept when he realized he had blown the most important by-election of the century (all by-elections are the most important of the century) and could forget about ever being allowed to stand for a seat again. Even as a parish councillor.

He or she is then given the hard-cop–soft-cop routine, taught to all newspaper journalists, who ask press conference questions and hunt in packs, seeking one wrong soundbite they can headline about help for the disabled and whether they needed more or less money than single mothers.

Then the hacks go doorstepping for a vox pop, asking the local punters in this test if they are going to vote for an idiot who was daft enough to say some single mothers should get more money and some disabled should get less. Or the other way round. Or vice versa, or whatever slant the tabloids wanted to put on it.

Friendly tabloid journalists strip the candidate naked of all confidence by asking him a series of other questions designed to show how little he knows of the EC set-aside subsidies for farmers, the EC human rights legislation and its Objective One Status, compared to Objective Two, to show him what a gibbering idiot he will be unless he starts cramming. Because he is never going to join the Party's officers' mess in Westminster if he doesn't.

Lots of Party members can busk it on a platform with a merry quip sounding off about local schools and bus stops. It brings in votes and is often highly successful for the Liberals, who are never going to form a government, and never have to defend anything, but it doesn't work if it's your lot causing the problems. Shutting down the works and losing the jobs, or letting rents and rates and prices rip while holding back pay rises might be good for the economy, it's disastrous for by-elections.

The public in the streets, and all voters, automatically think that any and every MP should know every detail of every local school, street, train, job, farm, pension or hospital, right down to how the defibrillators in the hospital intensive care unit work.

All politicians envy those jobs where a teacher gets a degree in French, teaches it, and nothing in his job ever changes. In politics, the subject changes by the hour, every single day, and instantly. From A for the Age of Consent to Z for Zimbabwe, politicians are expected to go on television or answer questions in the street to explain what it's all about. They can't. All they can do is busk it without music until nowadays the daily fax arrives from Party Headquarters. In 1968 we hadn't even got colour television, never mind mobile phones or faxes. Even the motorway only reached Nottingham and Yorkshire television was just two months old, with Richard Whiteley and Austin Mitchell as its new presenters.

Training for a by-election was like training to be an astronaut for the moon-landing which was to come a year later.

Candidates had to work during the day to earn a living. They'd be out drumming up helpers and supporters until ten every evening, then studying until two to master the Government's proposals to solve the economic crisis on the EC butter mountain. In the meantime, Alf Robens, the former Labour Cabinet minister now in charge of the National Coal Board, decides to influence the Government coal policy by closing the newest pit in Bassetlaw during the election campaign. With the council house rents doubling too, of course, it looked hopeless.

Even more hopeless when the Prime Minister, Harold Wilson, sent for me at the Blackpool Labour Conference. The previous day, miners protesting about pit closures had stormed their way off the street, on to the floor of the conference, to tremendous cheers from the delegates.

Harold asked me up to his room at the Imperial Hotel, gave me a long pep-talk about the political situation, waving his pipe, and solemnly said, in his special broad Yorkshire accent, 'It's all down to you now, Joe lad,' and then told me that the date of the election would be the last day of October, after the opening of Parliament.

I thought, thank you very much, Prime Minister, although I didn't like to say that in the usual Labour Party Smith Square Headquarters cock-up he had chosen a day the week after the clocks were put back, so we would have an hour's less daylight to get the punters to turn out. Hallowe'en looked very daunting.

But the kid had to fight. The Party agent then was a fighter too. Jim Smy was a miner who had actually left his job as a farmworker in a tied cottage in Suffolk to move to Worksop, the biggest town in Bassetlaw, and go down the pit shaft to earn more money. He and his wife Joyce were wonderful, honest, decent country people, who hated the landed gentry and were not going to let them win at any cost.

The Tories were clever too. They chose a man named Jim Lester as candidate. He came from Nottingham, and his father was actually a Labour Alderman on the City Council there. Later, Jim became the MP for Beeston in Notts from 1979 to 1997.

Pits were closing in the Sixties because many of them were

worn out or had geological problems in that the seams, while thick, didn't run straight. Which made it much harder to modernize them with power-drive cutters and conveyor belts. They were old pits with pick and shovel and push-carts, which had at one time had ponies. Pits where the miners dug out 'hand-got' coal as it was known. Where every shovelful had to be hewn and carried by sheer sweat and toil.

Jim Smy said, 'The only chance we have, mate, is to go for hand-got votes.' He was right. Every one would count.

In those circumstances it is kill-the-candidate time. Flog the willing horse over the jumps until it makes the winning post or collapses in the race.

In 1968, outside TV broadcasts were very expensive, needing a crew of five to set up the equipment – hand-held cameras didn't exist. In the entire four-week campaign, I only made one TV appearance. Nowadays, candidates can reach 20,000 local houses in a minute – and win or lose 20,000 votes in the process.

Then it was all legwork on the street. Opinion polls were banned from newspapers until the week of the election, and as Mr Wilson told me, a week was a long time in politics, and as there hadn't been a by-election for several months, there was no reason why we shouldn't win it.

Elections then were much rougher than now. There was rarely any apathy in politics. Feelings ran high. The voters got excited and public meetings in the evening were invariably packed, even if it was only to bait the other side's candidate and upset the landed gentry by booing them on the Tory platform.

Every day me and Maggie would be up at six to drive the fifteen miles to Worksop (we couldn't afford to stay in a hotel there, not even on election night) and study the morning papers (no Breakfast TV) to try and guess what the twenty or so journalists from the national papers would grill me on at nine o'clock. They were all working for Tory papers, and so obviously screwed me first, before then going to see the Tory candidate and offer him a few underarm lobs and take photos of his family with their dog.

After that, it was nine hours on the road with a van owned by Lincoln Labour party and driven by its agent Pat Mulligan, to make literally seventy loudspeaker speeches in seventy different streets, shopping districts, at factory gates, or anywhere four people stopped to listen.

We would stand the van at the side of the road, and belt it out to women bending down toiling to pick potatoes in the fields, and tell them what rotten bosses they had. With a friendly wave in return. We'd hector bus queues, bus depots, supermarkets, factories, kids and mums from school. Maggie would give out thousands of newly invented sticky lapel badges to their youngsters, or their mums, on streets which had never seen a real live politician before.

Bill Clinton still does it today in the USA. So do I in Bassetlaw.

There is simply no substitute for pressing the flesh in the streets. Forget all the boring nonsense of canvassing every door and spending twenty seconds on each doorstep asking for support. Today most voters are too clever to tell the truth.

But a five-minute blast on a pedestrian precinct followed by a wave and big smile and chat does a world of good. It's an acquired talent of cheek, chutzpah, chat-up and grin. Especially to women young and old, who all love it if you say what lovely, smashing kids they've got and can you give them a badge, and ask the youngster its name and whether they have got their new teeth. Let's have a look at them, and how one day you will be a big girl and look just as lovely as your mother and grandma.

It's bullshit and blarney and every punter knows it. But in an election it's old-time hustings razzamatazz and the voters love nothing better than seeing their MP, or future MP, earning his votes and his living.

But it's hard work.

In those days, believe it or not, there was no daytime television and nothing to do in mining villages for those on night shift. Kids were always on the streets everywhere playing football or hopscotch.

Any politician knows that if the kids are happy and enjoying themselves, then their mother and dad are happy too. There was another old Labour Party song which the lads had brought back from the First World War, 'Tramp! Tramp! Tramp! The Boys Are Marching', which the troops sang and changed the words to, 'Someone put the kibosh up the Kaiser'. It featured extensively in *Oh What a Lovely War*, a very popular film and stage show in the Sixties.

We'd take the van round the streets playing the music and then line all the kids up in ranks to sing:

> **Tramp! Tramp! Tramp! The boys are marching!**
> **Someone's knocking at the door!**
> **If it's Labour let 'em in. If it's Tories, kick 'em out**
> **'Cos we don't want the dole queue any more!**

Then the second verse:

> **Vote! Vote! Vote! For Joe Ashton!**
> **He's the man we're voting for!**
> **Ashton is our man and we'll have him if we can**
> **'Cos we don't want a Tory any more!**

Next day, half the kids in school would be singing it just like they sing TV advertising commercials today. Back then all we had was word of mouth, and in those days it still worked.

By six the candidate would be shattered. The pounding old-fashioned five-foot-long steel loudspeaker sent me totally deaf. I could even hear my own voice in my sleep. We fixed up a ten-foot-long lead on the mike, so that I could stay well away from the sound, and one idiot in the market-place rolled it up and garrotted me with it.

Other clever mischief-makers would pull the plug out. Or take the handbrake off the van and push it down a hill. We needed bodyguards everywhere. The 'Us Versus Them' speech appealing to Labour loyalty at a time when the Party needed it most, enraged local farmers and snooty landowners.

They had never had a working-class city oik from Sheffield stirring up trouble and strife before. The farmers and landowners retaliated by putting up thousands and thousands of Tory posters in every field lining every mile of every road. It was the worst thing they could have done. The posters infuriated reluctant Labour voters, who went out mob-handed at night, and wrecked them. All politicians thank the Lord for their opponents' own goals.

If the green wellies had just kept it quiet and low-key they would have sneaked home, but turning it into a class war was just what Labour needed to stir up all the old memories. Brothers, we were on our way.

Parliament wasn't sitting in October, so MPs from everywhere were drafted in to man villages as the word spread that Labour might not, just might not, be annihilated, and the neck-and-neck struggle caught the public mood. Places like Bassetlaw rarely ever saw big-name politicians and loved the opportunity of packing village halls to hear them speak.

In Langold, which has a thousand votes, Manny Shinwell pulled in a crowd of 400. Elsewhere in villages Barbara Castle attracted 500, George Brown 600 and Enoch Powell, grim-faced and booed but cheered to the rafters by the gentry, faced a crowd of 650. All in small towns and villages with a mob of journalists reporting every word.

The one opinion poll of the campaign, two days before the election, showed Labour with a lead of less than 2 per cent. And opinion polls were notoriously inaccurate then.

For a few days there had been rumours that the Government was once again in deep financial trouble. After the devaluation,

Chancellor Jim Callaghan had moved to become Home Secretary and Roy Jenkins had taken over. With the parties neck and neck, the Tory press began to scream loudly that as soon as the votes were cast, another squeeze and freeze would be announced.

At every meeting, furious Tory voters and journalists would demand to know if an economic crisis was being delayed for two days until the votes were cast.

Barbara Castle, a truly magnificent orator, who could bring in Labour votes, especially from women, by the thousand, smiled sweetly and announced firmly that there was no truth in it whatsoever. That it was a malicious rumour being spread by the Tories to damage the Labour Government and they ought to be ashamed of themselves in talking the pound down. At 3.30 p.m. on polling day, the Tories raised the matter in the House of Commons and were told it just was not true.

On polling day, every Labour Party worker for thirty miles around poured into the rolling square miles of Bassetlaw. At 6.00 p.m., we all knew from the returns sent back to the headquarters from the old age pensioners sitting outside the school polling booths that we were losing. It had started to rain (the first time for three weeks) just when Labour voters traditionally turn out on their way home from work or before they go to the pub. The polls then shut at nine. If they didn't set off before nine, we had had it.

We poured every single helper on to the council houses where rents had been a major factor and told them to knock anywhere, but don't stop knocking until the nine o'clock news came on. They didn't.

Later, at one o'clock in the morning, it was announced from the Town Hall balcony in Retford to a wet, packed crowd below that we had held the seat.

On a recount. By just 740 votes. Two years earlier the Labour majority had been 10,600.

The whole of Bassetlaw were still up watching television

waiting for the result as Maggie and me were carried shoulder-high in a beer-swilling booze-up that lasted until four o'clock in the morning. The *Titanic* had stopped sinking. Mafeking had been relieved. If the church had been open, some of our supporters would have rung the bells. It was Glory, Glory Hallelujah time 'cos the Reds Go Marching On. We sang 'The Red Flag' and 'Jerusalem', and Maggie was kissed by a thousand miners.

It was to be eighteen months before Labour held another by-election. And that was in the Gorbals in Glasgow, the safest seat in Scotland, where Frank McElhone scraped home.

Just ten hours after the Bassetlaw result was announced, Parliament was staggered to see Tony Crosland, the President of the Board of Trade, walk to the Despatch Box and announce a squeeze and freeze. It was Friday morning and the House sat at 11.00 a.m. then. Crosland announced higher hire purchase charges for cars, a 40 per cent deposit to be paid over two years, higher interest charges, etc., and a whole host of other measures which would cut jobs. There was an immediate uproar, cries of 'Cheat', and a furious Ted Heath denounced ministers for lying in the Bassetlaw campaign.

Every single newspaper on Saturday and Sunday cried that MPs who always call themselves honourable members should not accept the result, and that Ashton, in particular, should not take his seat, but should stand down and fight the by-election again. Labour should be ashamed, said Ted Heath, and *The Times* reported Tony Crosland as protesting that he had been abused in a most extraordinary manner. It was not a freeze, he said to the furious Labour left-wingers representing car-making and other washing machine and fridge seats, it was simply a mild chill.

It was Barbara Castle who took the real flak, however. The papers howled for her blood and resignation. Barbara simply smiled sweetly and said she hadn't lied at all. When she said that 'There was no economic freeze on the way', she had simply done what the last Conservative Chancellor, Harold Macmillan, had done in three previous Tory by-elections at Gainsborough, Hereford and Taunton, and if it was good enough for Conservative Governments, it was good enough for us.

It was Old Labour at its finest.

Six

THE WORKING CLASS CAN KISS MY ASS, I'VE GOT THE MP's JOB AT LAST

THAT's what the lads in the pit and on the shop-floor would sing to the tune of 'The Red Flag' and laugh, when any union MP went back to visit the wages slaves he had left behind. Well, it did beat clocking in every morning. On the first day I arrived at the House of Commons, an old miner, Bill Blyton, took my arm and said, 'Just take a look at this place, kid. There's no watter. The walls are solid and straight. You can breathe fresh air, the money is in the pay packet every month, it's the best pit I've ever worked in. And if ever you get fed up and miserable, just remember there's thousands outside who are ready to step into your shoes.' Very sound advice.

Later that evening a distinguished august messenger of the House in white tie and frock-coat came up to me, hissed and whispered, 'Which end of the 'Cliffe does tha come from? I come from Brompton Road. Did tha ever have to go for a shower at Maltby Street School?' He had joined the navy to climb out of Attercliffe and finished up a high ranking officer and eventually in the Serjeant at Arms' office of Parliament.

Three weeks later, the MP for Attercliffe bumped into me and asked, 'Don't I know you from somewhere?' It was typical. I had only been a leading light in his constituency party for several years but he didn't know, and hadn't turned up once at the by-election.

Meanwhile, the world outside was in turmoil. Eleven days after the by-election Richard Nixon was elected as the new Republican President of the USA. In Paris, a Trotskyist student leader called Lionel Jospin actually persuaded ten million workers to come out on strike. He is of course now the Prime Minister of France. The Russians had just invaded Czechoslovakia and sent their tanks into Prague, and here was I, the only Labour winner of a genuine election anywhere in Britain. No wonder Harold Wilson was waiting on the steps of Downing Street to welcome me as his hero bringing news of the Relief of Mafeking.

And what was the one thing I wanted to ask Harold? When do I get paid, that was what I wanted to ask him. Just like any other genuine worker would. All the riots in the world don't put bread on the table. Maggie and me had lost a month's wages in the campaign. The next pay day for MPs was 1 December and who was going to pay the mortgage, never mind the bed and breakfast in London, plus all the other expenses?

We were broke. Stony broke. As all Labour MPs were. There were no credit cards in those days. MPs' pay was abysmal. My first pay packet was £202 for a month. Less than £50 a week. By working-class wages it was magnificent. But MPs in 1968 didn't receive one penny in any allowances of any kind. We even had to pay for all our postage stamps. All the phone calls we made to the constituency or to our homes were paid for in cash. We had to find the money for any office equipment. Newcomers didn't even have offices. Not even a desk. They had to fight for a small space in the library to work on a table and if he left the seat, another MP would immediately dive in.

We had no phones either. At the end of a long corridor next to the gents was a room equipped with a dozen telephone booths and an operator at the entrance. He would dial the number, plug in the long-distance phone, and I would tell him to wave when the bill reached five shillings, then cut me off. We had to hand over the cash before we walked out.

Today, MPs have secretaries, researchers, word processors, faxes, computers, e-mail, an excellent allowance for renting a flat in London, allowances for renting an office in the constituency and to buy the equipment, and a superb back-up service of information, analysis and details of current legislation and issues of the day. MPs then had absolutely nothing or nobody to help them in their job, or even any cash or training for it. They were simply pitched into a bewildering maze of echoing corridors, unintelligible gibberish of legal phrases in Parliamentary bills, lawyers, jargon, procedure, ways and means, statutory instruments and clause stand part. Any new entrants in the class of '66 could at least learn from each other. A by-election winner in '68 was a loner until the next General Election.

It was the equivalent of throwing a Painless Potter travelling showground dentist into a modern hospital operating theatre and telling him to get on with the surgery.

It was done that way for a specific purpose. Just as the ancient bishops fought tooth and nail against translating the Bible into English, simply because they were the only ones who knew Latin and could understand what was going on, so the civil servants in Whitehall kept control by keeping back-bench MPs and the public totally in the dark. Mushroom men, as we were called then, kept in the dark and smothered in bullshit.

The country was run as it has been since King Lear, by the 'Yes, Ministers' of the Civil Service, as all MPs very quickly found out. These mandarins didn't want training courses for new MPs. The Proletariat might then start telling civil servants and ministers how to do the job, and deliver what the folks in the streets wanted, not what the Lord High Poo Bahs wanted to give them.

The warlike British upper class designed everything for combat. Every situation had to have a framework of two sides against each other. In an adversarial court of justice, it was two lawyers against each other. Our politics is virtually eyeball to eyeball, with a system of political parties either in government or opposition, and totally different to other legislatures where their chamber is a semi-circle with right wing merging into left. Everything in our Parliament is yes or no. Us versus Them. There is no maybe or perhaps. No fence to straddle or clench buttocks on, no matter how much the Liberals have tried to do so, and ultimately the voters demand a for-or-against decision for their for-or-against votes.

Only the Speaker is neutral. And when she shouts, 'Ayes to the right and noes to the left', it is not a gurning competition as viewers might think. She has to do the job of compère, panel chairman, selector, croupier, crap-shooter, lightning-conductor and weather-man, all at the same time. She can (and does) send players off for not shutting up or sitting down when she tells them to, and carefully keeps a balance and pecking order, with the best spots on the show reserved for the biggest stars.

Politics is a greasy pole, as Disraeli put it, where no official qualifications are needed except a thick skin and a majority of votes, and where the best way of advancement is undoubtedly greasing up to the person who can hand out promotion. Advancement, like the casting couch of Hollywood, more often than not depends on who you know and sleep with, and not what you know and where to sell it.

Early governments introduced exactly the same sort of fagging system as the public schools, and Labour Prime Minister Clem Attlee carried it on after the war, which the half of his Cabinet who went to public schools thoroughly approved of. Nowadays, the fetchers and gofers would be called minders, not fags, but the system is the same.

The pecking order starts on day one. No seats are allocated, but old-timers will claim certain perches as their own on big occasions. Old-time Labour MPs like me reckon the system is just like the Town Hall council house waiting list. Those who have been on it longest get the first pick, in the same way as lifers in prison get the sunny side of the exercise yard. Tories reckon that a handle of a 'Sir' or ex-Cabinet minister is equivalent to *droit de seigneur*, and claim their seats ruthlessly.

It does not take long for the euphoria of new MPs in winning a seat to vanish and the traumatic shock of survival in the herd to set in. New arrivals go through a culture shock, equivalent to a gaol sentence, national service square-bashing, or old-time public school thrashing and debauchery.

New MPs who were senior adults with top managerial experience in industry, or university professors, or media stars, have been known to suffer nervous breakdowns, and then vanish into oblivion, shuffling round the building anonymously, like a punch-drunk ex-prize fighter, while others from the pit face with nothing but thick skins, dominant, confident egos and the quick wits of a snake-oil salesman, have flourished and found their niche in life.

The disillusion sets in on day one. All the fond dreams of standing up in front of the green leather bench proudly speaking to an enraptured audience of the Cabinet and packed House evaporate as the new MP realizes that there are 650 other MPs in the place as well. All ambitious extroverts joining in the clamour to be heard. And all having the same boring problems of Little Twittering schools, jobs, roads, hospitals, houses, etc., which nobody else in the place gives a damn about, because every single one of them too is struggling to get out of the chorus. Hollywood bimbos, who climb by lying on their backs and gripping with their heels, have it easier.

Every single MP is a big noise in his constituency, trumpeting weekly newspaper headlines. In Westminster nobody cares. The first advice is from the whips, who tell him that if he wants to get his name in the newspapers, he should go out in the street and take his trousers off. Which is good advice. They tell him the old story of the local MP at a public meeting, who claimed that in the last session of Parliament he had put down more questions than any other member and a voice called out, 'Cor! Ain't you bleedin' ignorant!' If the time available for question and debate is divided out equally among all the 550 back-bench MPs it works out at just over an hour each per year.

New MPs can sit there for hours, even days or weeks, waiting for a chance to put their case, like hopefuls waiting for tickets for *Phantom of the Opera*. Even questions are balloted for, with over 250 going into the random selection every day. The law of averages says that a back-bencher might see his name pulled out about once every four or five weeks to put a question to a minister, and only once a year to the Prime Minister.

Government ministers are not daft. They know how to get their minders to hand out pre-written questions to willing ingénues and pack the ballot with underarm lobs praising and congratulating the Government on the excellent work it is doing, and to minimize the fast bowling from the opposition, or from his own hostile supporters behind him.

Back home, the voters tell their MP they never see him on TV. Why are the benches empty? He is bloody useless. They are not interested in how many committees he has to spend long hours on upstairs. Don't give a toss that the Chamber has been debating the abolition of the House of Lords for six weeks, and every other subject will be ruled out of order. Just go in there and shout and bawl, and tell them what a load of prats they are, like Dennis Skinner does.

It soon dawns on the chorus that there are only two career paths in politics – The Ladder or the Limelight. MPs can play the role of willing, time-serving committee stalwarts with a safe pair of hands, making no fuss, leading no rebellions, but carefully mastering the details of a department and specializing in farming, or defence, or the Treasury, etc., and climb the ladder, or greasy pole, year by year, amendment by amendment, clause by clause, knowing that over a hundred MPs lose their seats or retire at every election, and it might just be their turn next to become Parliamentary Secretary at the Department of Social Security signing thousands of letters, staying up late at night grinding our legislation on disability benefits, hoping that virtue brings its own rewards.

Occasionally it does. As it did for Mrs Thatcher. But for every one like her who gets the Field Marshal's baton from her knapsack, there are a hundred in the poor bloody infantry who will never get past trench warfare.

The real politicians go for the Limelight. Administration bores them. They want to be performers in the front line. Rebel characters loved by TV producers everywhere. Ministers and whips don't like them because they make life awkward, but the public love them, and no matter how obstreperous they are, how many lost causes or minority cases they pursue, these snipers and hand-grenade lobbers never seem to have any difficulty getting elected. Whereas in a General Election landslide massacre, the loyalists and back-pack carriers in the trenches get slaughtered on the barbed wire.

Just as certain footballers stand out on television, usually because they attack the referee, score own goals, have a daft haircut, or get sent off, or can turn in a good soundbite from a sweaty dressing-room corridor, and always have the crowd on their side whatever the result, so a couple of dozen back-benchers in every Parliament invariably make a national name for themselves.

Quite often, working on the Lyndon B. Johnson advice that it is better to have the awkward squad inside the tent pissing out, rather than outside the tent pissing in, they are offered jobs to keep them quiet. Not many accept. They know that a merry quip can bring the house down and destroy any minister's argument. They know, as any top comedian does, that the secret of heckling is in the timing. They wait for the right one-second break in a speech, or if a minister is daft enough to ask the House a question, then pounce.

*

When I entered the Commons, the £50 a week simply didn't cover the cost of living and doing the job. I could have bought a house in down-market Islington for £5,000 which today could fetch £500,000, but it was just as much out of reach in 1968 as it would be now. MPs went from 1965 to 1972 without any pay rise at all, and received not an ounce of sympathy from anywhere. The party workers in the constituency, who hadn't the foggiest idea of what London living costs were like, thought £50 a week after tax a magnificent sum, and expected MPs to buy drinks all round every night in the pub, to shell out for every raffle prize and every sponsored school walk, to wine and dine them on their visits to Westminster and run a constituency office and their car solely for the local party. And anyway, if MPs were hard up it would do them good and teach them what survival was like for the poor and the underpaid.

The Tories in Parliament at that time consisted mainly of retired wing commanders, farmers, landed gentry with private incomes, merchant bankers in the City, or lawyers, earning a guinea a word in the Old Bailey before turning up at Westminster after a good lunch at their club. They were smart enough to realize that low wages for MPs was one way of keeping out the ragtag and bobtail from the best club in London, and so they wouldn't do anything either.

We stayed in the cheapest, scruffiest, rat-ridden, bug-infested hotels in London, mainly at the back of Victoria Station or King's Cross, costing about £1.25 for bed and breakfast. They were horrendous. Noisy and filthy and unfit for human habitation. The sort of places where innocent tourists get trapped for one night, and then wisely prefer to sleep in the park, or on a bench by the river.

Some of the MPs who had won marginal seats in 1966, and knew that they had no chance of holding them at the next election, tried desperately to save some money, simply because there was no redundancy pay for MPs. We didn't even get paid for the month before the election, when the House prorogued until polling day.

However, we did get free rail travel to the constituency and back. And there were sleeper services then. So often hard-up members would ride up and down the country on overnight sleepers simply to save a night's hotel bill, and stagger round the building absolutely exhausted.

Maggie and I converted our back bedroom in Sheffield into an office, and the firm I worked for kindly gave me the battered old chair I had sat on as a leaving present and sold me a secondhand typewriter for £30 (half a week's wages), which Maggie's mother bought for us. Then Maggie quit her secretary's job at the Co-op to become mine. For no wages at all.

The previous Bassetlaw MP, Captain Fred, had never bothered replying to a letter unless it enclosed a stamped addressed envelope. Then he would simply send back a xeroxed reply, which read, 'Dear Sir/Madam, Sorry I can't help you. Please go and visit the citizens' advice bureau on Newcastle Avenue and tell them I sent you, Yours sincerely'. Even that reply was very rare and something to treasure.

The railway warrants were priceless. It didn't cost the taxpayer anything, because the nationalized railways lost a fortune and we were only taking up an empty seat anyway, but there was strong resistance from the Treasury to paying a car allowance. How anybody could be expected to cover an area of 300 square miles without a car was just blindly ignored, but in Parliament, as elsewhere in life, it was the 'Haves' versus the 'Have-nots', and even though the Have-nots were in a massive majority, the Haves were always a damn sight smarter and meaner and had inherited the earth. Eventually, after strong protests, a car allowance equivalent to the train fare was brought in. From London to Sheffield it was £6 return, but at least Maggie could now travel with me in the car.

Maggie and me had moved on from sharing an outside lav with neighbours, but not very far. One night, on her birthday, I took her to see *Fiddler on the Roof*, and we could just about manage to pay for two seats in the Upper Gallery. Way down below, in the third row of the front stalls, sat Ted Heath, the Prime Minister, which summed up the distance between us.

One or two old-timers, not having the cash for a decent bed and breakfast, never mind a flat (especially at the rate they supped ale), simply found a friendly widow woman in one of the council blocks of Westminster, or the local Peabody Buildings, and lived 'over the brush', as it was called, with her. So called because centuries ago in mining areas with no vicar, young couples pledged their troth by holding hands and jumping over a broomstick.

Some of the 'widow women' didn't even know that their lodger/lover was actually an MP. They simply thought he had a job out all day driving a truck, then taking it up to Manchester or Birmingham every Friday to come back on Monday.

The wife in the North didn't know either. Parliament wasn't televised. The old union lads were very rarely asked to do a TV interview; even then it was down the line to their region, which wouldn't be shown in London.

There was a golden rule, strictly observed by every Lobby correspondent of every newspaper, that they could only report what they heard, and nothing of what they saw. All, on both sides, MPs and journalists, followed the agreement religiously. The 'widow women' got their name when two Ulster Unionists, naive souls who had never been to London before, got elected and arrived at the opening of Parliament to be sworn in. They then found out MPs didn't get paid until the end of the month.

They had no money. So they just went and knocked on a few doors of the terraced houses opposite, behind Westminster Abbey (today worth a million pounds each and very posh even then), and asked if anybody knew of a kindly widow woman who could take in a couple of God-fearing MP strangers for the night.

As you might imagine, somebody did.

Others in similar circumstances had been known to knock on the door of the Mothers' Union building in nearby Chandler Gardens and ask for a bed. They got one too. Around the corner, in Rochester Row, stands a Salvation Army hostel, where until very recently, at least one teetotal working-class Lord and another MP had their own key and room for late-night sittings.

The 'widow women' were well known by everybody. One railway man in his fifties, who never expected to win a seat in the Labour landslide of 1966, realized it would be a short life in Parliament, so why not make it a merry one?

'Sydney' was the spitting image of Les Dawson. So was she. They looked like a double act. He had a wife in the North-east who never came to London, and every evening by half past six the pair of them would be in two corner bench seats in the old Strangers Bar downing whisky chasers, and brandy with Babycham.

By the ten o'clock vote she would be shouting, 'Let's have your glasses please' and helping the staff to wash up before belting out all seven verses of 'Somewhere my Love' from Lara's Theme in the film *Dr Zhivago*, and gazing fondly at 'Sydney' as though he was Omar Sharif. Then she'd slobber kisses on all and sundry and clear the Strangers Bar faster than any whip chasing a three-line division.

Not a word was ever mentioned in a gossip column or outside the House. The Mafia law of 'Omerta', the code of silence, and the brotherhood of the union prevailed. Silence. We are not our brothers' keepers, and what one member of the Party gets up to is not the business of any other. Even Cabinet ministers had girlfriends.

The only danger was if the real wife ever came down from the constituency. Then, if a mischievous neighbouring Tory knew her, he would walk up to the Labour MP smiling broadly, and charmingly say, 'Good morning, Bill. Why is it that every time I see you in here you are with a different lovely woman?' Then cheerily wave and walk away.

Of course, wives weren't daft. Fortunately for the men, wives, or 'spouses' as the civil servants called them, only received three free railway tickets a year. These were supposed to be for wives based in London to travel north for the constituency mayor making or civic dinner, etc. Although there was nothing to stop Northern wives using the warrants in the other direction for an invitation to Downing Street or the Royal Garden Party.

Several years later, when John Biffen, Tory Leader of the House, was in trouble because he was refusing to pay out the full increase in the MPs' pay rise, he decided to restore his popularity by announcing the number of warrants for wives would be increased to fifteen. There was an absolute uproar. 'Three is too many as it is,' the back-benchers yelled. 'Who is going to stay at home to look after the kids and answer the phone?' they shouted.

Fortunately, the row received little publicity in the papers. Like all MPs' pay rises and allowances debates, it was timed to start well after ten-thirty at night and go on until three in the morning to make sure the news was too late for the early editions. So fortunately, from the old lads' point of view, not many wives in far-flung constituencies got to know about it.

Sad to say, in 1969 the dreaded Boundary Commission produced its report which reorganized all the Parliamentary seats, particularly all those in inner-city Labour strongholds which had seen massive slum clearance forcing traditional council house voters to move away to the suburbs. The dwindling population meant that some safe seats, held by the unions for a lifetime, were merged or vanished.

What a dilemma. Not only were the union lads going to lose their jobs at the age of fifty-five, they had to choose which woman to stay with, the one in London or the one back home. Some time later I bumped into an ex-MP who was working as a lift operator in a multi-storey government building. It was a hard choice, he said. But there were no jobs for a man of his age in Glasgow. The shipyard had closed. There was no MPs' redundancy pay or re-settlement grant then either.

We tried renting filthy bed-sitters, and after spending one night on Clapham Common in our old Ford Escort, because we had had rats and mice running all over us in an attic, Maggie said she had had enough of waiting in some dump for me to come home at two in the morning, or hanging around in the Commons bar and then standing for an hour for the all-night bus, because we could never, ever, afford to ride in the empty taxis going past. So she went back home, while I spent fourteen hours a day in Parliament and six in beds worse than any Blackpool boarding house.

Nevertheless, there were marvellous consolations for our bed-sitter grime in the early days. I have never known anybody, whether it was Muhammad Ali or Diana Dors, who ever refused an invitation to speak to a meeting, or a dinner in Parliament. Regularly, as Chairman of the All Party Football Group which has over 150 MPs and Lords, I invite top managers, players, club owners, TV commentators, etc., to come and speak and then have a pint, and all of them think the place is magic.

Kevin Keegan, the England manager (a brilliant mimic), Alex Ferguson and Martin Edwards (Man. United), Alan Sugar and Sol Campbell (Spurs), Ken Bates (Chelsea), Arsene Wenger (Arsenal), John Motson (*Match of the Day*), and dozens and dozens of others, have all played the Palace and had a marvellous evening and there wasn't one single leak to the press.

Back in the Eighties, I was writing a column for the *Daily Star*, which was then a shooting-star newcomer with a circulation approaching 1.7 million, nearly as high as the *Daily Mail*.

Diana Dors was the paper's agony aunt. For thirty years she had been a top British pin-up, the UK's answer to Marilyn

Monroe and Brigitte Bardot. She had appeared in several Hollywood cheesecake pictures, played Las Vegas with Liberace, Dean Martin and Jerry Lewis (she called it Lost Wages because so many entertainers there gambled away all their salaries and finished up working for nothing), and she had had the usual show business career of three marriages, a bankrupt husband, *News of the World* headlines, etc., etc., but fading or not, she still undoubtedly had star quality, and had had it since she won her first beauty contest at thirteen.

Believe it or not, her real name was Diana Fluck, a name of German origin. It was a hoary old Labour Party legend that as a young rising personality in Swindon she had once been asked to open a gala. The local councillor, who was to introduce her as our own, our very own, Diana Fluck, was told he had better make sure he got her name absolutely right, otherwise he would be in big trouble. So he practised. And then stood up and proudly introduced her as our very own Doris Klunt.

Over the years, she grabbed many, many more headlines, nearly all bad, even more than the Diana who came later, but whatever she did, the public loved her.

The paper used to have public relations lunches at the Boat Show at Earl's Court where 'Star Stunnas' like Linda Lusardi would be on parade, but few of them were as sharp as Di. One lunch just happened to fall on the same day as British Rail launched a nationwide advertising campaign with ads yelling, 'British Rail – where the customer comes first'. As we chatted at lunch I said to Di, 'I've seen that advert before somewhere.' She replied, 'I have too,' and then pulled a book of matches out of her handbag with 'Stolen from Mabel's Whorehouse, Las Vegas – where the customer comes first' stamped on it. It's an old joke now, but the next day British Rail dropped the advertising immediately.

Would she like to come to lunch at the House of Commons? Well, of course she would. And a guided tour for her son? Why not. 'You are very lucky,' said Alan Lake, her husband, 'Di doesn't usually get out of bed for less than two hundred quid.'

I told the copper on the gate that I was expecting Diana Dors for lunch and he gave me that sort of look, and long pause, and said, 'Certainly, sir,' just as he would to any other nutter. The Dors family arrived in a stretch limousine, and by sheer chance, there was a television crew at St Stephen's entrance interviewing a top politician. At least they were, until they saw Diana stepping out, looking better than a million dollars does these days, and giving me a smacking big kiss. Then it was on every newscast that night, with every Bassetlaw voter saying, no wonder he can't find time to get our lav mended. All he is fit for is kissing bloody film stars.

Her third, much younger husband, Alan Lake, a smashing bloke from Stoke on Trent, and her young son Jason looked very nervous. 'Little Jason nearly died of shock coming across the Westminster Bridge,' Alan said. 'He saw Big Ben and shouted, "Ma! It's the income tax!" and dived under the seat.'

Naturally I had asked my missus along too, and naturally she is called Maggie. I took Di's arm and told her Maggie is waiting for us inside. Of course she thought it was Maggie Thatcher, the Prime Minister, 'Ooh, I didn't expect that,' Di cooed, as her eyes widened, but she carried it off with an Oscar performance when she met Maggie.

Bobbies fought each other to do the security check in case she was carrying two bombs for the IRA under her sweater. 'There is no need for a body search,' I had to shout at them. It was smiling courtiers all the away. Extra tickets? No problem. Best table in the dining room? Certainly, sir. Then came the phone calls from the gossip columnists. How long had we known each other? Where did we meet? She had headlines in every paper. Even *The Times* gave her the full back-page treatment and more coverage than Mrs Thatcher. 'A rose-red creation only half as old as Miss

Joan Collins,' it described her, 'who sailed majestically to her seat and obviously approved the way Mrs Thatcher handled men.' It even referred to me as the 'Labour cultural attaché'. Sarcastic sods.

There were not many women then who could outshine Mrs Thatcher in her own backyard, and have every face in the Chamber looking up at her in the Public Gallery instead of at the Prime Minister at the Despatch Box, but Diana Dors did.

Fortunately, Cinderellas that we were, we nevertheless got invited to some wonderful balls. Invitations would pour in for dinners at the Dorchester (not for Maggie), for the Institute of Mechanical Wibbling Tools and Sprocket Wrenchers Society, who just loved having an MP present at their table. There was always some embassy somewhere just begging Honourable Members to attend their National Day celebration, when the Ambassador would be delighted at your honourable presence at the official reception.

New MPs quickly learned which National Days would be a boring two-hour film about the grape harvest and how much concrete the peasants had shovelled for a million new flats, followed by wine made from pure alcohol, with six pieces of salt fish, and which would have champagne at Ladbrokes, or Crockfords and the Jockey Club.

So, acting on the sound advice that there was nowt too good for the working class, and it was always possible to enjoy the education without kissing ass and betraying socialist principles, life as an MP could be endured.

For one thing, the crack was good. Annie's Bar had just been opened as I arrived in Parliament and called after its first barmaid, and for the first time the press could openly drink with MPs without having to have a formal invitation. No public were allowed in. It was tucked away down an unknown corridor, and like all rooms in Parliament, had a well-known history of once being the secret place where the Irish rebel leader Parnell would meet his lover Kitty, when she arrived in her cloak at the side entrance, eventually giving up his career for her.

Many others have done the same in Westminster, although at that time there were better stories every day of the week. Journalists like Simon Hoggart, Michael White and David McKie of the *Guardian* were keen, sharp, witty young hacks. Other experts such as Ian Aitken, Bob Carvell, Chris Buckland and David Wood could spin a yarn, latch on to a leak, and at one in the morning, when other papers had gone to bed, be on the phone making a major headline story out of a chance remark or whispered gossip. Add to that crew a few astute, cynical young soundbite politicians like Gerald Kaufman, Neil Kinnock, John Prescott, Gwyneth Dunwoody and Tory Ken Clarke, and Oscar Wilde himself would have struggled to keep his end up.

It was magic. Who cared if the bedbugs bit, and, when the division bell rang for the last time, it would be a cold wait at the bus stop for the 2.20 a.m. to Clapham? There were some great, heady, sparkling late-night sessions. The beer was cheap too. Especially when the Lobby journalists were all on unlimited expenses.

Upstairs, for those who could afford it, was a magnificent dining room where for seven and sixpence (less than 40p), it was possible to have three courses with superb waitress service, and dine next to Roy Jenkins, the Chancellor of the Exchequer, Jim Callaghan, the Home Secretary, Barbara Castle, Dick Crossman, and half a dozen other Cabinet ministers too.

Although it was not a very happy experience. All of them had first-class degrees at Oxford or Cambridge and regarded their twin round tables near the River Thames window as the Government's officers' mess. Like all university tutors, they would listen politely to any contribution from outside their ranks, then dismiss it with a patronizing smile and a pat on the head, as though they had just tied a little boy's shoe-laces. Then they would calmly

proceed on to another idiotic policy of prices and incomes policies, EC butter mountains, rent rises or trade union and wages
restraint, all of which would lose the Labour Party another
million votes.

The opinions of Fred Bare, Issy Lewis, Sid Dyson or me were
neither sought nor heeded. Although the company sergeant
majors who ran trade unions' battalions had to be acknowledged,
and listened to before being ignored.

Who cared? It was only two and ninepence (14p) for pie and
chips in the cafeteria anyway. And there I could listen to John
Parker, the old MP for Dagenham, who told me how he once
chaired a meeting at the Toynbee Hall where Stalin and Mussolini
sat on the same platform. Or Bob Edwards, the MP for Bilston,
Wolverhampton, who could stun any Communist or Militant in
his constituency by listening patiently to their ranting then blandly
replying, 'That's not what Trotsky said to me.' Bill was a Spanish
Civil War veteran, who had actually been in Russia in 1917 as a
student and was at the Moscow conference when Leon Trotsky
denounced Stalin from the platform. 'I watched Stalin's face,' said
Bill, 'and I knew straight away that Trotsky was a dead man. He
fled the hall, but they chased him to Mexico and killed him with
an ice-pick through his head.'

Charlie Pannell, the Cockney MP for Leeds (the union Mafia
spread its wings everywhere) could also make better conversation
than any Oxford don. He had once held the job of Vice Chamberlain of the Royal Household when he was a Government whip.
'I used to chat to them all at the Palace, yer know,' Charlie would
say. 'All the nobs and the hangers-on and the Yeoman of the
Guard and the gentlemen-at-arms. They would tell me everything.
All about the Duke of Windsor. The only man in history to give
up a throne because he finally met a woman who could make his
cock stand up. It's true, you know. All true. The old Queen had
him tried with every daughter and blue-blood gal of every earl,
viscount, lord and marquis in the British Isles. Not one could do

the trick. There ain't a pub in the land called after a local baron what the Palace didn't cross the name off.'

It was fascinating stuff. For two and ninepence there wasn't a better chat show anywhere.

In summer it was even better. Then we could sit outside on the Terrace overlooking the Thames. Where is there a better pub in London? There aren't many warm evenings in a British summer, but when there are, a midnight pint on the Terrace beats any starry night anywhere in the world. Just ask any guest who has been there.

It is said that Parliament was built on the river so that it couldn't be surrounded by the mob, like the Bastille in Paris during the French Revolution. In Victorian days the MPs would toss pennies to the mudlarks below. The little kids would dive in and burrow down into the mud and filth to dig up the coins to the delighted cheers of the Honourable Members above. The tormenting still goes on, even today. Security is cast-iron because of the IRA threat. The press are not allowed in and there is no access to the public.

Regularly MPs would wait for one of the tourist boats to sail past just a few yards from the Terrace wall, and as the punters took pictures and waved, a Tory MP would run up to the river balustrade flourishing a foaming pint of beer and shout, 'Come on in, bruvvers. It's all free!' Which it certainly wasn't. On the return trip a Labour MP would then pick up a wine glass, point at the tourists, and shout, 'Get back to work, you idle swine.' Which so infuriated one young bloke, he promptly turned his back, dropped his jeans and showed his bare arse to the whole parade. That's when both sides yelled, 'It's no good doing that. All the Liberals have gone home.'

On winter nights, when we hadn't got any invitations and money was tight, we'd sit in the Tea Room and spin yarns to compete for the annual 'Keeper of The Cloth Cap Award'.

This went to the Labour MP who could show he had the

most impeccable poverty and hardship credentials. It was a very popular pastime. Later, of course, when Parliament was taken over by the sons of the toilers, who had all been to polytechnics, the tales of families which had nobbut one clog between two feet produced hilarity and ridicule.

But then Roy Mason, from Barnsley (now Lord Mason of Barnsley), would tell us how he went down the pit at fourteen, when he was no higher than a pit pony, and I'd get a few brownie points about Attercliffe and the fact that there had been two murders in our neighbourhood when I was a kid, but eventually the first prize went to one Frank McElhone, the MP who had won the by-election for the Gorbals in Glasgow.

Frank had actually won a by-election a year after I did, which again was hailed as a great victory for Labour, because it was the safest Labour seat in Scotland, nothing but slum tenements, and butt and bens full of Rab C. Nesbits.

Frank's boyhood was spent in a tenement flat above a couple who fought like rottweilers. One night, the bloke had had enough, so he strangled her. Then, not knowing what to do about the body, he cut it up and put the pieces into a sack to tip them into the canal or the River Clyde. Unfortunately, while he was carrying the bits and pieces down the street, an arm swung loose out of the sack and a stray, hungry dog jumped up and ran off with it.

The Glasgow bobbies had seen a lot of things in their time, including razor gangs carving up faces, and it is acknowledged that body-snatching was an ancient Scottish tradition. But nevertheless, they thought it was a bit much to use nagging wives for dog meat. Fortunately, as the arm had a wedding ring on the finger the butcher was captured.

With such a tale, and especially the way it was told in a rasping Bill Shankly, Frank Carson accent, Frank won the award unanimously.

For five years Frank and I shared a basement flat in Kennington on the street where Charlie Chaplin grew up, and we never had a cross word, except two nights a week, when because he wore thick pebble glasses and was blind as a bat, Frank would step in the dog shit on the steps outside and then tread it all over the flat while walking about trying to find out what stank. We lived like the Odd Couple. I had to boil the eggs, because he couldn't even plug in the hoover, never mind light the gas. So I'd get revenge by telling him I'd seen spiders in his room and he'd sit up all night afraid to drop off.

Before Frank became an MP he had run a street-corner fruit shop. After a row with his boss on the railways about the time he was taking off for the local council, he took the plunge by scraping and borrowing every penny he could from his large Catholic family to buy the run-down shop from an old guy. As he proudly handed over the money, it dawned on Frank that he had none left to buy any fruit and veg at the market.

'Don't worry,' the old man said, 'my credit is good. Meet me at six on Monday morning at the market, and you pay later when the money rolls in. They will give you three weeks to pay.' So Frank turned up and waited. And waited, and waited. The wholesale market traders didn't want to know. Frank became the only entrepreneur in history to open a fruit and veg shop with three pounds of potatoes and one bunch of bananas.

But never underestimate working-class know-how and ingenuity. Frank soon realized that none of the Glasgow councillors, or MPs in safe seats, ever gave a damn about getting housing repairs done, or chasing up bad landlords, or getting communal toilets repaired.

So Frank simply got the priest, and his mates and family, to put it about that the best way to get any action was to go into Frank's shop, buy some spuds, and he would write down all the details on a brown paper bag while his missus stood out front wrapping stuff up and taking the money.

Business boomed. And when the ancient sitting MP for Gorbals finally coughed his last, who was the most popular man and councillor and who should be the next MP? Frank McElhone.

His proudest moment was when his son's pop group, Altered Images, got a record in the charts and Frank rolled up in his dinner jacket and ministerial chauffeur-driven car to see them play at the Hammersmith Palais. Unfortunately, the bouncer refused to let Frank in and told him that Grab a Granny night was only on Thursdays.

At the age of fifty-three, Frank collapsed and died of a heart attack while on a march supporting a nurses' pay rise. The lives of all working-class heroes are not measured by the size of their obituary columns, but by the number of people who turn up at their funeral. Over two thousand were locked out and stood in the pouring rain at Frank's.

It was said afterwards that one Rab asked another, 'Who's deed?'

The other one replied, 'The minister.'

'He must have been a popular minister,' said Rab. 'What church was he at?'

'He was the Minister for Social Security,' mourned Rab, 'and Scotland will never have another as good as Frank.'

After about a year, I found a desk in an office down Whitehall in the traditional Parliamentary way, which was to listen carefully for any by-election death announcements, then ring up and ask where the dead MP's desk was (or even where he lived, if his bedsitter was better than the bug huts), then hurtle down and establish squatters' rights before anybody else could.

That's what I did – and landed right next to Bill Price. The Artful Dodger himself, but with a West Country Forest of Dean accent. Bill had started life in one of the ancient pits in the Forest of Dean, but was a natural spin-doctor twenty years before the term had ever been heard of.

By a miracle, he had managed to win a Tory Midlands seat in Rugby by about 400 votes, and was determined to hang on to it.

As a lad he'd quickly left the pit wages office for a job on the local weekly paper and knew every trick going to get publicity. When he led the local carnival riding a penny farthing bicycle, and the local TV asked him why he was doing it, he said, 'Because I've got a majority of 400 and I can't find a pink elephant.'

Bill did mailshots by hand, congratulating everybody in the local paper who got married, had a birthday, won a raffle or a dog show, and spent hours every day rattling off hundreds of letters to delighted and astonished constituents.

And he too was stony broke. But very smart with it. At that time all television companies and the BBC knew how hard-up MPs were, and would pay us a professional fee for travelling out to Shepherd's Bush to do an interview, or driving up to Leeds or Birmingham for a studio punch-up, and me and Bill became experts at it. Like a pair of scriptwriters dreaming up sit-coms, we'd hatch out cracking ideas which would guarantee ten quid from *World at One*, or *Newsnight*, or whatever the equivalent programme was called then.

How about if we ask the Chancellor to put the same tax on fox-hunting as he does on bingo? That'll get 'em going for the Budget. And we did. Isn't all this advertising of toys on ITV at Christmas a disgrace? Kids tormenting hard-up mothers who can't afford to buy them new shoes? Let's ban it. Let's abolish all the army bands, I'd say. Tell 'em the miners will play for nowt at the Royal Garden Parties. That's worth ten quid any day from Yorkshire Telly.

And what happens to the cash all those silly buggers chuck into the pond to make a wish at the Jewel Tower opposite the House of Lords? Bet you the security man nicks it at midnight. Nice royal scandal, it will make a very good headline about three quid in the fountain. When we heard that Danny La Rue was cracking dirty jokes about Sir Gerald Nabarro and his handle-bar moustache, we'd slap down an early day motion of outrage and indignant fury. We invented rent-a-quote before it was ever heard of.

Ten quid was ten quid. It would take me and Maggie into the gods with enough for fish and chips in a paper bag after. Cash for questions? Or questions for cash? Not really. Nobody asked us to do it. And it was poverty-driven, not greed.

Bill had a little earner in the summer escorting American students to Russia. The only way they could get there in the Cold War was to get visas through a British MP who would guarantee they would not go off spying somewhere. Bill's job was to smooth the paperwork path for those rich, spoiled future leaders of Uncle Sam, who once they were away from Mom simply shacked up together for the rest of the trip.

One night Bill woke up to a hammering on the door and a posse of KGB guards demanding he went and stopped the enormous drunken racket from the party they were having. Bill admitted afterwards he was terrified. He had visions of them all going to the Gulag with the fat cat kids bailed out and Bill left languishing for twenty-five years.

Leave it to me, he bowed and scraped and grovelled to the guy with the Kalashnikov. Then he shut the door and whispered to the teenagers, 'Listen. I'm not daft, I know you are going to fuck like rabbits all through this trip, but fuck quietly. Otherwise we are all going to finish up with shaven heads and your mummies and daddies are going to be very angry. Especially when I write the story for *Newsweek* and it's all over Washington.' After that Bill said he had no more trouble.

A few years later, the American Embassy started approaching MPs to see if we would take on an American researcher for free, to work in the office. The Embassy said it would pay £40 a month for expenses. Tony Benn and the other Tribune Group members said, as you would expect, 'It's all a trap. They are training young spies. It's being run by the CIA. They will be bugging your phones. You will all be caught in compromising circumstances with infra-red cameras then blackmailed into working for Herbert Hoover.'

'Oh well, in that case I'll have one,' said a brave soul, 'but only if she's got big tits.' The American Embassy sent a stunning girl round the very next day – and she had. After that other MPs rushed to enlist. We later found out that the poor girls themselves were paying the £40 for the work opportunity, and some came from very hard-up families too.

Unfortunately, none of them had a clue about Britain or politics, or even knew what a constituency was. They couldn't even research the underground map of the Tube stations, never mind a spy network. Most of them would spend a month putting down written questions about the waiting list for verrucas and haemorrhoids in Slagthorpe Hospital, each costing about £200 to answer, and the local Labour parties thought their MP had gone barmy.

But we gave them glowing testimonials when they left, so everything ended happily.

Bill Price had an astonishing piece of luck when a constituent came to see him with an incredible tale that he had saved Harold Wilson's life on his holidays. Bill laughed like a drain and thought he was one of the usual harmless nutters MPs have to put up with, but then the bloke got out the holiday snaps to prove it.

The Prime Minister had gone out sailing in a dinghy on his own with his dog Paddy, who jumped overboard and couldn't get back in. Poor old Harold tried to rescue him and he fell in the sea too.

Nobody knew a word of it, but the whole world did when Bill got the photos and shared the cash with the man who took them.

'Serves him right,' said Bill. 'Miserable bugger won't give us a pay rise because it will lose votes before the election. So what else can we do?'

Bill loved all animals passionately. Not just dogs who fell in the sea, but any others made to suffer cruelty. He was a leading advocate for the League Against Cruel Sports, and persuaded me to accompany him to a tucked-away field near Huntingdon, to infiltrate a hare-coursing meeting.

The live hare is let loose across a ploughed field to slow it down, while two greyhounds chase it and compete to catch and kill it, often by both getting it in their jaws at the same time and literally pulling it in half while it is still alive. The screams from the hare are horrendous. There had been many private bills in Parliament to outlaw it but none were successful.

Unfortunately, along with a photographer from the League Against Cruel Sports, we were spotted under our caps and mufflers. An ugly mob manhandled us to throw us into the frozen duckpond, until Bill whipped off his cap like Sherlock Holmes and yelled 'Stop in the name of the law! We are Members of Parliament!' The thugs recognized us, then shouted, 'He's not,' pointing to the cameraman, and gave him a severe buffeting. Although we did keep him out of the pond.

Later they were quietly fined for assault in the local magistrates court and pleaded guilty, to produce just a few paragraphs in the local paper.

Sadly, Bill died of leukaemia in 1999 after losing his seat in 1979. A great journalist and stuntman, he never achieved a minister's job despite holding his seat for four elections against all the swings. Parliament used to be full of lively committed campaigners and characters like Bill. It's a dull place without them.

In the summer of 1969 we even had to sleep on camp beds in Parliament because the flea-pit hotels wanted our beds for more gullible tourists who could pay higher prices than we could in winter. MPs bunked down on couches and settees all over the House, after it finished about 1.00 a.m., but all night long Big Ben would boom out to remind us Cinderellas of how privileged we were, and at five the anvil chorus of the cleaners came round banging on tin buckets with their mops and shouting to each other.

After a year in Parliament, I got the best job in the world. Bag-carrier, errand lad, gofer, minder and Mr Fixit for the Minister of Sport, Denis Howell. Officially known as his Parliamentary Private Secretary.

For a year the whips had been sending me round the country as a lucky mascot carrying a rabbit's foot guaranteed to bring victory at any by-election. It never worked once. But in Birmingham, at a by-election in Ladywood, where the local party actually had only two paid-up members because the rest had deserted, I stayed with party workers and they must have sent word back to Mr Birmingham himself, Denis Howell, famous ex-football referee and a Brummie natural at wheeling and dealing, who knew everybody who was anybody in the sporting world. He knew I was football daft, because I kept asking him questions in Parliament about betting and match-fixing and bribery, including three Sheffield Wednesday players who had gone to gaol.

Which suited me fine. We went on official business to ringside seats at all Henry Cooper's big fights, Wimbledon tennis, the Derby at Ascot, and never travelled to Wembley Stadium unless we were accompanied by screaming motorcycles with blue flashing lights to halt the traffic and take us to the back door by a secret route. It still happens today to stop the IRA practising target shooting. In those days everybody thought we were royalty and saluted.

There was a downside to the job. All too often I would have to sit next to some foreign ambassador's wife who would natter all through the game about 'Oo ees is that good-looking number six, hey? The boy with blond 'air and so strong legs.' It got on your nerves after a bit. Spoiled the whole match.

Although the troubles in Ireland had just started, security then was non-existent. There were no passes, no checks, and, like any groupie following the band into a Rolling Stones concert, I'd just walk behind Denis Howell and say, 'I'm with the minister' and that was it.

When it was the 1970 Cup Final replay at Old Trafford, Harold Wilson insisted on going too. I just tagged on and said, 'I'm with the Prime Minister.' Anybody could have done it. Matt Busby shook me by the hand, put a glass of champagne in it, and I sat next to Harold Wilson at the game.

Harold was no mug. He knew how popular football was even then, and loved it when the Labour Party members bragged how England only won the World Cup under Labour, as they had in 1966. 'Two world wars and one World Cup!' our fans would chant at the Germans on Costa Brava beaches. The 1970 World Cup was just six weeks away in June, and Harold was going to hang on to its handles and milk the feel-good factor for all it was worth.

Leeds were playing Chelsea and Mick Jones scored for Leeds. As a professional Yorkshireman, Harold was absolutely delighted. 'He comes from Rhodesia, that lad,' I told him, and Harold's pipe nearly dropped out of his mouth. Harold Wilson had had terrible trouble in Rhodesia with the white settlers refusing to accept black democracy. 'Don't worry,' I cheekily cheered him up, 'it's Rhodesia near Worksop in Bassetlaw.' When they sank Steetley pit, the manager was called Rhodes, so he named the village Rhodesia, after himself.

Harold said nothing until two minutes from the end of extra time, with both teams level at the crucial climax of the game, and then turned to me and said, 'Go downstairs and ask my driver to phone the Foreign Office and find out how Manchester City have gone on in the Inter City Fairs Cup in Budapest. The game will be over now. If they have won, tell him to send a message of congratulation from me and tell Joe Haines [his press officer] to make sure the Press Association know about it.'

'Can't I wait to see the end of the game?' I asked.

'Do as you are told,' Harold said. 'I'm the Prime Minister and you are the errand lad.'

When I got back Chelsea had scored and Leeds were out. Serves him right, I thought, secretly glad that I was a Sheffield Wednesday supporter, who had just been relegated and sent down by Manchester City.

Then it got even worse. Harold Wilson was famous for wearing a daft-looking rubberized mackintosh with black lapels which sold in C&A for about £4. It was made by a textile firm in Yorkshire owned by a Hungarian refugee called Joe Kagan, who Harold later put into the House of Lords, before the guy was sent to gaol.

Harold was proud of this new material made by the white heat of new technology and wore it everywhere. Although I never saw anybody else wear one, because the rubber made your body sweat like a pig.

Except for one old guy who not only just happened to be at the game that night, but was also a guest in the boardroom. When he left wearing that mac, I followed him out and said to the bobby, 'Stop that man! He's pinched the Prime Minister's famous mac.' So the bobbies arrested him. I had to make humble apologies to the old gent, and at the end of it had to keep quiet, and couldn't even manage a few quid from a television interview for a top gossip story.

A few weeks later Harold made a stupid decision to call an election in June instead of waiting until October. The economy was picking up fast and we were actually winning by-elections again. Chief Whip Bob Mellish went canvassing in the Tea Room and asked every single Labour MP when the election should be held. Every single one said October. So Harold went in June. Right in the middle of the World Cup. Too daft to realize that in politics sod's law will always prevail. If anything can go wrong, it will, and at the worst possible time.

England were favourites. The Swinging Sixties, Carnaby Street fashions and British pop music were in demand all over the world. British films and our theatre were winning accolades everywhere, and Harold the gambler was on a roll, intoxicated with success.

But Harold's luck was cracking. Goal-keeper Gordon Banks dined out on the Mexican food one night, instead of sticking to the rigid English diet, and two days later, with a substitute goal-keeper, England were out.

And so was Harold Wilson as Prime Minister, Denis Howell as Sports Minister, and me as the working-class bag-carrier.

Seven

THERE'S NOWT TOO GOOD FOR THE WORKING CLASS

Nothing upsets the British taxpayers, and especially their newspapers, more than politicians going on foreign trips. Even a fact-finding tour of the miserable Falkland Islands or Afghanistan will produce instant wrath, never mind Hollywood, Barbados, Hawaii, Hong Kong, the Virgin Islands, New York, Dallas, Sydney, Soweto, Acapulco, Tokyo, or even Katmandu. All of which I have toiled in, doing service on behalf of Her Majesty's Government. Often at great personal inconvenience and jet lag.

Our embassies abroad are adept at avoiding awkward headlines back home when our MPs do go abroad. Their main job is to swamp the delegation with so many meetings, tours, visits, receptions and discussions about the late rum and banana production, well away from any beaches, pounding waves, swimming pools or dusky maidens, that all the delegation will ever want to do is fall into bed at nine, suffering from severe sunburn, alcohol and jet lag.

Immediately the delegation comes down the Club Class ladder, half asleep and hung over, the bombarding, briefing and bumf will begin. With, of course, some more gin and tonics or Campari or even Pimms in the hot sun before the reception. When it's, please don't mix up the President with the Opposition Leader, or even worse, their wives, otherwise it may start another civil war or coup. And if you see this scruffy giant following you around, who can't speak a word of English, ignore him. He's not a beggar, he's the James Bond of their police force acting as your bodyguard in case you get kidnapped and held hostage.

Please don't go near any of the young women, or boys either, they have all got diseases. The local hooch is dreadful. The embassy will supply all your needs in that respect, but you will be expected to drink a glass of holy water at the ancient shrine on Thursday. We will be standing by with these black bombers, as we call the pills, and a car to rush you back to the hotel, when the holy water immediately evacuates your bowels. Rather a nuisance, I'm afraid, but it would be a deadly insult not to drink it. There is an allowance of £20 a day for expenses, but we thought you might like to purchase these rather nice Wedgwood ashtrays and porcelain dishes to give out as mementoes, so we have deducted the cost of them from your allowance. The bus leaves in ten minutes, so you will have time to change, shower and study your brief for the next session, followed by the pineapple plantation, the local gaol, hospital, children's concert, dockyard, war veterans and police.

So what's the point in going? It is simply to chat to the locals over a beer at night, and find out the real story of where a lot of the overseas aid money is hived off and why the local Lord High Poo Bahs are driving around in Mercedes, while little pot-bellied kids are going hungry and are full of disease, with no schools or school books, medical care, or any hope at all.

The Oxfam people there will tell us the truth. So will the man who sweeps the streets (if he can speak English and knows we won't shop him). He'll tell us how much he earns, how much he has to kick back to keep the job, whether he ever eats chicken once a week, or once a year, and so on.

My first trip in 1973 was a top-prize eye-popper to Japan. Back in the early Seventies, Japanese cars, motorbikes, televisions, cameras and transistor radios were pouring into Britain and closing our factories everywhere. There was still a very strong opposition to anything Japanese from veterans of the Bridge on the River Kwai, and our other old soldiers who had suffered terribly in Far East prison camps in Burma and Singapore.

All over the world, countries were furiously imposing import taxes, quotas and restrictions on Japanese goods, which were being sold abroad at half the price they were in Japan. The British trade unions resisted Japanese imports fiercely and demanded trade sanctions against them.

Those nice men at the Foreign Office said the Japanese really are sorry for what they did in the war and would like to make amends and we shouldn't be beastly to them. So could the Labour Party Whip's Office perhaps arrange for one or two trade union MPs to go to Japan on the usual fact-finding tour to get the real story? And perhaps even take a bomb-damaged stone gargoyle from the blitzed Houses of Parliament to Hiroshima, to show that London was bombed too? Would I like to go? It was like asking would we like to win the pools. And it wouldn't cost the British taxpayer a penny.

The Japanese Government paid for first-class fares all the way on JAL airlines and the best hotels in the world. A seventeen-hour flight with champagne non-stop, except for refuelling in Alaska, and all in the company of three good mates. These were ex-miners Joe Harper MP, the well-known piano player at the Pontefract Miners' Welfare, Eric Varley from Derbyshire NUM, a serious lad from Chesterfield, now Lord Varley, who could collect all the statistics and do the talking, and Walter Harrison MP, an electrician from Wakefield, the hardman to keep us out of trouble, because Lord Lambton had that very week been involved in a story published in the *News of the World* about a call-girl. One or two Conservatives went as well to help keep the stiff upper lip on behalf of Her Majesty.

Walter's job was to make sure we were all tucked up in our own beds by 11.45, and right on the minute he would telephone our rooms to check. Unfortunately, we would drive him barmy and ruin his sleep by deliberately not picking up the phone, until he finally stopped bothering.

The first problem we had was finding a bomb-damaged gargoyle. Nobody knew what had happened to these important pieces of Blitz history until we finally traced the old guy who had been in charge of Parliamentary rubble-shifting, and he looked over his shoulder and admitted he had actually borrowed a few bits for posterity, which were still on his garden wall. He packed a lump up and it went first class with us.

It was doubtful whether any back-bench MPs had ever been to Japan before 1973. So they laid on the full red-carpet, bowing-and-walking-backwards tour of hospitality. Our first weekend had to be spent Japanese style, wearing only Japanese clothes, eating their food, sleeping on the floor, listening to their music, and we would be spending it in a ryokan, or ancient inn, in Kyoto, a city of Buddhist temples, beautiful gardens, perpetual rain, and rooms with paper walls. Nothing there has changed for a hundred years.

First of all, you have bath, they said. Go in the little room, find tap on wall with basin, sluice, and wash down all over. Get in bath. The maid will then come in and wash and massage you. Put on kimono and slippers and nothing else, then come down to dinner.

Well, we had all been in the army or RAF or pit-head baths before and we were all starving hungry, so we each walked to our little chamber. Joe Harper reckoned it couldn't be anywhere near as bad as Russia, where all the pit-head baths were manned by twenty-stone Russian women, carrying three-foot-long scrubbing brushes, and the miners' union had stopped sending delegations, because they could only find one public schoolboy at the pit to volunteer.

The wooden bath measured three feet square and three feet deep and was steaming. There must have been a gas ring under it. One degree hotter and it would have bubbled. So I had a sluice off the wall and then came the knock on the door. I put the kimono on as fast as I could and there stood the maid with a dish of green tea.

She was at least four feet tall and eighty-one years old.

They like their little jokes, do the Japanese. So we all of us made our excuses and left, as they do in the best tabloids, because as good trade unionists we objected to the exploitation of older people in sweat-shop conditions.

True, all true. But we did cheat with the kimonos and wooden sandals, which stopped at size seven. The trouble for us working-class, wide-legged Northern blokes is that kimonos swing open in the middle right up to the top, and it takes a certain art to walk and mince with knees together, never mind slink down on the floor with knees bent, in front of a foot-high table.

The Japanese do it. But British lads down the pit and on building sites squat with legs wide apart like all ale-suppers do. They wouldn't know how to slink. So the British showed the finest array of C&A, and Marks and Spencer Y-fronts ever seen in Kyoto. It didn't half make the geisha girls laugh at the dinner.

Then the geisha girls served us a twenty-seven-course meal using chopsticks, lasting four hours. Raw kidney beans, raw fish, raw eggs in suki yaki stew, seaweed, gherkins, squid, octopus, even 100-year-old carp. The geisha girls loved that so much, we gave them ours too. We were that hungry we even ate the dandelions and chrysanthemum leaves they had trimmed the plate with.

The geisha girls are not good-time girls, of course. They are there just to fill the saki cup, sing a song or two, perform an occasional dance, and play ying-tang, ying-tong songs on the square banjo. Plus telling fortunes, fanning us when we swallowed a lump of raw ginger, thinking it was parsley, and giving us all a neck rub every half-hour to keep the cross-legged circulation going.

It was very boring. Old Joe Harper was a natural comedian

as well as a piano player. 'Do you know any good jokes?' he asked the interpreter. 'Did you hear that one about this young couple sitting in the empty pictures in Pontefract, and it's bitter cold, so she's snuggling up to him when this funny-looking bloke comes in and sits next to them, holding his pet ferret inside his trousers to keep it warm. After a minute or two, the lass nudges her boyfriend, and she says in shock, "Kevin, this feller next to me has got his thingy out." "Well, it's nowt you haven't seen before," Kevin says, "so do stop making a fuss." "I know," she said, "but this one's eating my crisps." '

Not a sound came from the assembled guests. Ah well, you see, they don't know what ferrets and crisps are in Kyoto. Joe shrugged. 'You don't happen to have a piano here, do you?'

Joe Harper got to his piano a couple of days later at an official reception at the embassy in Tokyo and insisted on playing 'La Paloma' and then 'Fascinating Green Eyes' to all the delighted guests, while the monsoon blew outside, and then persuaded an obliging Lady Antonia Fraser, who just happened to be a special guest that evening, to sing 'A Nightingale Sang in Berkeley Square', on a wonderful British occasion which just showed that the old Labour motto, 'There is nowt too good for the working class', is absolutely fine. The next time Joe bumped into Lady Antonia was at a reception at Buckingham Palace where he was the Labour Government Whip, officially titled Vice Chamberlain of the Royal Household. 'Does tha remember me, lass?' he asked. 'I played the piano for thi in Tokyo.' She did too.

The Japanese made us honorary members of their Parliament, the 'Diet', and were desperate that we should persuade our unions not to block their goods. They showered us with gifts, silk scarves, radios, and wood carvings, but it was obvious they were breaking trade agreements everywhere.

We soon fathomed out that the Japanese cars sold in the UK with a three-year guarantee only had a 10,000-mile guarantee in Tokyo. In the UK, Japanese cars came equipped with radios, heated rear windows and all sorts of extras for free, which had to be paid for in Japan.

Then, stupidly, British Leyland decided it had too many dealers in the UK, selling two or three cars each every week, and in an act of mighty folly took away their franchise. Overnight, Datsun (now Nissan) and Toyota moved in and took over 5,000 outlets from every town in Britain to flood our home market.

The retailers and wholesalers on Japanese high streets were all owned by the manufacturers. There was no competition, and our Scotch whisky exports could only be found at four times the UK price behind a large pillar on the ninth floor of a department store. Although they did sell a good imitation of their own at a quarter of the price.

The whole marketing structure was run by a tightly controlled Mafia of price rigging and feudal families, and the reason for Japan's success was that everybody worked a fifty-hour week, with unpaid overtime, retired at fifty-five, but didn't get any old age pension until they reached sixty-five. Which meant they had to save for the ten-year gap.

Who did they save with? Their own employer, who took in a massive 27 per cent kickback from the wage bill every week, to reinvest in the company. No wonder none of them ever went on strike.

Half of Tokyo wasn't even on mains sewerage, with highly paid skilled technicians still living with septic tanks, or pot and carry, in one room, or with their in-laws, no different to those conditions Maggie and me had lived in fifteen years earlier. In social terms, their prosperity was a total myth. Much of that is common knowledge now, but back in 1973, after years of the American Occupation which allowed them to build their new factories to put ours out of work, it was a revelation.

So that was why MPs needed to travel.

I came back from Japan half a stone lighter, full of rice and saki, bearing gifts for Maggie, and I brought another gift too.

We went off to the Lake District for a rainy weekend and guess what? Maggie was pregnant. Which was a bombshell to us, because we had by then been married sixteen years, with never a sign of a family at all. Not that we weren't a very healthy couple, who loved kids. It was just that our chemistry didn't work. And in the days before fertility clinics, etc., there was damn all anybody could do about it. Except perhaps spend three weeks in Japan.

There was just one more small snag. In two months' time, to make up for all my absences, and leaving her on her own every week from Monday to Friday, I had promised to take Maggie to America. A nice little drive from New York to New Orleans and back, calling at Nashville, Natchez, Atlanta, Cherokee, and, most importantly, Washington, DC. Where the Watergate hearings were taking place and where I could earn a few bob writing about them for the *Guardian* and *Sheffield Star*.

In 1973 very few people, apart from film stars and the rich, had been to America either. It cost at least a month's pay for an MP, just for the fare. Air fares were kept artificially high until Freddie Laker broke the cartel, but there was a way round it. All you had to do was form a club and charter the plane for private hire. Clubs even advertised. So we joined a flower club and paid £75 each return and that was it.

But now Maggie, aged thirty-four, and classed as an older mother then by the NHS, was in the middle of morning sickness. The Thalidomide scare was big news, and thousands of mothers who had taken it to help their morning sickness had ended up with severely abnormal children.

But she decided to tough it out. So we hired the smallest Ford Pinto car, stayed in twenty-dollar-a-night motels, and rolled 3,000 miles all over the South, listening to country and western and bluegrass, with car sickness all the way, through steamy towns with courthouses surrounded by Civil War cannons, and shops on one side of the street for whites, with the others on the opposite side for blacks. Segregation had been made illegal six or seven years before, but the Ku Klux Klan still advertised on huge highway hoardings everywhere.

We put on Basil Rathbone Sherlock Holmes accents, because that was the only one the chaw tobbacca-spitting gasoline attendants seemed to understand, without setting the hound-dogs on us in *Dukes of Hazzard* country, and we politely declined their offer to take food stamps for gas. 'You all ain't on the run from Watergate are yah?' they'd tee-hee as they spotted the hire-car number plate. They really did spit and slap their thigh.

But the real history was back at the Senate at the Watergate. Inside the Caucus room, Cecil B. De Mille could not have staged it better. Massive pillars from *Samson and Delilah* held up the ceiling, and folks from back home with Senators' passes, leaned, hung, craned, chewed gum and peered on tiptoe from every nook and cranny. Camera crews snapped and flashed just as they did in all those gangster films where the accused puts his hand over the mike, and then the lawyer says, 'My client pleads the fifth amendment.' All it needed was guys in white coats yelling and selling popcorn and hot dogs like a baseball game.

For a boring hour the director of the FBI read out fifty-one pages about how he burned all the documents, as the committee yawned, scratched, and muttered to each other in a Friday afternoon way. When he finally finished the Chairman, the very famous seventy-six-year-old Senator Sam Ervin, from South Carolina, called the meeting to order.

Senator Sam could have been chosen by Central Casting for the part. He actually looked like Charles Laughton or Burl Ives playing Big Daddy in *Cat on a Hot Tin Roof*, and we all thought – good. Now for some old-time politickin.

But Big Sam simply said, 'Am tarred. It's too hot for anythin' except fishing and it's Friday afternoon, so Ah am going to leave the rest of the questionin' until Monday,' then walked out before the usher even called 'All rise'.

The fans didn't like it. They felt short-changed and demanded a rain-check. I tried to get to him and tell him how much I admired his homespun honesty, but the nine-foot security guard grabbed me and threw me out.

With her morning sickness, poor Maggie didn't get to see him or much else either, except TV in the motel bedrooms. But she began to agree that MPs going on foreign trips wasn't always a picnic.

It was fifteen years later when I returned on another Select Committee trip to Japan in 1988. This time the Trade and Industry Committee was studying why the UK Government appeared to be about twenty years behind everybody else in using computers. As a result, crooked dole scroungers were still turning up at six or seven different DSS offices, in six different neighbour-hoods, claiming for six different families from six different Irish addresses, and getting away with it. Government offices lagged years behind in modern technology so we went to talk to the experts in Tokyo, Silicon Valley, San Francisco, Austin, Texas, Boston, and New York.

The problem was, we flew the wrong way round and went to Japan first. Japan and the attitude of its politicians and Govern-ment had changed unbelievably. No more humble kow-towing. This time we were the poor relations. Very little was laid on. This time, after a week of their no-fibre diet, and not filling my belly which was used to real ale and thick brown bread, the sushi and tempura gave me – for the first time in my life – haemorrhoids. Go on, have a good laugh. I used to do it until it was my turn. I can tell you that fourteen-hour flights from Tokyo to San Fran-cisco do nothing to help cure haemorrhoids.

By the time we got to New York, I was mincing down Broadway like one of the cast from the then smash hit *La Cage aux Folles*, singing 'I am what I am' and looking at the sky and asking, 'Why me, oh Lord? In a country with no National Health

Service, why didn't you choose a Tory instead?' Then I spent a sleepless night reading the New York Yellow Pages, past all the adverts offering abortions at only $500, or $450 without anaesthetic, then reading about laser-beam instant pain relief in very posh Fifth Avenue clinics for cripples like me. What the hell, I thought. This is an industrial injury, honestly acquired in the service of Her Majesty. Let the Embassy and the British taxpayer pay for it.

So the Embassy laid on a stretch limousine (that way I could lie down), and took me to Fifth Avenue. Would you believe it? Even the receptionist had the latest computer. But no laser. 'They don't work,' said the very expensive New York quack. 'The damn things just come straight back again. What's more, I am not sure your cheapskate British Embassy insurance covers anything but the economy budget. The best thing to use is this,' he said and held up a needle the size of a six-inch nail and shaped like the New York RKO radio tower which King Kong had climbed up.

'Just bust 'em,' he said dismissively. 'I busted 'em last week on a nice girl from Brooklyn going on honeymoon with her third husband, and it worked a treat.'

I should have insisted on the anaesthetic. Even for the other fifty bucks. Even to pay it myself. Because without it you bite clean through your bottom lip. To be fair, he only charged me (in 1988 money) $61 for the two-minute cure. And nothing at all for the paper napkin to hold inside my trousers with one hand to staunch the blood, as he turned me out on to Fifth Avenue and the stretch limo, where the chauffeur quickly found some newspaper for the seat. To be unfair, he also insisted on $32 for a tube of ointment which Boots sell over here for two quid.

And what did I learn on the trip? Well, I learned that I just cannot understand why the voters and press make such a fuss about MPs travelling abroad. It is so educational, and gives us such a valuable personal experience of private health care.

Trips abroad are also valuable because, despite the voters

thinking that politicians are best mates behind the scenes, the different parties rarely mix, or even have a drink together at the Houses of Parliament. As everywhere, similar people band together, and few Liberals from Eastbourne would sit down to eat and drink with a Barnsley miner, or a Tory knight of the shires, or vice versa.

On foreign trips, MPs have no option. On one trip to New Zealand there was a cock-up with the hotel bookings, and the delegation hit town on the weekend of a big convention and had to share twin-bedded rooms with Tories paired with Tories, etc. The problem was that Sir Jasper More, a lovely man, was a Tory with a terrible snore, and nobody wanted to share with him. Except Walter Harrison, the MP for Wakefield in Yorkshire, a notorious Labour Whip hardman and fixer who said, 'Leave it to me'. That night, just as Walter turned off the light, he cooed, 'Give us a kiss, Jasper,' and for the rest of the night Sir Jasper lay awake and never uttered a sound. And there was nothing in the papers either. Walter said afterwards that it's what the prisoners do to all the new arrivals in Wakefield gaol. It works every time.

In the Eighties our Home Office Select Committee was investigating the phenomenal growth of crack cocaine, and the trail from Mexico to El Paso to Dallas and Washington, long before the media were interested, or had ever heard of it. We studied the Fagin and Oliver Twist drug dealers there who used kids as pushers because kids don't get mandatory long sentences. So Washington had 2,700 addicts who looked after kids in foster care, many with AIDS from sharing heroin needles. We studied DNA testing too, many years before the newspapers cared, or knew what it was. In 1988 our Home Office Select Committee warned that by 1992 a cheap drug epidemic, mainly crack, would sweep Britain's council estates in poverty areas where drugs had never been seen before. Nobody took any notice. Then it did. But it wasn't until it happened that the media screamed shock, horror and demanded to know why it had been allowed to happen in our ghettos.

Why? Because prophets never have any honour. Any politician forecasting doom and gloom, or the end of the world is nigh, is labelled a boring nuisance. The media are only interested in what is NEW today. If it ain't yet broke, then don't fix it. Then when it breaks, blame the politicians.

We went to Prague, Budapest, Warsaw and East Berlin long before the Berlin Wall came down and were surprised how good the people's standard of living was. The cities were exactly like ours in the Sixties. No traffic, but no crime either. Good buses, schools and care in the community, good real ale and cheap food. It wasn't their ideology holding them back, it was their technology, because the Yanks wouldn't let them have the microchip for computers, and they could not develop it themselves.

We warned they would catch up fast if they ever got it. Now they have. But if Manchester United can beat them at football, who cares about the prophets and technology?

Meanwhile, in Katmandu, the little orphan kids we found freezing in doorways late at night are probably still there, shivering, but never mind, a few bob to a charity will stop us all worrying. Then we can all shout 'Absolute disgrace' at politicians flying out to try to solve the problem. Why don't they get the pavements mended on our streets?

It was ever thus.

Eight

A SWIFT KNEE IN THE GOOLIES

U NTIL 1992, there was never more than the same percentage of women in Parliament as there was in prison. About 5 or 6 per cent. Which just goes to show where the rogues and villains of the world come from.

Two of the very first women whips in the 1974 Labour Government were no less than Betty Boothroyd, who eventually became Madam Speaker in 1992, and twenty-six-year-old Ann Taylor, who later, in 1997, became Leader of the House and then Chief Whip herself – the very first women in 600 years of history to be awarded the honour. Back in those days they had to put up with the daily ribaldry of other macho shop-floor MPs who automatically put all women into categories ranging from Linda Lusardi Page Three girls to Sloane Rangers from Chelsea.

When the Labour Government was hanging on by a thread in 1976, old-time MPs would try every trick in the book to get a night off for a big game at Wembley. They would furtively sneak into the Whip's Office and beg Jack Dormand, the pairing whip, to allow them to take the evening off, because really, honestly, Jack, it's our twenty-fifth wedding anniversary, and the missus has come all the way to London for it, and we've got tickets for *Evita*.

And really, Jack, I've got a firm pair, with a Tory MP who also wants to be absent. Without even taking his eyes off the BBC six o'clock news, Jack would simply shake his head and say, 'The only firm pair in this office tonight is over there on Ann Taylor. Now bugger off.'

Labour Government Chief Whip Bob Mellish walked into Annie's Bar one night in 1970, shaking his head in despair. Bob was a typical old-style Irish Cockney who represented the Bermondsey part of Southwark just across the Thames from the House of Commons, and who had taken a rare hour off to make his annual visit to one of the local Party meetings.

He sank a large whisky and said, 'I've been married twenty-five years and had a house full of kids and I swear I will never understand women. There's this young bird at the meeting and she stands up and asks me what our Government is doing about the Agricultural Farm Price Review this year. "Farm Price Review?" I says. "Farm Price Review? What are you worrying about the Farm Price Review for, darling? The only cows we got here in Bermondsey are those in the Co-op Women's Guild." She went bleeding bananas,' Bob said in amazement. 'What was wrong with that?'

Twelve years later Bob Mellish quit his seat in despair. The times had changed so much that a Gay Rights campaigner, Peter Tatchell, was chosen to fight the by-election and lost an 11,756 Labour majority to the Liberals in a working-class seat, which has never been regained since. The Labour vote slumped from 19,300 to 7,700, but that's another story.

Ex-colliers like Joe Harper, the MP for Pontefract, who had never worked with a woman in their life, just could not understand why any woman would want to get to Parliament. 'It's a damn sight easier to marry an MP and then tell him what to do than it is to find a seat yourself,' Joe would declare.

Joe reckoned the best form of three-line whip ever invented is a swift knee in the goolies, just as the MP is dropping off to sleep. 'It works every time. It's not the hand that rocks the cradle which rules the world,' he used to say, 'it's the timing of the knee on the knackers in the night.'

Joe would claim that every Friday when the lad on the motorbike delivered the envelope with the whip instructions outlining next week's business to his house, his wife would get hold of it and say, 'Widow's pensions on Monday, don't forget to vote for that. Equal pay for women – just make sure you are not missing then.' 'Anything to do with the kids, schools, animals, hospitals I have to be there,' he'd say. 'As for the little things like Vietnam or the unions, I can please myself.

'I just mentioned the other week,' said Joe, 'that this new woman Tory leader, Mrs Thatcher, was announcing that second wives should get more of the bloke's wage packet and divorced first wives should get less, because she was a second wife herself, and ever since then my balls have been black and blue.'

And it is true. Joe Harper was right. There has never been a world leader yet that hasn't had to respond to an unexpected up-and-under. Not even Tony Blair or Bill Clinton. Every politician needs a candid friend, and a candid friend is a pain in the balls. Which is why wives and partners, who have a vested interest in the family business, give the most honest advice. Wives and partners know that when you have got men by the family jewels, their hearts and minds will surely follow.

And even in those distant days of Miss World beauty contests, Benny Hill chasing Bunny Girls across the fields and over the stiles, and *Carry on Camping*, with Barbara Windsor catapulting her bra into space, no one ever really doubted that it was women who ran every establishment from Buckingham Palace to the Rover's Return. Basil Fawlty never ran Fawlty Towers. Nor did Alf Garnett run his house in Wapping either.

It was their daughters who changed it all. They started to read books. The first working-class daughters began to leave university about 1970 and the educated Ritas soon followed.

Lecturers introduced them to Germaine Greer's *The Female Eunuch*, and Erin Pizzey showed them that domestic violence did not have to be suffered.

It was a Labour Government that brought in legislation to outlaw racial discrimination, after Enoch Powell's 'rivers of blood' speech in Wolverhampton. So why should it not be a crime too to discriminate against people on the grounds of their sex? Why should women be paid less than men? Why shouldn't women read the *Nine O'Clock News* on television? Or the football results? Or drive buses and Tube trains? Or even become MPs? And when a Labour Government is in power, is it not much easier to change Government policies through the block votes of the unions, where thousands of women are members?

Another feminist leader who burned her bra at the time was film star Jane Fonda. She caused outrage and fury all over the USA with her open hostility to the Vietnam War and Lyndon B. Johnson's handling of it. The American press stuck the nickname of Hanoi Jane on her and the title followed her right round the media globe. In America there were attempts to have her charged with treason, and violent demonstrations everywhere she spoke. To make amends and apologies for her earlier Hollywood sex-bomb films based on pin-up science fiction fantasy, like *Barbarella*, she had started dressing in old jeans, black T-shirts and a scruffy dark woollen donkey jacket, like those worn by cement-mixers everywhere, which quickly became a feminist fashion statement. Her fame and notoriety were worldwide. She couldn't appear in public without being mobbed by TV cameras, photographers, politicians, protesters, fans, autograph hunters and the sort of crowd that used to turn out for Princess Diana.

There was a very large, powerful body of MPs in Parliament at that time who campaigned furiously against this American war. Practically every week, they led large crowds through London to march on the American Embassy in Grosvenor Square, and inside minutes there were fists flying, women screaming, horses stampeding, and riot police charging and using truncheons as the protestors fought back with their banners.

All over America, too, students such as Bill Clinton were refusing to register for military call-up or finding ways to opt out of it. So it was in great secrecy that the Tribune Group of Labour MPs, which was very left-wing then and consisted of thirty-seven of Westminster's hand-picked puritan socialists, managed to persuade Jane Fonda to come and speak to them at their regular weekly meeting in the House.

She agreed on one condition. There must be no publicity. No mention of it to the press until after she had left. She had to be met outside, escorted in through the back entrance, straight upstairs and then out again immediately afterwards. In all seriousness, she was genuinely scared of some nutter taking a shot at her as they had at President Jack Kennedy, Bobby Kennedy and Civil Rights leader the Rev. Martin Luther King just a few years earlier, and John Lennon a few years later.

The details were fixed. She would be met in the St Stephen's Tavern pub, just across the road (which has now been pulled down) and brought in through the pedestrian subway from Westminster Tube station.

But who would recognize her? None of the old farts in the Tribune Group had been to the cinema since George Formby was a lad. Every single one of them could have lined up in the Praesidium next to Stalin, Brezhnev, Bulganin, Beira, Gorbachev or Yeltsin, and been totally identical in exactly the same jacket, trousers, hat, haircut and glasses. After due discussion it was unanimously moved and agreed, that the newest, youngest recruit of the group, Comrade Dennis Skinner, just six months in Parliament, would be the one most likely to recognize her, and he should be sent as delegate to deliver fraternal greetings and escort her to the meeting.

By sheer coincidence it was St Patrick's Day, 17 March 1971. And the whole of the Fleet Street newspapers were on strike.

Naturally young Dennis was wearing a shamrock, to show solidarity with the workers of Ireland in their class struggle against the forces of worldwide capitalism and so that Miss Fonda and her companion would recognize him. Anxiously, Comrade Skinner searched the St Stephen's Tavern, but could see no sign of the great Jane. The time was ticking away and here he was on his first mission from the Westminster Parliamentary Politburo and unable to deliver. Finally, he approached the barmaid, and asked, 'Excuse me, missus, but I'm looking for Jane Fonda. Has she been in yet?'

The Cockney barmaid gave Dennis a long cool look and said, 'Not been in yet, dear. But usually she sits over there and has a Guinness.' Dennis did another quick tour of the three floors of the pub, which was pretty full by now, and thought – what if she is in the Ladies? Quickly he ran downstairs and said to the barmaid, 'No, really, I am looking for Jane Fonda. Honest. I promised to meet her in here at half past seven. Could you just have a look in the Ladies and see if she is in there?' The barmaid stared at Dennis, put down her towel, and wearily replied, 'Jane Fonda? Jane Bleeding Fonda? Why don't you just piss off, you Irish bum, before I fetch the police.'

So Dennis did. I bumped into him ten minutes later anxiously searching the Central Lobby and asking every copper if they had seen Jane Fonda, and then he asked me too. I couldn't tell him for laughing. Dennis knew at that time I wrote a column for the local *Sheffield Star* and he begged me not to write it. 'I'll never live it down with the lads at the pit,' he pleaded. 'No,' I said, 'the papers are all on strike anyway.' (So I didn't. Until the following Friday. Then I kept out of his way for a month.) 'What shall I do?' he asked me, a veteran of two and a half years' service in the House. 'Just go back up to the meeting and say she never turned up,' I advised. They will never know. So we did.

But there she was, about five feet three inches tall, in full flight, holding all the old Cold War warriors breathless and agog.

Not because of any words of fire or wisdom or knowledge, but simply because she had taken her donkey jacket off and excitedly kept pulling her thin black cotton T-shirt down hard, at every verse end, with nipples sticking out not like chapel hatpegs, but at least as good as any topless Page Three girl, which the *Sun* launched shortly afterwards. A few weeks earlier the famous feminist 'Burn your bra' battle-cry had resounded round the world, and here was a beautiful young Hollywood star actually showing British MPs she had done it.

It was the only time the Tribune Group ever clapped a speaker at the end because they were too stunned to ask questions. Even to ask Dennis how she managed to get past the bobby on the door.

The women who did get to Westminster not only had to be smart in a macho man's world, they had to learn to adopt that innocent, double-edged guile where the cat easily outwits a pack of howling dogs then sits on the roof and smiles. Quite simply, in any group of 650 people, if twenty of them are women, they can get away with anything. And every single woman MP knew it. Few women MPs in those days campaigned to get more women into Parliament. The ones already there wallowed in their exclusivity. Need an instant column for the Sunday papers outlining a woman's angle on television, sex, clockwork orange films, abortion or birth control? Certainly. How many words? Don't worry, we'll sub it, and is £50 okay? Well, considering MPs were on only sixty quid a week, and no expenses, it was very nice thank you.

Dame Irene Ward, the Tory MP for Tynemouth, was a classic. Without changing a hair, she could have done an impersonation of Margaret Rutherford leading the Belles of St Trinian's to war. Totally unconcerned, she would sit in the middle of the top bench of the gangway (which has no seat in front of it), legs splayed wide open to hold her enormous handbag, exposing long-legged hand-trapper shiny silk knickers (as we called them when we were kids) with tight elastic at the knees, as blithely relaxed as Hyacinth Bucket at a Ladies' Circle cake-making meeting.

Naturally, she was nicknamed the 'Mouth of the Tyne' rather than the MP for Tynemouth, and prided herself on being a doughty campaigner for naval affairs and women. Once, when the Government decided to issue new-style uniforms to the navy, she stood up and furiously demanded to know why the men's uniforms were being handed out first.

'Is the Minister saying that all the Wrens' clothing has to be held up until every rating and officer has had his turn?' she asked innocently. She knew exactly what she was doing. As the House roared at the Minister's bumbling reply, she went on, 'The Minister has had me down on this one already in committee, but he's not going to do it again on the floor of the House.' It was pictures and headlines in every newspaper the day after.

Just as Diane Abbott's picture was, on the very first day she took her seat for the Queen's Speech when Parliament opened in 1987, because she was the first black woman MP elected. It also happened to be the first time that Parliament had been televised. Although the rules said TV cameras only, hordes of photographers turned up in the gallery to take still pictures of Diane carefully posing on the benches to powder her nose from her compact. It even beat the shots of new MP David Blunkett, with his guide dog, and Bernie Grant in an African robe.

On that day, the press photographers invaded the Chamber long before business started, and began snapping away. A picture of me appeared in nine daily newspapers showing me with my feet up, reading *The Times*, with row upon row of empty benches around me. Actually I had got there early to claim a good seat and was simply reading the paper while waiting for the show to start. Ever since then, whenever MPs ask for a pay rise or want to alter their long hours, it has been wheeled out to show a picture of idle layabouts skiving at work. Despite many protests and even serious threats to sue, it is forever more a classic, like

Marilyn Monroe with her skirt flying high on a windy New York subway.

Of course, the women loved being televised. It meant that any woman MP wearing a bright red or blue outfit and big hat immediately stood out in a sea of grey or black suits and was instantly recognizable to her voters. Even one or two of the scruffy men started to smarten up.

And why was the House being televised for the very first time? Because the very first woman Prime Minister, Mrs Thatcher, instinctively knew that TV pictures of howling ruffians shouting down a poor little woman who was trying her best to run the country and stop the bully-boy unions from going on strike, would appeal to every floating woman voter in the country. She was absolutely right, which was why the smart, experienced male politicians among us consistently voted against televising nine times before it was finally carried on the votes of one or two vain male loonies, who could not live without the daily narcotic of media adrenaline. And were daft enough to think it would make them, and not just the front-bench faces, famous.

Mrs Thatcher, a grocer's daughter from Grantham, had been totally anonymous in Parliament for fifteen years, even as she rose to become Secretary of State for Education in the previous Tory Government, until she was daft enough to advise housewives to stock up on tinned food during the miners' strike and energy crisis of 1973. Then showed the TV cameras her well-stocked Chelsea larder with a year's supply of cans all neatly labelled. Which went down very well with poor pensioners shivering at home with no electricity for heating or oven. Later, she became nicknamed Mrs Thatcher 'Milk Snatcher', after cutting the school milk budget, and after that wisely decided to lower her profile and keep away from TV.

After Ted Heath lost the second General Election in October 1974, he tried to cling on as Leader of the Tory Party, knowing that the other front-bench leaders couldn't agree on a challenger to plunge the knife into his back. When Mrs Thatcher bravely stood alone to take him on, nobody gave her a cat in a dog's kennel chance. By an amazing fluke, she got the prize because a future Labour MP's wife, and a Labour-supporting TV programme, scored a massive own goal.

Sometime before she threw her handbag into the ring, Mrs T. had agreed to do an interview with Linda McDougall, a young producer from New Zealand, married to Austin Mitchell, who was also a TV presenter at Yorkshire Television at that time, and who was later to win a famous by-election at Grimsby when, against all the odds, he held the seat after Tony Crosland's tragic death. Linda hung the interview on a peg that she too was the mother of boy and girl twins and oh, what a pair they are when they are together.

But when Mrs T. bravely climbed under the ropes in February 1975, and into the ring, it quickly became a Granada TV *World in Action* special for a notoriously hard hitting investigative programme which had attacked the Tories on many occasions. But this time *World in Action* were too clever by half. They decided to do a programme which would send up this housewife, married to a millionaire, living in a posh house just off the King's Road in trendy Chelsea. With deadpan faces, they treated Mrs T. like royalty. They took her onto building sites, with a minion to run forward and kneel in a puddle to brush every speck of mud from her shoes. It showed her a million miles from the hard world of strikes, unions, pay rises, poverty, crime, slums, council-housing tower-blocks, and all the other serious problems of politics. Which, of course, she was.

But that didn't matter because the only votes she was after in that programme were not those of the viewers, but those of the other Tory MPs. On that Monday night, by sheer chance, there were no votes in Parliament, and a very large number of Tory MPs, plus their wives, plus the chairman of their constituency party's wife (enormously influential in the Tory Party) actually sat at home and watched *World in Action* and loved her.

'She's just like the Queen!' they gasped. 'Such poise, dignity and charm. So beautifully eloquent and capable. She's just what the Party needs.'

Later, in at least a hundred Tory beds, knees were going into goolies.

The next day, Mrs Thatcher pulled in enough votes to see off Heath, and then went on to beat another five ex-Cabinet ministers. Linda McDougall has made many fine TV programmes about women in politics since (usually they show how women effortlessly beat the male system) but none has ever had the same long-term effect on history.

The election of the first woman Leader of the Opposition was classed as a joke by both Labour and Tory male MPs. It was a stunt. A gimmick. A desperate gesture by the Tory Party to try to cash in on the growing demands of the women's protest movements and pull back the women's votes which Labour had picked up from Tories in the 1974 elections with promises to bring in equal pay and bump up child benefit allowances. Together with new laws on sex discrimination and sexual harassment at work.

How could a woman Prime Minister run the country? How could she wheel and deal standing shoulder to shoulder in the Gents, whispering out of the corner of her mouth, alert, careful, looking under the cubicle door to make sure nobody was listening? That was how disputes among men had been settled since urinals were invented and the cavalry stopped approaching the Indians with a white flag to pow-wow. Every guy knows that trying to do deals with women leads to nightmare rows. They change their minds every day. There is no such thing as a verbal contract. How could she get the unions back to work?

Men work in teams, they said, they hunt in packs. From day one at school it's the TEAM that counts. That's why the unions are there. Women are loners. Individuals by nature. Little

Sharon's trip to the dentist will always be more important than moving reference back of the resolution opposing workplace ballots. Of course Mrs Thatcher is an exceptional woman, we admitted. She got two degrees, in both chemistry and law, conveniently had twins to save time, and studied her courses while carrying them.

Brilliant. A magnificent achievement. But when did she ever play for a team?

All right, all right, we said. If there were to be two Prime Ministers, with a bloke naturally responsible for the big stuff, like jobs and industry and wars and the police and the departments where men work in gangs, with another woman Prime Minister looking after hospitals, kids, pensioners and those committees where they instinctively know that it's daft to put kids and prams in high-rise council flats, then it might be sexist, but it would be what nature intended, and could be feasible in government.

Even if all the other nations had women leaders, it might work, we said. They could start off the summit in Moscow getting the photos out of their handbags over a cup of coffee, and pointing out how the twins didn't look a bit like each other, then a trip round the Gumm store sales, and with a bit of luck the nuclear missiles might never be used, except for May Day parades.

But an Iron Lady taking on the miners and hitting Arthur Scargill with her handbag? We couldn't wait to see it.

The reason sports broadcasters on Sky TV or any other channel don't put microphones on players in action is that every other word would be a bleep. Brutal, searing, personal sarcasm about the other guy's looks, background, earning capacity or physical deficiencies are all part of the team rat-race culture and taken for granted. The arena called the Chamber of the House of Commons is no exception. The BBC, who handle the Parliamentary broadcasting, are absolutely terrified of being sued for libel or accused of trivializing the House in any way. The Chamber at Question

Time sounds like feeding time at the zoo to the listeners and viewers because all the wisecracks, heckling and abuse from the back-benchers in the arena are deliberately jammed.

No wonder the viewers are puzzled and can't understand why the MPs suddenly roar with laughter and point at each other. If the words of the speeches are recorded in Hansard then these are privileged and can be used by anybody without the fear of a writ. But nobody as yet has been to court to sue for any other libel, slander, insult or innuendo made as an aside which isn't privileged or protected. And the BBC have no intention of setting a precedent.

It is particularly daunting for women. The best, like Mo Mowlam and Clare Short, can certainly meet wisecrack with wisecrack, holding a handful of smart ripostes ready, because they know what to expect.

One or two of Labour's New Women, christened Blair's Babes, were devastated when they had to face the arena after the last Election. Reading MP and former BBC producer Jane Griffiths, who can speak four languages, protested strongly that a Tory MP opposite raised both hands, palms upwards, in front of his chest, then moved them up and down, shouting 'Melons' every time she got up to speak. Jane got very little sympathy from Madam Speaker Boothroyd, who had lived with it for twenty-five years. Old Labour women MPs would have taken it in their stride. They would have held up a limp little finger, slowly wiggled it up and down and gently sung, 'Chipolatas'.

Another new woman MP, a doctor of philosophy, seriously suggested that all heckling and interjections should be banned because it was not fair to women. Their voices are not strong enough to carry. Their skins are not thick enough to stand the abuse, and it would be much fairer just to clap when a clever debating point is made. Rather like a bowling green, instead of Highbury or Old Trafford. But with 400 MPs packed into a very small Chamber, almost as tightly as in a crowded Tube train or on a Spion Kop terrace, it is not going to happen. The professionals know that one wisecrack, expertly timed, can devastate a Prime Minister in mid-sentence, and he knows it too. Like Shirley Bassey or Bernard Manning on a Saturday night at the old Glasgow Empire, if they can't handle the hecklers and haven't learned their trade, then they shouldn't be on the stage. Public speaking, debating and television jousting with an interviewer as sharp and as tough as Jeremy Paxman are absolutely essential skills.

When Mrs Thatcher became Leader of the Opposition and had to joust with Jim Callaghan, the Prime Minister, at the Despatch Box, he would patronize her like an elderly uncle talking to his favourite niece. 'I welcome the Right Honourable lady to her new post as Leader of the Opposition,' he said, 'and I am sure the House will join me in hoping she retains her position there for a very long time.' Mrs Thatcher would smile sweetly, without realizing that the words had a double meaning, while the back-benchers hooted sarcastically.

Mrs Thatcher had many skills and talents, but she lacked one of the most essential for a politician. She had no sense of humour. Unlike Barbara Castle, the outstanding Betty Boothroyd, Edwina Currie, Theresa Gorman, Clare Short, Mo Mowlam, Margaret Beckett (who can bring a pub audience to its knees when she sings ''Tis better to be a whore than a housewife'), Ann Taylor, Diane Abbott, Virginia Bottomley, Gwyneth Dunwoody, Lin Golding, Harriet Harman, Gillian Shephard and dozens more, she just couldn't understand a joke at all.

It seemed as if the only way she knew how to talk to men was rather like a schoolmistress addressing unruly boys in the playground who need admonishing because they were enjoying life too much. It was pretty soon apparent that she needed a top public relations adviser to alter her image, her hairdo and her strident voice, and coach her in fireside TV chats and how to give Jimmy Young a chance to say something on his own show.

But humour? When her advisers said it was important in a major speech to impress on the punters that Prime Minister Jim was nearly ready for his old age pension, and she ought to start referring to him as 'Moses' and tell him to keep on taking the tablets, she chortled from the platform, 'And what's more, I do hope he keeps on taking the pills.' Then stood there baffled when nobody laughed.

Like slip fielders standing around a batsman, half a dozen of the Labour boot boys would place themselves within fifteen feet of her, and fire verbal bullets every time she appeared at the Despatch Box to put questions to Prime Minister Callaghan or make a major speech. They would do it in voices just loud enough to carry to her at the table, but not for the microphones to pick up. There is no place on earth more exposed than the Despatch Box of the House of Commons where ministers have to stand alone.

It is putting it kindly to say that the new woman Leader of the Opposition struggled. She was certainly no Iron Lady then. We would crack sexist jokes, wolf-whistle and growl – 'Ooh, she's an exciting woman,' just like Compo does to Nora Batty in *The Last of the Summer Wine* or Les Dawson used to do to Roy Barraclough in drag. 'They reckon she does the work of two men,' I'd feed to Dennis Skinner on the opposite side of our gangway, and he'd yell back, 'Yeah. Laurel and Hardy.' When the great guffaws went up poor Mrs Thatcher would panic.

Concentrating hard on her typed speech, she would often not quite catch what we had said and wonder if her own words contained some double meaning or innuendo, and lose the thread of her argument in the uproar. Sometimes she would make the fatal mistake of trying to ad-lib and respond. Which is about as wise as a batsman trying to answer back to a wicket-keeper's taunt in the middle of a fast bowler's attack. Very, very few Parliamentarians have the wit, steel nerves and aplomb to carry it off with the impeccable timing it takes.

Eventually she learned to grow cloth ears and take no notice whatsoever of any jibe or bait, however tempting. In fact, as Labour tore itself to pieces with internal battles with the unions, hanging on to votes every night where the majority could be counted on one or two fingers, she blossomed with confidence. She managed to conceal her anger and fury, even when the rough boys succeeded in tripping her up.

In 1978 she went to the Cup Final at Wembley Stadium, which was probably the first football game she had seen in her life, and had the cheek to do a TV interview after the match saying that the Ipswich player, Trevor Whymark, had been the best player (well, she had to, because Ipswich was a highly marginal seat and Arsenal wasn't).

Unfortunately, whoever had primed her before the game forgot to check whether or not Whymark was fit to play. He wasn't and didn't. The following Tuesday, the bovver boys were ready to ask Prime Minister Jim whether he would make sure she could sit next to Denis Howell, the Minister of Sport, in future, so that he could show her how to read the programme. Which went down very well.

By this time, Mrs Thatcher had learned to keep her cool and just smile sweetly and say nothing. A technique perfected years later by Virginia Bottomley and Harriet Harman, who could deflect the most difficult question by answering it like Mary Poppins doling out a spoonful of sugar to make the medicine go down.

Labour women MPs had grown up among the rude wise-cracks, abuse, fury and fire of picket lines, union meetings and Party Conferences, and learned to live with it. It was very different for upper-middle-class Tory women used to being treated with deference by staff, husbands and family. Open sarcastic defiance made them furious. What they couldn't stand even more was the old adage that hell hath no fury like a woman scorned.

And that was just the strategy which the Labour bovver boys

used next. They ignored Mrs Thatcher. They simply sat back, or turned round, and chatted to each other whenever she rose to speak. They argued loudly with their neighbours about last night's match on TV, or the quality of different beer, or the price of new cars, and just let her carry on trying to make a point over a hubbub of loud conversation. Any public speaker, night-club singer, after-dinner comedian, or even teacher in a classroom, knows that the most difficult audience to face is one which talks to itself and pays absolutely no attention to what is happening out front.

When the Tory back-benchers tried the same trick with Michael Foot, he simply let them get on with their chattering, then shouted abruptly, 'Right, then. That's settled. How many of the Tory members opposite actually agree with what their Leader has just said? Put your hands up now!' Few of the Tories had been listening and only about five or six raised their hands in the air. The Labour benches roared with mocking laughter, and a bewildered Mrs Thatcher looked round (she had been chattering herself), absolutely livid at what she saw, as Michael Foot quickly moved the vote.

Cruel to women? Of course it is. Unfair and downright dishonest? Absolutely. Mean, beastly, spiteful barbarism? Dead right.

But here was a woman who, if she won the election, would turn out to be totally hostile to every request to help old age pensioners, the sick and the poor, the three and a half million people whose jobs she would eventually take away, and have no pity or sympathy at all for that half of Britain which depended on heavy industries for its living. Until eventually, when she could win elections no longer, her own side got rid of her. And went back to gentle persuasion by the goolies.

Now, of course, Parliament has 119 women MPs, 108 of them Labour. A quarter of all Labour MPs are women. Ten years ago, in May 1987, there had been only twenty-three women MPs in total.

It has a Labour woman Speaker, Betty Boothroyd, who simply laughs when she has to chastise a rowdy young male MP and the old guys shout 'Smack his legs, miss, get your ruler out and smack his legs,' as though she were a primary school teacher. Parliament has a woman Leader of the House, Margaret Beckett, formerly President of the Board of Trade, a woman Leader of the Lords, Baroness Jay of Paddington (daughter of Jim Callaghan), and a Chief Whip, Ann Taylor.

The cool Mrs Beckett, who possesses a regal dignity and bearing which often remind people of Princess Anne, is nevertheless wickedly funny at the private dinner parties held by Madam Speaker in her magnificent apartment deep in the Houses of Parliament. Invitations for these evenings are as highly coveted as any for Buckingham Palace. It is black tie and jewellery. The food and wine are superb and politicians, especially the women, let their hair down and perform their party pieces.

Margaret Beckett, with perfect aplomb, literally brings the House down with a little song called 'Don't Get Married, Girls'. It's twenty-one verses long, and here are just a few of them:

> Don't get married, girls. It's very badly paid.
> You may start off as the mistress, but you'll end up as the
>   maid.
> As he thinks that you're his mother, and lays his head upon
>   your breast,
> So you try to boost his ego, iron his shirt and warm his
>   vest.
> So don't get married, girls, for men are all the same.
> They just use you when they need you, you'd be better on
>   the game.
> Be a call-girl, be a stripper, be a hostess, be a whore,
> But don't get married, girls, because marriage is a bore.

Change your lover every Friday. Take up tennis, be a nurse. But don't get married, girls, for marriage is a curse.

The women MPs have made great progress in cutting down on the late-night sittings which led to late-night boozing (to say nothing of other pastimes to pass the night away) and the futile tired battles and friction of government. They have introduced healthier food. Fewer Friday sittings, so that men don't have an excuse not to go home and see the family and their constituents, and they are even arranging for Parliament to have a week off for the school's half-term break in February, when dads can see the kids.

Not only does the place look nicer, it smells better on the back-benches too, with perfume replacing the stale ale and tobacco which gained the place its ancient name of Halitosis Hall. Women have been an enormous civilizing effect on Parliament and politics. Two of them even bought me an anniversary cake and card when they found out I was celebrating twenty-nine years in the House. It was the only time I have ever been at a loss for words. And they were not after my safe seat either.

Meanwhile, as usual, all the scandal is still caused by men. Every embarrassing headline is still about the monstrous regiment of males caught in the headlights of the cruising tabloids. Whilst three of the women MPs were humbly and deeply apologetic, because they had switched their pagers off to listen to a tape of classical music in their office (and sip a glass of sherry as well, would you believe) and missed the ten o'clock vote.

Whatever is the political world coming to? It is beginning to look as if the most effective form of whipping has had its day.

Prime Minister Tony Blair appeared on the *Des O'Connor Show* to confirm proudly that every time he goes on holiday with Cherie, they always take his mother-in-law along with the kids (nothing new in that, we used to do the same at our house).

'My mother-in-law is my closest political adviser,' he told

Des. 'She is the one person of absolute common sense.' Well, of course she is. She is sixty-five-years old, her husband abandoned her with two small children, and she brought them up in Liverpool in her own mother-in-law's house to become successful lawyers.

Obviously Gail Booth has seen it all, suffered it all, wept for it all, and is now justly proud of it all. And even though the London trendies jeer at the Nanny state of Labour, it couldn't be in better hands than that generation of Gail, Betty, Ann, Margaret, Mo (short for Marjorie), Clare, and all the others with Swinging Sixties names who turned out to be a damn sight smarter than we macho hounds of the Elvis, Sinatra and Lennon era.

Probably because they don't have goolies.

Nine

SOME MPs GOT HIRED – I NEARLY GOT FIRED

B Y February 1971 MPs had not had a pay rise since 1964. Seven years of pay freeze under six years of a Labour Government which insisted that MPs should set an example to the nation, and in particular to the unions, by not asking for, or receiving, any extra money. As usual, the public and the unions took not a blind bit of notice and kept up their own demands.

It is a fallacy to think that MPs can ever vote themselves a pay rise. They can walk through the lobbies, of course, but after the vote their pay cheques have to be signed by the Chancellor of the Exchequer and approved by the Prime Minister. So even if they do vote for it they get sod-all money. Simply a huge heap of wrath from newspapers and voters alike.

In those seven years everybody else's wages and salary had gone up by 67 per cent. An independent survey showed MPs were working sixty-three hours a week and paying for London bed and breakfast and all other expenses out of standstill wages. So, inevitably, in those seven years a moonlight or black economy developed.

Conservative MPs at that time were invariably landed gentry or affluent somethings in the City. Or barristers, farmers, retired wing commanders, all of whom, like prospective Guards officers, had to produce evidence of a private income before being selected for the seat. None of them were too keen to make life easier for hard-up Labour MPs. Many of the Tory pinstripes supplemented their salary with part-time work in London in the mornings, but a toolmaker from Salford could hardly be expected to set up a lathe in the bowels of Parliament to do the same.

However, the one thing any MP could do was to get publicity. Any campaign by an MP, however daft, would be seized on and highlighted by the newspapers and television. The public relations industry was in its infancy in the late Sixties but was smart enough to know that a question in the House of Commons was a lot cheaper than buying an advert, and more people would read about it too.

Within weeks of my arriving and while I was still wet behind the ears, a friendly hand dropped on my shoulder and said, 'Joe, my old pal. You've got plenty of slagheaps in Bassetlaw, haven't you?' When I nodded in my simple, gullible way, he went on, 'There's this friend of mine who shifts slagheaps to make hardcore for motorways but the local councils keep charging him rates on the tonnage of the slag and not just the outbuildings. He wants us to kick up a fuss, put down amendments in the Budget and get it stopped. What's more' (wink, wink, nudge, nudge) 'he is willing to pay.'

Politely, with a sharp four-letter word followed by a three-letter word, I told him how to remove himself. But a few days later questions were being put down to harass the Chancellor, claiming that this financial impediment to improving the environment should be abolished.

Other fund-raising activities were just as blatant. At a time when MPs were being paid £80 a week with no expenses and allowances, public relations firms were handing out over £350 a week between two MPs, one from either side, simply to host whisky receptions in the House of Commons dining rooms on Budget Day. Supposedly to protest against tax increases on alcoholic drinks, with as much free booze as MPs and their friends could swallow. Whisky galore had arrived in Westminster.

Some charities paid handsomely for questions in the House to show their supporters how important it was to leave them money in their will. And every year the contestants in the Miss World contest would be paraded and photographed on the terrace over lunch with the dozen most handsome young trendy MPs, to get a lot of publicity for Mecca, who organized the contest.

Few back-benchers then could afford to take continental holidays, but nevertheless, although Spain was still run by a Fascist government which garrotted its political prisoners under the regime of General Franco, Albert Roberts, a Labour mining MP from Normanton, Yorkshire, regularly took groups of MPs from all parties on a visit to Spain to look at coal mines there. Greece had a similar Fascist government run by army colonels. The birthplace of democracy gave its citizens no votes at all. Yet at least one Labour MP was paid by the colonels to push their cause at Westminster. Other MPs were offered free trips to Iceland of all places, to listen to the Icelandic version of the cod war, and rows over fishing rights which were destroying British trawler jobs.

The franchises for local commercial radio stations were being awarded and very lucrative prospects were up for grabs. So the order paper was flooded with immensely complicated enquiries about waveband frequencies, and catchment areas.

A common stunt was for three MPs to form an 'All Party Group' which contained just one carefully chosen member from each party to become Chairman, Secretary and Treasurer of the All Party Group for Rambazania. Followed of course by free fact-finding trips, then the usual questions, delegations to ministers, adjournment debates asking for overseas aid or other cash favours. Most of which would go straight into the current dictator's back pocket, or on military weapons, while half the babies in Rambazania did not reach the age of six months.

Decent, honest back-benchers on all sides (and literally 99 per cent of all MPs despite their poverty were decent and honest) found that if they brought in a Private Member's Bill to protect the public in any way from being abused or ripped off by a large corporation, then the bill would be blocked late on a Friday afternoon, in an empty House, by some paid front man. All he had to do was shout 'Object' from behind his hand, without his name even going into Hansard, and the bill would fall to the back of the queue.

I introduced a Football Betting Levy Bill to make the highly profitable football pools industry pay for improvements to our ancient football grounds following the Ibrox stadium disaster in Glasgow which killed sixty-five people. The Tory MP for Southend, Stephen McFadden, paid by the pools promoters, blocked it for months on end simply by shouting 'Object'.

Two years later, under a Labour Government, Sports Minister Denis Howell and I persuaded the Government to back it and set up the Football Trust. When faced with compulsory legislation the pools promoters paid up voluntarily and since then it has worked magnificently. Especially for football ground improvements following the Hillsborough disaster in 1989, when ninety-six young fans were crushed to death, and all-seater stadiums were introduced.

Earlier, in June 1965 the new Labour Chancellor, Jim Callaghan, had made a speech in Swansea, saying, 'When I look at the Conservative MPs opposite, I do not think of them as the Honourable Member for X, Y or Z. I look at them as Investment Trust, Capital Speculators, or is that the fellow who is the Stock Exchange man who makes a profit on Gilt Edge? I have almost forgotten their constituencies but I shall never forget their interests. I wonder sometimes who they represent. Their constituents, or their own, or friends' particular interests.'

There was an uproar from Tory MPs and Chancellor Jim was hauled before the mighty Privileges Committee to apologize humbly and give his assurance that 'Nothing in my speech was intended to be derogatory in any way to Parliament.' The Committee then let him off the contempt charge.

It even got to the stage where huge pyramid-selling organizations, ripping off thousands of pensioners, were brazen enough to defend themselves at lavish lunches in the Parliamentary dining rooms to show MPs what wonderful organizations they really were.

Dammit, it even reached the point where one day a guy came up to me in the Strangers Bar (and how these touts ever got admission into the place we never knew) and whispered, 'Joe, I need your help. All I want is for somebody to arrange for that small wooden door at the foot of Big Ben to open for two seconds and we will be very generous to any guy who can arrange it.'

I said nothing.

'What we want to do is to film a cocky little man walking over Westminster Bridge, whistling on his way to work, going down the steps off the street, looking at his watch and straight through the door. And then the voice on the commercial will say "THE MAN WHO WINDS UP BIG BEN WEARS A TIMEX WATCH".' It was a great idea. Whether somebody else tried to do it I don't know, but I never saw the advertisment on television, so maybe they lost that one.

For some years ever since the Callaghan row, there had been a large number of MPs, particularly the hard-up Labour backbenchers, who demanded not just decent pay and office allowances to put the job on a proper full-time basis, but also to establish legally a register of members' interests where every MP would be compelled to declare any outside income, and where the money came from.

Which was, of course, vigorously opposed by practically all Tory MPs, and quite a lot of Labour ones too. The Tories ceaselessly pointed out that many Labour MPs received a cash sponsorship from the trade unions, who paid their election expenses and some office expenses. Although they never pointed out that none of this money went into the MPs' personal pocket. All of it went to the local Labour Party.

Of course, those MPs who strongly opposed a compulsory register said they wouldn't mind if a 'voluntary' register was introduced. Well, of course they wouldn't. They wouldn't bother putting their names and little earners on it, would they?

Without a majority, it began to look as hopeless as votes for women had done until the First World War broke out.

When Ted Heath won the election in 1970, many more new Tory MPs came into the House from a generation who hadn't got private incomes. They too demanded better wages and office allowances. Ted Heath set up an independent committee under Lord Boyle, a former Tory Cabinet minister, and, glory to God, Boyle brought in a report which said MPs' pay and allowances for back-up staff was a disgrace. Nothing had really changed since 1911 when MPs first got paid, and we should all receive a pay rise of 38 per cent plus office expenses, a proper car allowance and cash for living in London. Ted Heath, to the eternal surprise and gratitude of Labour back-benchers, and the only Prime Minister ever to do it up until today, accepted the independent report in its entirety, without trying to seek cheap popular votes by cutting the award.

Naturally, as has always happened in every MP's pay rise, the usual handful of hard left Labour MPs voted against it. Then, of course, as they have always done, they quietly took the money and stuffed it into their back pocket a few weeks later when their sackcloth and ashes gesture to the poor had been milked of the applause for their being the only genuine socialists in the House.

There was now no excuse whatsoever for any back-benchers to try to make a bit on the side by under-the-counter methods. The new attitude adopted by an overwhelming number of Members was that if MPs wanted to make extra money, their constituencies and local parties should know about it. Then they could face the consequences at the next election, or the wrath of their local party meetings on Friday nights.

Unfortunately, and very sadly, the pay-offs still continued.

The same handful of half a dozen names were still prominent in pushing certain issues and causes. Usually these causes were non-party, non-political and even non-controversial. Consequently they attracted little attention from party activists, or the press, at a time when Irish terrorist problems were exploding, the 1972 miners' strike was blacking out the country, the unions were marching through the streets, house prices were rocketing, and the Arabs were fighting the Israelis. So who cared very much whether cigarette manufacturers were paying cash to MPs to campaign against the ban on tobacco advertising?

The 'shot at Sarajevo' came in 1972 when the Arabs rocketed the price of oil, pushing up inflation and interest rates, and the booming property market collapsed.

So too did an architect called John Poulson, who over the past ten years had built up a long string of Labour Party connections, particularly in the north-east and Yorkshire, where his firm was based. Poulson's eventually became the biggest architectural firm in Europe, employing over 750 people, and he had connections in local councils and local health authorities throughout the country. He was very close to a man called T. Dan Smith, the former leader and in effect city boss of Newcastle, who titled himself a 'public relations adviser', plus Albert Roberts, his local MP, and none other than the Conservative Home Secretary, Reggie Maudling.

In February that year, an innocuous piece of legislation was introduced in the House by Home Secretary Maudling to allow the nationalized Tote to set up betting shops on the High Street and not be restricted to the race-course. NOBODY, BUT NOBODY in public or Parliament was interested.

Except the bookies.

It is not generally realized that gambling in Britain was then one of the biggest industries in the country. Added together, the betting turnover of horse racing and football pools in 1972 would proportionally be equivalent to the cash laid out on the National Lottery today. The pools provided the big jackpots of about £100,000 and the bookies paid out the small two or three quids.

Gambling, especially for the working class, has always been frowned on by politicians. Especially Labour politicians, who had seen it cause so much back-street misery and poverty. Bookmakers at the tracks often did a runner with the bets before the last race ended and in the Thirties razor gangs regularly fought pitched battles at race-tracks to get the best spots. Illegal backyard bookies in slum areas made a fortune without paying tax and took up an extraordinary amount of police time. To say nothing of police corruption. The rich, of course, had always been allowed to bet on credit over their telephones. Consequently, in 1960, the Tory Government passed legislation to allow the bookies to set up official shops on High Streets, so that the Government could collect the tax, and at the same time get rid of the back-street gangs.

Practically every other country in the world, even today, even in the free enterprise citadel of the USA, refuses to allow private bookmakers on race-courses. Virtually every single country only allows betting by a Tote. That way, all the bets are placed in a pool and shared out on a non-profit-making basis at the end of the day, with a percentage going back for prizes and improvements at the track. But in Britain, the Sport of Kings, as horse racing is rightly called, has political connections right through the noble ranks of supporters in the House of Lords and up the ladder to the Royal Family itself. So private bookmaking on the tracks was never outlawed. Even more so as the bookies regularly gave huge donations to the Conservative Party funds at election time.

For ten years the poor old Tote struggled on, confined to the course and not allowed to trade in the High Street. Then the great

British public was allowed by Parliament and the Home Secretary to receive daytime television. Hour after hour of cheap TV, usually from racing, filled the screens. And especially the screens of the newly installed TV sets in betting shops. Instantly, book-makers' profits boomed. From 1968 to 1970 the profits of Ladbroke's, William Hill and Coral rocketed by increases of between 600 and 700 per cent. Meanwhile, the attendances at the race-tracks plummeted and so did the cash coming into the Tote, despite the fact that the non-profit-making Tote always paid better odds, sometimes 50 per cent higher than Ladbroke's. What's more, the Tories' hatred of all nationalized industries meant that the poor Tote was handing nearly 4 per cent of its turnover to the compulsory betting levy for prize money while the fat cat bookies got away with ½ per cent. No wonder the Tote was dying on its feet.

The former Home Secretary, Jim Callaghan, said the Tote must survive to stop betting from falling totally into the hands of the bookies. Ted Heath, the Tory Prime Minister, agreed, much to the fury of his back-benchers, who were absolutely against helping any nationalized industry.

With their ten-year head-start, the private bookies had nat-urally snapped up all the best shops in the best places on High Streets everywhere. They already had 14,000 private betting shops in prime sites. The Tote wanted to set up 200. Yet for some reason the bookies put up a ferocious, unbelievable campaign against this 2 per cent competition.

Over a hundred MPs from all parties were invited to the best restaurants in London to hear the wounded pleas of the book-makers. The Conservatives were wined and dined at the posh, very posh Mirabelle in Mayfair, while Labour were fed at the less expensive Hyde Park Hotel.

At the weekly meeting of Tory MPs called the 1922 Com-mittee, poor old Reggie Maudling, whose heart was obviously not in it, was given a roasting by the Tory back-benchers. The usual suspects among the Labour back-benchers, plus a few more gullible fools who were against helping gambling in any form, argued against it too.

The bill was introduced in Parliament on Thursday, 3 February 1972, to an empty House, with no vote. The world and Fleet Street took no notice, especially as British troops had shot thirteen civilians in Derry the previous Bloody Sunday, in the first big killings of the Northern Ireland terrorist campaign. Notwithstanding also that the miners were on strike against Ted Heath's pay policy, and on that day a miner was killed on a picket line when a lorry ran over him at Keadby Power Station near Scunthorpe.

Who cared about betting shops and bookies? Nobody.

So why then did a Parliamentary bill backed by both Government and Opposition take nearly six months to pass through its committee stage when it should have taken two weeks? Because certain back-bench MPs, including Labour MPs, filibustered for weeks to block it. And they eventually did, saving the bookies hundreds of thousands of pounds in profits and condemning a tiny nationalized industry to wither away.

The two Labour back-benchers who filibustered and put down dozens and dozens of new clauses and amendments were Mr Brian Walden, the MP for Birmingham All Saints, who later left Parliament to become a well-known TV interviewer and political pundit, and Mr Arthur Lewis, a Cockney MP for West Ham North. With the bookies and their legal advisers blatantly sitting next to the MPs in the standing committee, and passing notes and advice to them, the two MPs spoke for hour after hour, day after day.

During the second reading of the bill Brian Walden had stated, 'I have no financial interest, direct or indirect, in the bookmaking industry or any allied industry.' Arthur Lewis never mentioned whether he was getting paid or not.

When the bill finally staggered out of the Committee, still

complete with its help for the Tote, despite weary hours of filibustering, it lay in the Home Office for weeks awaiting a rubber-stamping third reading in the Commons.

Other Labour MPs like myself, John Golding and Arthur Davidson QC, who supported the Tote and the official Labour Party policy, were furious at the tactics of Walden and Lewis. We had been campaigning for a compulsory register for years, yet we did not know, nor could we prove, that any member of the committee was being paid by the bookies to kill the bill. In any case if they had, they would have been doing nothing illegal at that time, especially if they had said a few words indicating a financial interest, to stay within the rule of the House. There was no public register of Members' interests, neither voluntary nor compulsory, so technically they were doing no wrong.

On 20 July, with the House almost at the end of the session and weary MPs all ready to go on their summer holidays, the Prime Minister, Ted Heath, made a sensational announcement.

The Poulson bankruptcy papers had been sent to the Director of Public Prosecutions and Home Secretary Reggie Maudling had quit his job because technically he was in charge of the police and 'he decided it wouldn't be right for him to handle it'. Too right it wouldn't. The bankruptcy court investigations into John Poulson's firm of architects had opened the biggest can of worms politics had seen for generations. The *Daily Express* said at the time, 'The Home Secretary's resignation was a gesture without parallel in recent politics.'

Maudling was a very wealthy man, but greedy. Poulson had been paying him thousands of pounds, when the Tories were in opposition from 1964 to 1970, to use his contacts abroad to get contracts for hospitals in Malta and other places. Two other MPs, John Cordle, the High Christian Tory for Bournemouth, and Albert Roberts, were also named, although no arrests were made until a year later. Poulson's bankruptcy hearing showed that his firm had given the former leader of Newcastle Council T. Dan

Smith's public relations company £155,000 (today worth well over a million).

The bankruptcy laws allow gifts to be recouped if the cash can be used to pay off debts, and Poulson owed the Inland Revenue and other creditors £275,000. All in all, he had handed over £500,000 in bribes and backhanders for contracts and favours in towns stretching from Wakefield to Wandsworth and all the way to Malta and West Africa.

T. Dan Smith, a working-class lad and son of a miner, left school at fifteen to quickly set up a painting company employing 200 people, mainly on council contracts. He lorded it over Newcastle with his DAN 68 number plate on his Jaguar. He sent his three kids to private schools, and claimed there was nothing wrong in making money, at the same time claiming to be a committed socialist.

The police enquiries into the Poulson investigations had interviewed no fewer than 300 local and small-time politicians.

When Maudling quit, as if by magic, the Tote Bill was brought back before the House for what should have been its virtual rubber-stamping, on the very last day Parliament sat in full session, Thursday, 7 August. Lo and behold! It had been emasculated by the Government and new Home Secretary. The bookies had won. The heart of it had been torn out.

By a miracle, half a million pounds had been found to rescue the Tote and wipe out its debts. The special clause to let the Tote set up shops on the High Street would only come into force if and when the new Home Secretary introduced a statutory instrument which he would lay before Parliament as and when, if at all, he thought fit, which meant never.

At 9.30 p.m. that August evening, Mr Brian Walden began his welcoming speech by declaring he did now have a financial interest in this matter, and thanked Mr Arthur Lewis for his assistance (even at that late stage Lewis had put down another sixty-seven new clauses and seventy-two amendments).

To say that the Labour Members were furious, never mind breathless at the blatant effrontery at it all, would be an understatement. Even future Tory Cabinet minister Norman Fowler demanded to know why the Government had changed its mind to help the bookies. The new, now worthless, bill was finalized in the small hours of Friday morning in the last day of the session, when practically every MP had left for the beaches.

The few Labour MPs on the Committee, including me and Arthur Davidson, were incensed but powerless. The regular Parliamentary Labour Party meetings would not be held again until the House returned in October, but we were determined that if Labour were to win the next election, after all the Poulson stain and stigma, it had to include a *compulsory* register of MP interests in its manifesto.

The bookies had saved an immense amount of their profits with the help of Labour MPs, while the Tories, supposedly in favour of competition and free markets, had bent a bill to save the bookies from such fair competition.

The Poulson enquiry had dragged on to reveal more and more disreputable stories of Labour councils in the North giving suspect planning agreements for Poulson's projects and it was all causing the Labour Party great embarrassment as the 1974 General Election came closer. After the 1973 summer recess, Labour backbenchers banded together and sixty-seven of us presented a signed petition to the Labour Shadow Cabinet demanding a Party debate behind closed doors, to force the Cabinet and the Conference to include a compulsory register in our next election manifesto. In a packed meeting over 250 Labour MPs demanded its inclusion, and that a committee be set up immediately to draw up rules for a compulsory register.

Only one Labour MP, John Stonehouse, objected. He stormed out of the meeting, protesting and ridiculing the whole principle. Two years later, he vanished off a Miami beach leaving behind his clothes, debts of over £1 million (with another £100,000 tucked away in a Swiss bank account), a twenty-five-year-old mistress and twenty bankrupt companies. He was later sentenced to seven years at Her Majesty's pleasure in Wandsworth.

Because of my vociferous complaints, I was elected to serve on the Register Committee chaired by the Deputy Leader of the Labour Party, Ted Short, who was a Newcastle MP. The Committee also included Eddie Milne, the Labour MP for nearby Blyth.

Eddie, a very brave Geordie, had been campaigning against T. Dan Smith on Tyneside for a very long time, since Poulson designed Blyth's new town centre. Eddie's reward for challenging the feudal closed shop of the then North-East politicians was to be deselected out of his seat by his local party at Blyth.

Amazingly, Eddie courageously took the local party on and stood as an independent on an Honest Eddie ticket in the following 1974 February Election. He won by 6,000 votes, although he lost the following October when the Blyth local party chose a fox-hunting barrister, John Ryman, to oppose him; Ryman himself went to gaol a few years later.

Our new Committee quickly brought in a report recommending a compulsory register which was accepted unanimously by the Party's MPs and then by the Labour Party conference. The Party workers, who often lived in miserable houses doing rotten jobs, were furious at the newspaper revelations on Poulson and the whispered rumours about Labour MPs, especially as MPs were no longer underpaid. The Party members wanted it all cleared up.

T. Dan Smith, formerly a director of Tyne Tees Television, had friends in very high places. Even the Labour Chief Whip, Bob Mellish, Chairman of the London Labour Party, was close to him, and campaigned regularly that contracts for council houses on the huge estates should not have to be put out to tender.

Following the arrests of Poulson and Co., the whole issue of corruption became *sub judice* and the campaign for a compulsory register cooled as the winter of 1973 and 1974 saw the Conservative Government in terrible trouble. The miners' strike led to power cuts everywhere, until Heath surprisingly called a snap election on who runs the country – the Government or the unions. Much to the surprise of Harold Wilson, Heath lost.

Labour were back in, but only as the largest party, without an overall majority. They were put there by a suspicious electorate, who didn't know whether Labour could be trusted, but were fed up with television sets being switched off at ten-thirty every night to save electricity, and actually thought the miners deserved higher wages anyway.

In the General Election of February 1974, Labour won only fourteen extra seats. It had no overall majority, with only 301 MPs out of 635, and it was obvious that another election would be called later in the year, probably October.

In a matter of four or five weeks after that February election, the slagheap scandal appeared once more.

On 4 April the new Prime Minister, Harold Wilson, was under ferocious attack from the whole of Fleet Street. There were serious allegations that Tony Field, the brother of Wilson's secretary, Marcia Williams, had earlier bought a quarry in Lancashire and a slagheap in Wigan to sell off the waste. Field had also managed Wilson's office as an unpaid aide.

His company, which included Marcia Williams as a director, made a profit of £250,000 on the deal, which Wilson defended as 'land reclamation' for industrial development and not speculation for profit. Eventually, both Harold Wilson and Marcia Williams had to issue several writs for libel, and the following November the man who bought the land, Ronald Millhench, was charged with forging letters and theft of Downing Street notepaper, and sentenced to three years in gaol.

The next five weeks of that spring of 1974 were to rock the new Labour Government walking its tightrope more than any financial oil crisis could ever do, as the Tory press in Fleet Street went hysterical. The Foreign Secretary, Tony Crosland, actually had to take a silver coffee pot, which had been given to him as a memento, to be valued at Sotheby's to show it was worth less than £40 and not the thousands the newspapers had claimed.

As the Poulson trial drew to a close, and the hysteria about MPs' interests mounted in both the press and the Party, I happened to write my regular column for the Party newspaper, *Labour Weekly* and coined a phrase which not only went down in history, but exploded like a match to a gasometer. The words were 'MPS FOR HIRE'.

The column read:

> It is likely to be announced in the House very soon that in future MPs will have to enter on a register any outside jobs, fees, gifts, free trips or perks they might get for launching campaigns in Parliament.
>
> Let's be perfectly clear. It doesn't go on to any great extent. The number of Labour MPs who can be hired can be counted on the fingers of one hand. And the rest of us know who they are. But often their constituents and constituency parties don't.
>
> The new Government now has the chance to compel all MPs to declare any source paying them more than £50 a year, or all gifts of more than £50 in value. If necessary, we should put it before Parliament, and be defeated, then let the electorate decide.

With the impeccable timing of many other events in my life (well, I was named after a kid accidentally run over by a steamroller), it appeared on the morning of Friday, 26 April, at exactly the same time as John Poulson was being sentenced to seven years in gaol and T. Dan Smith to six. Five other men also received prison sentences.

The verdict meant that all the restrictions on press reporting which had been held back for many months since the arrest were no longer *sub judice* and were lifted. Now, every newspaper, TV and radio programme could virtually say what it liked.

And they said plenty. By sheer chance, Jimmy Young asked me to record an interview earlier that morning for his lunch-time radio programme before the verdict was announced. I did my duty and defended the Labour Party, saying, 'I don't think that out of Labour MPs we have more than five people who are doing it. Just over one per cent. Yet it is so damaging to Party morale.'

Immediately Fleet Street screamed 'NAME THE GUILTY FIVE!' I had also done a similar broadcast for the BBC on *World at One*. The uproar was incredible.

Understandably. Here was a Labour MP in a Government which was on a life-support machine until October, with the Tory Party in disarray, and now the agenda had instantly changed from the miners or the unions to corruption.

For me, things had never looked blacker. My wife Maggie had given birth to our Lucy just five weeks earlier, after a gruelling, freezing election campaign in which she went out with me on the streets every day. As a then 'older mother' aged thirty-five, she spent eighteen hours in labour with a very difficult pregnancy and a 1974 emergency caesarean operation. I had to stay in London, even when she gave birth (I couldn't even get up there to sign the necessary permission form for the operation), with the other MPs who were propping up the Government's non-existent majority, and she was alone every night without sleep seeing to our new daughter.

Harold Wilson was still giving out jobs to his new junior ministers and a bright young MP might well have expected a corporal's stripe for valiant service. Now it looked like I could be court-martialled from the regiment instead.

Twenty-five years ago, Parliament was a very different place to what it is today.

Parliament had its own grand code of 'Omerta', the Mafia word for silence, which was paramount. MPs could do anything they liked (and some did) providing they did not bring the House into disrepute. To do so was a grave 'Contempt of Parliament'. Parliament was, and still is, a club. The lucky members can only be admitted by the votes of their constituents, but once in they are 'Members' and they can be expelled at any time by the other Members. Some indeed have been, and for offences a lot less serious than mine, which alleged that some of the 'Honourable Members' of the club were on the take and no better than crooks.

As expected, the Tories, despite the overwhelming majority of their Members having outside jobs, seized the opportunity. One of them, Sir Harmer Nicholls, the MP for Peterborough, had held his seat in the February election by just twenty-two votes. He was a certainty to go out next time and he knew it (he did so by 1,800 votes but was soon rewarded by a seat in the Lords), unless of course he could pull off some spectacular coup.

When the Commons met on the Monday, following a stormy weekend of press headlines, Sir Harmer stood up in the House and moved that my column and interviews on radio should be ruled 'Contempt of Parliament' and referred to the Lord High Executioners of the Privileges Committee, the highest Star Chamber court of the House, consisting of ex-Prime Ministers, Home Secretaries, Attorney Generals, etc., etc., who could, if they felt like it, throw me out. Providing of course the other MPs backed their decision with a majority vote.

Sir Harmer read out the offending article and transcripts of the broadcast to a packed House, and the day afterwards the Speaker ruled that the mighty Committee of Privileges should investigate the allegations which the whistle-blower (me) had had the cheek and effrontery to make against the mother of all Parliaments, renowned throughout the Commonwealth for its honesty, integrity and incorruptibility.

The day's delay gave my lifelong friend and eternal saviour, Arthur Davidson QC, who had been the Labour Party front-bench spokesman on the Tote Bill, a chance to visit the condemned man and draw up his defence.

The old boy network in Parliament, like all professional bodies, whether they are lawyers, doctors, army officers, or the Press Complaints Commission, etc., always know how to nod and wink their way out of such internal dilemmas. The standard practice is to kick the can of worms upstairs to a committee, which will meet in private, then several weeks later when the offender has gone down on his knees to grovel, promising never to do it again, the chairman will slap him on the wrist. Then the verdict will be quietly made public a few months later, when all the fuss has blown over. The problem in this case was that a few months later, there was to be another General Election.

The tried and tested routine is what the full House of Commons expected when it met the following day. Except that oh my God, the awkward bloody whistle-blower, me, stood up and refused to play their game and politely told them to get stuffed. Though not in such blunt words, of course. Arthur and me and scores of other back-bench Labour MPs had not campaigned this hard and long to capitulate now.

I told the Speaker in legal terms drafted by Arthur that I would 'substantiate the allegations – though I fear that this may bring the House into even greater disrepute than the article I wrote', which naturally caused another uproar. Here was a brave daft fool carrying a can of petrol through a forest fire and threatening to spill it.

Arthur's advice, and he had been the *Daily Express* libel lawyer before becoming the MP for Accrington in Lancashire, was to put in a 'defiant defence'. Hadn't the Committee itself ruled in 1967 that 'it was not contempt of the House if the issue was fair comment, written in the public interest, in the belief that it was true, and published in a proper manner'?

The words I wrote were true. They were written in a proper

manner, in a proper Party newspaper, not on a lavatory wall, and spoken on the BBC. They were without malice, in the public interest, and what's more I could prove what I had written and said. And I could too, with a dossier of names, dates and deals two inches thick.

Many of us were furious that two weeks earlier Simon Hoggart had reported in the *Guardian* that the Deputy Leader of the Labour Party and Leader of the House, Newcastle MP Ted Short, had indicated that the new Government was going to rat on our manifesto commitment for a compulsory register and simply introduce a voluntary one instead. Which was why I had written the piece in *Labour Weekly*. There could be no backing down now.

A horrified House immediately voted by 283 to 94 to kick the whole matter upstairs and out of sight. Except for Dennis Skinner, Leslie Spriggs, John Mendelson of Penistone, and David Steel, the Liberal MP for Roxburgh, Selkirk and Peebles, who demanded the debate should be held there and then in full view of the public.

Two days later the flames were fanned even higher.

The Poulson trial had revealed that Ted Short, the man who would actually chair the Privileges Committee enquiring into my allegations, had himself received a payment of £250 for his office expenses in his Newcastle constituency from T. Dan Smith.

It should be said right now that Ted Short, now Lord Short, was, and still is, a very decent and honourable man, but at that time there were simply no allowances paid for office help or research for Opposition parties. Labour leaders, including future Prime Ministers and all Opposition front-benchers, had no option but to accept cash from friends and supporters to staff their office.

In fact later, when Ted changed the system to give grants to Opposition parties, the grants were promptly called 'Short money' and still are. Today the main Opposition party, the Conservatives, could receive over £3 million in Short money for research, expenses and travel. The Liberals could get £1 million. William Hague gets £500,000 to man his office. Poor old Ted had to manage on a £250 handout.

The headlines that week were enormously damaging. The first month of the new Labour Government had been a nightmare. President Nixon was still embroiled in his own Watergate problems when he visited London that week, and here too was our new Government with headlines of politicians on the take. Voters expected it from the Conservatives, but not from Labour with its history of Methodist Chapels, Temperance banners and pride in its Pilgrim Fathers' sanctity and honesty.

Then, incredibly, it got even worse.

Two weeks after my article was published and I had been sent before the hanging judges, Simon Hoggart wrote a front-page piece in the *Guardian* on Saturday, 11 May headlined, 'MP GOT £25,000 [worth about £200,000 today] AS BOOKIES' ADVISOR' and went on to say that Mr Brian Walden, the Labour MP for All Saints, had accepted a contract – £5,000 over five years – while he was conducting a vigorous campaign against a Parliamentary bill which threatened bookmakers' interests . . . The sum works out at exactly £500 a year more than Mr Walden's Parliamentary salary'.

On the same front page David McKie reported that 'The Leader of the House, Ted Short, has now formally notified all the other Party leaders that the Government would introduce a COMPULSORY REGISTER BY THE END OF THE SUMMER RECESS'.

We had won our campaign! But only after a terrible, bloody, grievously mutilating, suicidal battle in the worst traditions of Labour's usual self-inflicted wounds.

In the same week the *Leeds Evening Post* carried banner headlines that Labour MP Albert Roberts had been taking £2,500 a year from the bankrupt Poulson. Which, when he had signed the contract with Poulson some years earlier, was actually more than his annual salary. Albert had also served on the Tote bill.

Nevertheless, the plain indisputable fact was that no MP had broken any law of the country, or even the rules of the House of Commons. They had declared their interests verbally, but not said how much, or who from, and as there was no official registrar's office to check or keep any record for publication, Mr Walden had every right to argue he firmly believed the Tote should not be allowed to set up betting shops to compete with the bookmakers, and subsequent events may have shown him to be right. The Tote still exists and thrives and in fact the 1997 New Labour Government very soon had plans to sell it off.

Inside six weeks of the new minority government and two weeks after my article in *Labour Weekly*, the Government took fright, did a massive U-turn and announced it would introduce a Select Committee to set up the new compulsory register and run it. The move was still opposed by the Conservatives, but many abstained, and a majority of over a hundred MPs voted it through. The Select Committee would also decide what punishment would be handed out to Reggie Maudling, Albert Roberts and John Cordle, who had been named in the investigations. But nothing was said about me. My trial as whistle-blower would continue, if 'trial' was the proper name for it.

The Committee of Privileges investigating my allegations would sit in private. It would consist of seventeen very long-serving, high-ranking, grand Members of the House, who even included the famous left-wing leader, Ian Mikardo, doyen of the hard left Tribune group, and a great supporter of nationalization. Unbelievably, Mikardo had opposed the new Tote shops at every turn – unbelievably, because he too was a great gambler, who offered odds to other MPs every day on events ranging from by-elections to beauty contests. What's more, the Committee would be chaired by Mr Ted Short, although I quite openly said that in

Top left: Little Uncle Joe, aged three, in clogs – later to be run over by a steamroller; my mother aged eighteen months – note the steel tips on the hand-me-down shoes; and Aunt Delia, aged five. The photo was rescued from the Blitz in a tin box.

Top right: Little Joe, aged eight, proudly shows his teeth after the Attercliffe school's wooden hut clinic had cleaned them and pulled out the molars.

Right: First election for Sheffield City Council, 1961. I got 3,500 votes, more than any other Labour candidate, and still lost.

MUNICIPAL ELECTION
THURSDAY, 11th MAY, 1961

NORTON WARD

J. ASHTON

FOR

LABOUR

The South Yorkshire Navigational Canal, Attercliffe, 1971. MP Jim Marshall and Sheffield City Council leaders Dame Grace Tebbut, Sir Ron Ironmonger and I all grew up within a hundred yards of this spot.

The steelworks rolling mill at the end of the street crashed and thumped all night. Even the sparrows coughed.

Left: We bought the offices next to the gasometer in Worksop for £3,000 in 1971. Harold Wilson opened it. It's a listed building now worth a fortune.

Top right: Guess which one is the politician and which one getting ready for a swift knee in the goolies.

MP's visit to Manton Colliery, Worksop. Horny handed sons of toil. Labour's finest.

This page:

Top left: Still a striker!

Top right: Highly secret three-line whip. Shadow front bench spokesman on energy, 1980.

Right: It's the clock that is leaning. Not me. 1981.

Opposite page:

Top: You can't beat kids and cats on election addresses.

Middle: The Prime Minister, Jim Callaghan, meets Lucy Ashton at the opening of Retford Labour Party Headquarters, 1978.

Bottom: A rare day off, 1976.

Lunch with Diana Dors, Britain's answer to
Marilyn Monroe and Brigitte Bardot, 1984.

Benn, Ashton and Skinner, October 1998. 'Clegg, Foggy
and Compo' celebrating thirty years in the House.

view of his integrity and probity, I had no objections to him doing the job.

But, but . . . it would sit in private. There would be no Hansard record of who said what, or when, or where. The 'jury' would not get their business over and done with in a few days but would sit one afternoon a week only. No record would be kept of any absentees from this jury (they were all very busy men), but at the end of the proceedings, which might take months, they would all still be allowed to vote on the verdict, even though they had not heard all the evidence, and had nothing in writing in front of them. I would not be allowed Arthur's legal representation either.

What a farce! It was an ancient Star Chamber court of the worst kind, run exactly as they used to be 300 years ago, when politicians could have their heads chopped off for opening their mouth too wide, or simply having the wrong religion. The same sort of court as Lenin, Stalin and Khrushchev had been conducting for years. There was a Russian dissident writer at that time, called Solzhenitsyn, who exposed the system in the USSR, which promptly got me nicknamed by my mates as 'Solzynashton'.

Politely the Committee asked, would I like to appear before them in person for cross-examination? Or merely write answers to their questions? Arthur Davidson was adamant. 'Joe,' he said, 'if you opt to face a large group of lawyers who are experts on cross-examination, they will skin you. Tell them we will do it in writing.' So we did. And what a boring, lengthy procedure it was. The Committee would send questions to me, and I would reply by mail, followed by further questions until no doubt the election was over.

As the summer months dragged on, a lot of my mates in marginal seats, decent, honest MPs who had never taken a penny in their lives, became anxious. There was no redundancy pay then for MPs, and some of them were hanging on by a thread. In a few towns with two MPs side by side, one MP could be named and the honest John next door was understandably worried that the voters' backlash would rebound on him too.

The Committee never once asked me to name names, but they did refuse permission for me to prove my defence by having access to the bookings for the wining and dining receptions in the private rooms. It was obvious that there was no way the whistle-blower was going to be allowed to win.

Reluctantly, accepting that this was indeed a time for all good men to come to the aid of the Party, I indicated to the Committee, just before the election, that I would apologize and withdraw the allegations.

Which led to enormous sighs of relief all round.

Two weeks after the election in October (when, incidentally, my majority soared to 13,000, the highest I ever had until 1997), the Committee published its report, once again to banner head-lines. The *Evening Standard* screamed on its front page:

MPS FOR HIRE. A SERIOUS CONTEMPT. This was the solemn verdict announced today by the powerful All Party Committee of Privileges. The man found guilty of this major Parliamentary offence is Joe Ashton, Member for Bassetlaw. Ashton said today if somebody has to be wounded in this campaign for a compulsory register, I am quite happy to be the one [which privately I wasn't, I was bloody annoyed].

The Select Committee, looking at the crimes of Maudling, Roberts and Cordle, sat for another two and a half years. Its report wasn't debated in the House until 26 July 1977, again, as always, just before Parliament went on holiday and the voters are thinking of nothing but sunbeds. The Committee recommended that Maudling, Roberts and Cordle should be expelled from Parliament. It vindicated everything I had alleged, that some MPs were for hire.

Cordle didn't wait for the vote a week later, he quit immediately. Maudling and Roberts decided to put their case to the House and plead for mercy. When the vote on Maudling's expulsion came first, some MPs abstained, but a very large number of Conservatives opposed the register and the penalties being inflicted on the Home Secretary. With the Tory whips openly herding their ranks into the lobbies on what was supposed to be a free vote, Maudling survived by 288 to 144.

This infuriated the Labour MPs, who promptly decided they were not going to see a situation where a Labour MP was kicked out while the Tory survived. So they promptly voted not to expel Roberts either.

By that time, nearly three years later, I had been paroled by the new Prime Minister, Jim Callaghan, and made a Government whip. Consequently, as a whip I was not allowed to speak in any debates or proceedings in the House and had to sit in sheer frustration while MPs decided merely to 'take note' of what Maudling and Roberts had done, without imposing any punishment at all. They were not even judged guilty of the 'serious and solemn offence of contempt' as I had been.

There was no pardon for me. No public apology. No amnesty. Nothing at all for the brave, mad whistle-blower. I was sore, and still am, at being saddled with the stigma of a censure, for doing something which had the approval of over 90 per cent of the public.

In future, I decided, I would keep my mouth shut and stop writing. A firmly held resolution which lasted all of about a month.

Twenty-five years on from those events, the Register of Members' Interests has developed into a Parliamentary Commission for Standards with its own department, run by a man above suspicion, Sir Gordon Downey, the former Auditor General, who was later succeeded by Elizabeth Filkin, a former Inland Revenue investigator.

It still has its problems. The 1997 election campaign was dogged by allegations of sleaze, with at least one MP, Neil Hamilton, the Tory Member for Tatton, losing his seat following stories that twenty-five MPs had at one time received cash payments on behalf of Mohammed al Fayed for Parliamentary services rendered without these being registered. Others, like Jonathan Aitken and Treasury Minister Geoffrey Robinson, were also alleged to have failed to declare directorships. Even today, the House of Lords register is still only voluntary, and the Commissioner has no powers to question MPs on oath about their activities as a judge could.

Like a political skin disease which keeps returning and refuses to clear up, there will always be some businessman somewhere who is prepared to pay for a favour. And some politician who is tempted to supply it.

Fortunately, believe me as a guy who knows, those politicians can be counted on the fingers. And if the public know what they are up to, then the public can, and do, and should vote them out.

Ten

BOG TROTTING, BOTTOM FLUSHING
AND BOVVER BOYS

WHEN Harold Wilson won the October 1974 election the good news was that Labour had 319 seats to the Tories' 276. The bad news was that the Liberals also had 13, the Scots Nats 11, the Irish Ulster Unionists 10, the Irish Catholic SDLP and Independents 2, and the Welsh Nats 3. Which totalled an 'odds and sods' score of 40, plus the Speaker, who does not vote. Which meant an overall majority of just 3.

Two years later, on 5 November 1976, the Tories had gained three seats in by-elections and Labour was in a minority. By March 1978 they had gained three more and the Liberals won another.

To make matters worse, two Labour MPs, Jim Sillars from Ayrshire and John Robertson of Paisley, defected to the Scottish Nationalists, another Labour MP, Tom Swain, was killed in a car crash, and yet another, Dr Alf Broughton, was too ill to come and vote.

By that stage in March 1979 the Party was in a minority of seventeen. Yet by some Parliamentary miracle, it was still staggering on through the marathon of a five-year term and existing on the wiles and guile, blackmail, gambits and checkmates of a bunch of Old Labour pros, most of whom, like me had left school at fifteen as soon as they were old enough to earn wages.

The architects of this episode, of this marathon stonewall of what was probably the most skilled piece of political craftsman-ship of the century, were nicknamed 'The Fixit Four'. They were the Leader of the House (who organized the business timetable) Michael Foot, the Chief Whip, Michael Cocks, commonly known as 'The Padre' because of his quiet, gentle, persuasive manner, Walter Harrison, Deputy Chief Whip and hardman, a time-served electrician, and Jack Dormand, the Pairing Whip, a genial but ruthless Geordie headmaster.

Foot, Cocks, Harrison and Dormand were commonly referred to as Footinit, Cockup, Harassment and Dormant by the other mutinous dogs on the lower decks. But they were the ones who ran the boiler-room of the Ship of State, and while they and the other whips often privately thought that the Prime Minister and Cabinet steering the ship from the bridge of Ten Downing Street were obviously barmy, they regularly organized about 308 Labour MPs to outflank the 323 others and send Mrs Thatcher to bed every night gnashing her teeth.

Getting their balls tickled was an occupational hazard for whips. For many years the votes in Parliament have been carefully counted in the Lobbies yet never shown on television. Those MPs in favour, the ayes (eyes), slowly file through half-open swing-doors in one lobby, whilst the others, the noes (nose), troop through the other Lobby on the opposite side of the Chamber. Even today the Government whip on duty stands and shouts 'One! Two!' and verbally counts as the MPs file through the two swing-doors, which were held just wide enough for big Cyril Smith to get through and to stop two or more MPs from rushing past together to beat the scrum and get to the front of the taxi queue. It was absolutely crucial that the whip got the count spot on.

Over a century ago, long before electric lights and the Labour Party were invented, lazy, drunken MPs who could not be bothered to stop playing cards downstairs would order their manservant to go upstairs and vote in their place. In the gloom of the candles the bogus runner would wrap his head in his scarf, wear a big hat and mutter his master's name as he checked in to be counted. He could go round doing it two or three times for other absentees if nobody noticed. So today, all MPs who vote have to give their name to a civil servant sitting at a high Dickensian desk, who crosses it off on a register. Every MP is still expected to lift his head high and show his face to the counting whip to prove he is not actually an impostor.

It was at that crucial moment, as the counting whip looked upwards too and shouted out the score, that mischief-makers like Ted Garratt, MP for Wallsend, would reach down and tickle his balls. Ted swore that he once saved the Labour Government by tickling one young whip, the startled bloke not only went all falsetto and blushed deep pink, but jumped from 168 to 179, saving all our jobs and another week's wages.

In the Whip's Office it was even considered whether whips should wear plastic jockstraps, or those boxes which cricketers use as protection against fast bowlers, to see if that would stop him. Or perhaps put a woman whip on the count instead. The problem was, which one would volunteer?

By-elections were lost with record swings of 22 per cent. The House of Lords blocked every measure it could, waiting for the Government to fall. Some treacherous, downright irresponsible and just plain loony Labour MPs would go off on their own star trek and become heroes of the working classes in the name of the Great God Socialism, by abstaining or voting against their own side, to retain their own personal purity or ambition. Which was of course more important than letting the Tories in and deeply satisfying at the time no doubt, as the taste of humbug usually is, but somehow the Fixit Four kept the ship afloat. Aided by the other whips, Ted Graham, Joe Dean, Peter Snape, Ann Taylor,

Frank White, Alf Bates, Jock Stallard, Donald Coleman, David Stoddart, Jimmy Hamilton, Jim Tinn and Tom Pendry, they knew every trick of the trade and even invented a few new ones.

They knew for instance that Scottish schoolchildren go on holiday earlier than English. No Scottish daddy likes to be away in London in August. If the controversial business could be held back until then, it was probably worth a couple of Scottish votes gained.

The Fixit Four controlled the dates of the Labour by-elections and could fix good news announcements, or a give-away mini-budget to coincide. Or simply delay bad news until the day after. Even international football games and results were carefully weighed up. Hadn't Harold Wilson lost in 1970 because of national gloom and doom when England were beaten in the World Cup ten days before the General Election? Nowadays it would be called sophisticated news management, but there is nothing new about spin-doctors in politics.

Many MPs headed home on Thursday night and travelled to Scotland, Wales or Ireland on train sleepers simply to save a night's hotel bill. So Thursday night was when the Four would Fixit for a difficult vote.

I once saw hardman Harrison grab hold of Eric Heffer by his lapels on the Commons Terrace and threaten to throw him over the wall into the Thames if he didn't get into the Chamber and effin' vote. Walter would scour the *Irish Times* every day to see if there were any big funerals which would prevent a couple of Ulster Unionists from coming in to vote. He would check the West Country papers for agricultural shows and prize livestock events, knowing that was where the local Liberal MPs would be away grubbing support.

He once asked me to phone Jeremy Thorpe's office (Thorpe was then the Liberal Leader) and pretend to be from the BBC, and ask if Jeremy would be available to do an interview on

Newsnight. When I asked Walter why, he said he had heard a rumour that Thorpe was going to be abroad and we might gain a vote. When I said, 'What if Thorpe says he's here and will do it?' Walter said, 'Tell him you'll ring back at six to confirm it – then don't.' Then he changed his mind. 'Forget it, Joe lad,' he said, 'your accent's too broad for the BBC. We'll get one of the women to do it.'

Walter knew every inch of the Guy Fawkes cellars, where treacherous dogs might be abstaining instead of voting Labour. He would post look-outs at the taxi rank and every exit to trap anybody bunking off, and to check if any tuxedo-wearing Tory gents were doubling back from their clubs to ambush the Government after loudly shouting goodnight to all the staff.

He had 'Deep Throats' in all the little odds and sods parties, who would secretly ring him up and whisper how many of their lot might be absent. Some of the Nats were in on a whisker majority, never expecting to get elected, having had to pack in a good job to become an MP. They were terrified of being booted out at a minute's notice on to the dole queue. They wanted a five-year Parliament more than anybody.

MPs have mortgages and families too, and nobody knew it better than us. Long before calculators were invented, headmaster Jack Dormand, the Tally man, kept the running total of the poorly, sick and lame, as well as the idle or famous who might be at the other end of the world when the vote came. If he added it all up wrongly – down we went.

He once gave me an eight-hour pass when my house got burgled. It was three hours each way on the train, but he left me just enough time to screw the front door back on. The Government's majority came first, and as I mentioned earlier, I had to be in the House voting on the day my daughter Lucy was born. It was a day later when I got up to Sheffield to see her.

Jack fetched Shirley Williams all the way from China to vote.

He made her come straight back on the plane after a seventeen-hour journey. She was not best pleased when we had a majority of five because some odds and sods had skipped off.

It was called 'teeming and ladling'. Every day the pairing whips would meet and negotiate one of our heart attacks, for the vote of a Tory fox-hunter who had fallen off his horse. The daily prayer was that if one of ours was rushed into hospital for an emergency cardiac arrest, it might happen at nine in the morning. Then it might be possible to bring him in an ambulance to vote at ten at night. Or alternatively ask the surgeon to postpone the operation until the following day.

One night, Leslie Spriggs, MP for St Helens, was rushed through the gates in an ambulance after serious heart trouble. The agreed rules between the parties were that the sick MP had to be on the premises to be 'nodded through' but was spared the pain of actually having to wince and stagger on foot through the Lobbies. The Tories would send their pairing whip with one of our whips to check that the body really was on the premises in the ambulance in New Palace Yard. So Joe Harper went along with the Tory to look at poor seemingly lifeless Leslie laid out silent and still. Without Leslie's vote it would be a tie, 315–315. 'How do we know he is still alive?' whispered the Tory whip. Joe Harper, well rehearsed by Walter, simply leaned forward, pushed the red button on the heart monitor, watched as the green beam swung round in an arc and said triumphantly, 'There, you bugger, 316. You've lost.'

That Whip's Office, without the help of any mobile phones, pagers, etc., simply because these things had not been invented, knew the whereabouts of every one of the 300-odd Labour MPs instantly. And if they did not they could damn well soon find them. Top and bottom flushers were the duties allocated to the younger whips. They were ordered to run round every toilet on the top and bottom corridors as soon as the bells rang to start the eight minutes count-down. There was even a woman's whip for the Ladies.

Their instructions were to look under every door for feet. If anybody was inside using it, the whip had to jump up, look over the top and see who it was. If it was Labour, then no matter what the circumstances, get him out to vote. If it was a Tory, then quietly steal away and leave him.

It was essential to carry a screwdriver and get the lock off if the Member was ill or drunk. Or fetch the bobby to help. Either way, or any way, pick him up under the arms and physically drag him down to the Lobby and through it, shouting his name to the teller to register his vote.

Would you believe that the Labour Government nationalized the whole of the aircraft and shipbuilding industries on one night, involving millions of pounds and nearly 140,000 jobs, on the vote of little Harry Selby, MP for Govan, Glasgow. Without his feet touching the ground once.

Harry was carried blind drunk past the tellers seven times, and he slept right through it. The only time he woke up was when the whips tried to put his jacket on him. He was only five feet tall, but four of us could not hold him down.

One of the younger whips, a gentle soul doing a stint in the office to get experience, summed it up admirably when he said, 'The future of the shipbuilding and aircraft industries, the strength of the pound sterling, the value of the Stock Exchange quotations, the level of inflation and pay rises, and the glory of the Labour Government, all depend on me doing the bog trotter's job and climbing up closet doors. I studied law at Oxford, fought two hopeless seats, made myself an expert on EEC taxation and subsidies and inflation-proof pensions, the Textile Tariff and Trade Multi-Fibre agreement, defence and weapons procurement, and will be on the dole next week if I don't get some drunk's arse wiped in eight minutes.'

The grizzled old pros like ex-miner Joe Harper, from Ponte-fract in Yorkshire, would simply look up from the sporting page of the *Daily Mirror* and say, 'Aye, lad, and when you jump down, just make sure tha doesn't land on the glass splash guards at the front of the stalls, because they shatter. So don't stand on 'em either. Take advice from a former chairman of the Pontefract Urban District Council Cleansing, Refuse, Baths and Public Uri-nals Committee. Those things were not made for standing on. They are put there to protect suede shoes, which can't be polished. What's more, all toilet doors have a safety outlet. If the lock says "Engaged", there will be a little screw somewhere which will turn from the outside to change "Engaged" to "Vacant". It is to let the attendant get out the heart attacks and suicides. If tha had learned that at Oxford, it would have done thi a lot more good in Labour Party politics.'

Every day in the Whip's Office, the proceedings opened with a roll-call of anybody died, gone missing, or found shacked up with a millionairess, who we ought to know about before we read it in the *News of the World*. The register would be ticked off, and invariably there would be ten or so doubtful, poorly obstreperous headline seekers, and mischievous, awkward bastards whose egos or ambition or conscience came first. Or who were just simply Jack-the-lad who was totally fed up with the whips crying wolf yet winning the vote, so he was going to chance it anyway.

'Edgar' was one of these. 'Edgar' is now dead and left Parliament several years ago. Like a few other MPs then, he had a wife 200 miles away, and a frequently changed mistress in London. For every eight-minute vote, he would arrive breathless and flushed with five seconds to spare, beaming and waving to the packed Lobby as they cheered him in before the doors slammed shut. If it got to Wednesday and 'Edgar' had not been seen, the whips did not panic. They simply rang his wife. She would say he had safely left home on Monday, and half an hour later 'Edgar' would come steaming into the office, breathing blood and fire, demanding to know who had phoned his missus. She always knew where to find him. Wives usually do.

Edgar even had it away on the premises. And the whips knew which room he did it in too. It was seriously discussed whether the top-floor flusher should go and bang on the door when the bell rang to hurry him up to run down and vote. The whip had his doubts. 'He's forty-nine,' he said, 'what if he has a heart attack and the majority goes? You can't rush a bloke at that age. It might take him a lot longer than eight minutes.'

At that time there was a hit show on in London called *Oh Calcutta!* It had run for a few years and achieved massive publicity because the actors sang, danced and performed in the nude, doing some very funny sketches. One of which was a masturbation race. Five guys sat in rocking chairs, going backwards and forwards, while watching a soft porn film as the *William Tell* Overture blasted out.

As the music went faster and faster so did the rocking chairs. The joke was that right at the climax, the film switched to the Lone Ranger riding his horse into the west and all five yelling 'Hi Ho Silver!' as they reached orgasm. One whip seriously said, 'We don't want to give him too much of a shock banging the door.' 'No, not at his age,' said another. 'So why don't one or two of us just stand outside and sing that Lone Ranger tune to speed him up a bit?'

And all this while the pound sank lower and lower.

By the time Harold quit as Prime Minister, in March 1976, the pound had dropped from $2.25 to $1.70. No wonder he had had enough. By this time Heath had gone too, and Mrs Thatcher was sitting there on the roof like a vulture waiting for the staggering invalid to fall and have his eyes plucked out.

In any war of attrition where both sides dig in for hard years of weary grind, there is always one big set-piece battle event like the Somme or D-Day, which is intended to settle the issue and lead to one side overwhelming the other. In this neck-and-neck Parliament it was the bill to nationalize the shipbuilding and aircraft industries. The Fixit Four tried to pass both together, at the same time, in one bill, and quickly, before Callaghan's majority died off, crumbled, ratted or just plain tuckered out.

Labour's Holy Grail, which the Party worshipped, was the famous Clause Four of its constitution, on nationalization: the means whereby the country and the taxpayers would 'own and control the commanding heights of the economy'. The workers' jobs would then be safe from company shareholders, foreign banks, capitalist running dogs, fat cats of the City of London and anybody else who had never had callouses on their hands, from doing night shift down the pit, or chilblains in a freezing open-air shipyard on Clydeside.

And wasn't it justified too, claimed the lads and lasses and shop stewards. In 1956, just twenty years earlier, Britain made half the ships in the world. Now, despite having hundreds of millions of public cash poured in, the yards were dying on their feet. Why shouldn't the taxpayer take them over? As for aircraft, two big firms dominated the industry. Yet their main customer was the Government buying planes for the nationalized British Airways or the RAF, or shelling out billions in new technology for Concorde.

It was simple working-class common sense for these to belong to the nation. Clause Four (the very first thing Tony Blair scrapped when he became the new Party Leader twenty years later) was carried on banners high behind brass bands, on every union and party demo and parade, right across Britain. And the nationalization of shipbuilding and aircraft was Clause Four at its finest. Every MP and party worker was expected to die to defend it.

But the Tory generals led by Mrs Thatcher had a secret plot to put a stiletto right through its heart.

When the bill was introduced in Parliament, Thatcher and Heseltine craftily allowed the preliminary skirmishes in committee rooms to go through 140 hours of debate and fifty-eight sessions of cliff-hanging meetings. Then right at the final vote they alleged that the proposed legislation was 'hybrid' and flawed. They claimed that the civil servants who drafted the bill had cocked it up.

To save time, the Government had not included mobile offshore drilling rigs. Well, who would? Rigs do not have captains. They do not have sails or engines. And in 1884, when the Maritime Acts were laid down, nobody had ever heard of oil rigs.

Ah. Ah. Ahem, coughed the highly paid legal 'Yes Ministers' in the best Civil Service tradition. Very sorry, Prime Minister, but it does appear that we have cocked it up. Still, no harm done. We will just have to start again and put it right.

Which would of course have taken another year, with the majority running out.

Except that the Fixit Four got round this by brazenly moving the goal-posts. They announced that if the civil servants had got it wrong, then we would simply change the standing orders of the House and say that in this case the rules about hybrid bills do not count. 'It's your fault,' they told Mrs T., 'you should have put the complaint in before the game started – not now. You did the cheating, not us.'

Imagine the uproar! Imagine the fury!

The two sides lined up for the full-frontal assault on 27 May 1976. It was the night before the House rose for the Spring Bank Holiday, carefully chosen by the Fixit Four in the hope that one of the Opposition would slope off a day early for the break, and Labour would gain a vote. One did. Despite all sorts of warnings one Tory, Peter Fry, MP for Wellingborough, left for a holiday in Corfu, but still the Tories were confident. All the odds and sods tut-tutted against the 'cheating' as they called it, and lined up against Labour. Even the Ulster Unionists too. Belfast had one of the biggest shipyards in the UK at Harland and Wolff, where they built the *Titanic*. Nationalization would have saved thousands of jobs there. But they were all Protestants, weren't they? If the shipyard was to become Government property, some of the jobs in the shipyard would have to be offered to Catholic workers. Which had never happened in its whole history. The Orange Order was not having that. They would sooner see the yard go bust than save the Government with their votes.

All day the House was packed. It was hot and sultry waiting for the vote. The bars did a roaring trade. Michael Heseltine led the charge for the Tories, with sabre held high, and at ten o'clock waited for the result as the votes were counted. Thatcher sat by his side, smug, prim and proper.

She smiled as an exultant Tory whip, John Stradling Thomas, rushed to her 'like a messenger from Aix to Ghent' as *The Times* described it, to whisper the result to her before it was announced in the House by the whips standing at the Mace.

It was a tie: 303–303.

There was pandemonium everywhere. Thatcher still smiled. She knew that under the rules, the Speaker would have a casting vote. And in accordance with long-standing precedent, he would have to vote to preserve the status quo. And therefore oppose the Tory amendment allowing the Government to move the goal-posts. If the next and final vote to nationalize the industry was also a tie, she would be in Ten Downing Street as Prime Minister inside a month.

Except, the slip between cup and lip happened.

As the whips lined up in total silence to announce the second vote, Joe Harper, with a deadpan face, announced 'Ayes 304 – Noes 303.'

Labour had won! Somewhere, somehow, Labour had plucked another vote out of thin air. *The Times* in its report said that 'wild disorder broke out'. Labour's back-benchers sang 'The Red Flag' as they waved their order papers taunting the Tories who were yelling 'Cheat! Cheat!' Parliamentary bovver boys hurled abuse, pushed, shoved and shook fists everywhere as MPs stormed off the benches and on to the floor of the House.

Michael Heseltine picked up the gold-plated Mace which lay across the table when the House is sitting, and swung it round his head, threatening to attack the traditional left-wing Labour front row below the gangway. Just like the Clydeside rebels had in the hunger march debates of the Thirties. Jim Prior, the Tory MP, wrestled with him to put the Mace back and then put it on the wrong way round, to great guffaws from Labour.

The Chamber was in turmoil with scenes rarely seen before.

The Times reported that punches were exchanged between Tom Swain, the mining MP from North-East Derbyshire, and Michael Spicer, Tory MP for South Worcester, with Andrew Faulds trying to separate them. The elderly Serjeant-at-Arms sitting with his sword in his high chair at the entrance, tried to calm things down in his usual austere, forbidding way, as one would expect from a former admiral. But he ended up using 'foul lower-deck language', according to Willie Hamilton MP, to try to stop the fifty-year-old drunken hooligans from wrecking the pitch.

There was no way the Speaker, George Thomas, was going to get any 'Order, order' out of that lot. So he announced he was suspending the business for fifteen minutes to have a cooling-off period. An idea which the previous Tory Government had made compulsory for all strikes, demos and workshop protests.

At five to eleven he came back and said that because of the scenes of 'grave disorder' he was going to adjourn the House until the following day. As a lifelong teetotaller, he probably knew quite well that this would close all the bars as well, and five minutes later the pubs over the road would be shut too.

So who was the mystery extra voter? The inquest the following day showed the extra vote had been recorded by a Labour whip, who hadn't voted in the first ballot. The Labour Whip's

Office claimed there had been a mix-up in the pairing arrangements, whereby the Opposition always agreed to pair any Government minister who had to travel abroad on official business. The whip was named but then successfully sued several newspapers for libel after they called him a cheat. Which soon settled the issue.

The Times reported that Fred Peart, the long-standing Secretary of State for Agriculture, had gone off to a meeting in Denmark, forgot to tell the Whip's Office, assumed his civil servants would do that, and went to bed. When it was found out he hadn't voted, the Tories alleged that the Labour Whip's Office had switched another name for his and gained one extra. Which they claimed wasn't allowed.

Heseltine humbly apologized for his hooligan behaviour and said it was the singing of 'The Red Flag' in the Mother of Parliaments which had inflamed him. And the guy who had bunked off on holiday early offered to resign.

But in cold fury, Mrs Thatcher got her revenge. She cancelled all the pairs and permanently opted out of the pairing system. In future there would be no minister who would dare to go abroad, or across to Northern Ireland, without risking defeat for the Government. The poorly, sick and lame would have to be dragged through death's door to keep Labour in office.

What's more, she had another ace up her sleeve. The House of Lords. The Tory majority in there, of peers who had never won an election in their life but who were descended from some of the worst and most famous rogues, thieves, whores, cheats and liars in history, would boot the bill out in the next three months. By then Labour might have lost another MP.

It did. It lost the vote of the liar, cheat and thief, John Stonehouse.

A month after Wilson was elected in October 1974, John Stonehouse was found alive and well in Melbourne after being mistaken for Lord Lucan, who was also on the run after allegedly bashing the nanny's head in thinking she was his wife.

The Fixit Four, and Harold Wilson, managed to persuade Stonehouse to turn up for votes, while he was out on bail, to avoid a by-election. Unfortunately, in July, Mr Justice Eveleigh at the Old Bailey gave him seven years at Her Majesty's pleasure in another abode at Wandsworth Prison, and not even the Fixit Four could unfix that. So things were looking bad for the replay of the Nationalization Bill when it came back from the Lords in November.

As expected, Stonehouse's seat was easily won in the by-election by the Tories, but to make things worse, the new Prime Minister, Jim Callaghan, decided he needed two more experienced Cabinet ministers in the Lords to beef up Labour. So, amazingly, he created two more by-elections in the so-called 'safe seats' of Newcastle Central and Workington, to send the famous Fred Peart there and also the Leader of the House, Ted Short.

The Whip's Office had severe doubts. Any politician knows that by-elections in Government seats mid-term where the sitting member hasn't died but has quit for a better job somewhere else, or to become a Lord, are a disaster waiting to happen. To hold all three on one day, 5 November, was tempting fate. The public resent being used for political wheeling and dealing, and often retaliate by giving their own side a kick up the bracket. Which is what the voters of Workington and Walsall promptly did by electing two Tories. Meanwhile, in Newcastle, they simply stayed at home and Labour got in by 1,840 in one of the safest seats in the country. It was an incredible own goal, which meant two votes less for Labour and two more for the Tories.

Two weeks later, on Armistice Day, the bill came back from the Lords with its heart torn out and Labour had to win again. Otherwise the MPs would be singing the funeral march from *Saul*, not 'The Red Flag', with a mournful chorus of 'Jerusalem' as the Party sank into oblivion.

There was just one consolation. In those by-elections the Liberals had been whacked out of sight too. There had been serious allegations both in the newspapers and in Parliament that their leader, Jeremy Thorpe, had had a long homosexual relationship with a young man, Norman Scott, and then plotted to have him murdered. Just before the big vote, Thorpe had resigned as Liberal Leader, but was eventually found not guilty of all charges. At Walsall North, Stonehouse's seat, they had even been beaten into fifth place behind the National Front and an independent candidate. It was coffin-lid time for the Liberals too. So they wouldn't be in much of a hurry to bring Labour down.

The crucial votes took place on Armistice Day 1976. The odds and sods knew that after the by-election results, they too would most probably be swept aside in any General Election. But as usual they wanted it both ways. They could not be seen to be propping up a busted government, but equally, as fence straddlers, they could not upset too many Labour voters if they were going to be asking for their votes in a General Election the following week.

So it was a day of chaos. To make it worse, some of the House of Commons' hot-food catering staff, though not the bars, were on strike too.

Nobody could forecast what would happen in the five votes that day.

All Labour could do was get everybody still alive through the Lobby when the bell rang. Young Helene Hayman (now Lady Hayman in the Lords) had won a seat by a tiny majority at Welwyn, an aircraft industry town. She was keen to vote, but her baby had been born just nine days before. And, like a modern mother in 1976, she was determined to breast-feed him as long as she could. Nowadays there would be no problems, but then?

'GOVERNMENT HANGS BY A NAPPY PIN', screamed the *Daily Mail*. Helene couldn't get out of the front door for photographers, TV cameras and freelance journalists. There were strong objections from Tory *grandes dames* when she took the baby into the Ladies' Room. The Labour whips begged Helene to make sure he had at least three nappy changes in there, without any air freshener, and a hundred volunteers from the Tea Room staff offered to hold little Ben and cuddle him when his mother had to go and vote. Little Ben was two and a half years old before Mrs Thatcher finally managed to get Labour out.

But the key vote was that of Frank Maguire, the invisible man.

Francis Meredith Maguire kept a pub in Linaskea and was the official Independent Republican Catholic MP for Fermanagh and South Tyrone, which is right on the border where Northern Ireland meets the South, and in the heart of the 'bandit' area.

The voters there always split right down the middle on religious grounds. Half Catholic and half Protestant. All vote the religious ticket. Frank had beaten Harry West, the leader of the Ulster Unionists, without making a single speech in the campaign, or holding a single meeting. He dared not. The other lot would have wrecked it.

Since then, he had never made a speech in Parliament either, or put down a question. Except of course in Frank's Bar in Linaskea, where he sounded off every night. He was a lovely, friendly, charming, big fat red-faced Irishman, who loved the crack (not to mention the Guinness and the Bushmills Whiskey), and who would, on very rare occasions, allow himself to be persuaded to come over and vote for a Prime Minister with a good Irish name like Callaghan.

It so happened that in the Labour Whip's Office was an ex-shop steward from Camden called Jock Stallard, whose wife, Sheila happened to know Frank's wife Philomena. Frank was a feller who was likely to be shot at any time, and who had nothing to gain from keeping a Labour Government in power. Except that if those Loyalist bastards, the Reverend Ian Paisley and his ilk, were voting against a Labour Government, then wasn't it the duty of a good Catholic MP to be supporting it?

Of course it was. And if he came over, couldn't he do himself a lot of good by visiting the Irish boys who had been locked up in English gaols for belonging to the Catholic IRA cause? Of course he could.

It was all based on Irish logic that I could never understand. All we knew was that 1,300 people had been killed in the Northern Ireland troubles.

Frank was a Republican who believed Northern Ireland should have been handed over to Dublin and not run from Westminster. He was not even a member of the Labour Party. He was a Catholic with half his mates locked up in the Maze Prison, put there without trial by a Labour Government, and by some crazy logic we were asking him to risk his life coming across to London to keep us in office.

God works in mysterious ways. Especially in Ireland.

Philomena was against, of course. Even though the whips tried to persuade her to come too. Didn't she know that all MPs' wives got three free travel warrants every year to come to London? No she damn well didn't, she said. Frank never told her nothing about free travel warrants for wives. You could be on the plane tomorrow, we said. Jock Stallard and Sheila will look after you. They will take you Christmas shopping down Oxford Street to see the lights. I'll think about it, she said. Philomena didn't fly over, but Frank did. Well, somebody had to look after the pub.

His terms were that he wouldn't have to show his face anywhere, or go into the Chamber or meet anybody. No bother, we said. Just sit in the Whip's Office and read the paper or watch Benny Hill on ITV. He did. Until about tea-time – but he had a terrible thirst. By seven he was in the Strangers Bar, commonly known as the Little Kremlin, drinking it dry of Guinness and anything else he could swallow, roaring out old Irish ballads and telling us how he was going to come more often because he had never realized what a good pub it was.

The Irish MP for Islington (when it was a working-class seat), Michael O'Halloran, who started life as a hod carrier, took him in hand, and Frank made a firm promise that next time he would bring his mandolin, because it was just what the place needed. Another Irish MP said he knew of a ceilidh band at Kilburn who were very good, and before he could stop him, Frank was on the phone asking them to come down and entertain a bunch of his MP friends. The band were very disappointed when they turned up in an old builder's van at the Houses of Parliament and the security-conscious police said they didn't believe a word of it, and could they search the van with a metal detector please.

Somehow the Government survived that night on majorities of 3, 4, 6, 1, 1 and a tie, and although Frank Maguire complained mildly that the Government kept locking up good Catholic boys in lousy conditions in the Maze Prison but never gave him anything in return, he had had a grand night none the less.

Frank McElhone, the good Catholic MP from the Gorbals with whom I shared a basement flat in Kennington helped me to smuggle him out there in the dark after the vote, then to Heathrow for the first plane to Belfast the following morning. Maguire drank our flat dry and kept us up all night with his tales, demanding to know why, if my grandad was called Maloney and came from Ballymote in Sligo, I wasn't a Catholic. Until he finally simply fell down on the carpet and slept until the alarm went off.

His place in the history of Parliament and the Labour Government is assured for ever.

Surprisingly, there was not a great deal of rejoicing by Labour when the siege of the Government was over. Simply a mighty relief.

Callaghan had delivered to the Party what he had promised. All he had to do now was hold on. With North Sea oil getting nearer every day, he could simply sit and wait until the bonanza came in and solved all the Government's financial problems. The Tories sat and fumed and Labour were actually beaten on thirty different votes, but nothing important. It was only a vote of confidence which could bring us down.

And with the Tories riding high in the polls, which of the odds and sods would ever, in the immortal words of Liberal David Penhaligon at the time, act like turkeys volunteering to vote for Christmas?

So what happened? Callaghan's own party committed suicide by slow amputation until eventually he too took leave of his senses.

In the next six months, Labour intellectuals Roy Jenkins, Brian Walden and David Marquand, who were offered other better jobs as an EEC Commissioner, a TV presenter and a professor at a top university, didn't hesitate to jump the sinking ship. They ratted on the Labour Party which had made their names. They ratted on Parliament and on the Government and left their mates to fight the by-elections their defections had created. To this day, they are loathed in Old Labour circles for the way they walked out on the Labour Government's crisis, plunging it into a deeper minority, with a loss of the 22,000 majority in Marquand's seat of Ashfield, Notts, and in another seat, Jenkins' at Stechford, Birmingham, although Labour did hold Walden's seat at Ladywood, Birmingham.

Other MPs simply collapsed and died under the strain of all-night sittings, having essential operations postponed for months until the recess. Or being sewn up and brought in on stretchers. The Foreign Secretary, Tony Crosland, exhausted from flying round the world every week, and then hauled back at a minute's notice to vote because of Mrs Thatcher's 'No pairs' decision, died suddenly from a heart attack. Frank Hatton, MP for Moss Side, Manchester, Millie Miller of Ilford, Alex Wilson from Hamilton, Scotland and finally, to our grief, Joe Harper of the Whip's Office, went under, from terminal illnesses, heart attacks or postponed operations. There were others like Alex Lyon, husband of Clare Short, who never entirely recovered from immediately returning from the operating theatre to vote, and suffered health problems for many years.

On one occasion Tally man Jack Dormand did his arithmetic and told the Chief Whip that the Government would lose the vote by one. The Tories had refused to pair Don Concannon, the Minister of State for Northern Ireland. It was twenty minutes to nine, with the vote at ten o'clock, and Conkers, as the huge six-foot four-inch ex-miner and Guardsman MP for Mansfield was known, had no chance of getting across the Irish Sea.

The Chief Whip, 'Padre' Michael Cocks, cool as a frosted glass, simply picked up a phone, rang Downing Street on the Prime Minister's top security number, and Jim Callaghan told the RAF to lay on a Hunter jet and get Conkers over. The planes are all on this side of the water, Jim was told. But we could strap an extra fuel tank on to a helicopter, then pick up Conkers and drive him fourteen miles from Northolt to Westminster in eleven minutes, with all the traffic lights fixed in his favour. Conkers straddled the tank and walked in with a minute to spare, bow-legged as John Wayne, to stupendous cheers, with a special wave, bow and smile for Mrs Thatcher.

The prize of North Sea oil was the Scottish Nationalists' prize too. They were content to keep Callaghan there until the jackpot arrived, providing he would give Scotland its own Parliament and let them get their hands on the money. It was also agreed that devolution and home rule for Scotland would be traded for votes. And with the oil pulling in £150 million in the first gusher at 1976 prices, there was enough for everybody.

But as always, Old Labour pressed its self-destruct button. The Tories tried to talk the Devolution Bill out. If they won the election they didn't intend to share the money with anybody. Least of all a bunch of red-neck, red-kneed, kilted caber-tossers from the Highlands, or the slum dwellers of Glasgow. Or give them a Scottish Parliament either.

Callaghan, however, knew he would have no problem hanging on and getting the bill through with Scots Nats support. Except. Except that his own 'awkward squad' of Eric Heffer, Dennis Skinner, Neil Kinnock, etc., etc., refused to vote for it. Nobody knew why. But the hard left said the Scots Nats were Tartan Tories in disguise, and they weren't going to give them anything. What's more, if Scotland could have its own government, what about the Socialist Republics of South Yorkshire, Merseyside or Tyneside having one too? It was suicide by stupid back-bench politicians.

In any case, although the Holy Synod of the Labour Party Conference had actually voted by four million votes to one million for a devolution policy, it had not actually voted for a guillotine, they said. So, unbelievably, the Labour Government lost the vote by twenty-nine. Some of them deliberate, own-goal votes of their own MPs. Two right-wing rebel MPs, Tam Dalyell and George Cunningham, on the other wing from Skinner & Co., voted against it and demanded a referendum, with no less than 40 per cent of the Scottish people having to vote in favour.

Still Callaghan patiently hung on. His 'peace and quiet' strategy was actually working on the voters, who had had enough of strikes, trouble and strife. Labour had been easily holding by-election seats in Pontefract, Penistone and Berwick, where sitting MPs had died in the struggle, and kept the sympathy of the public. The economy, with the oil in sight, was getting better by the hour. It was time to cut and run. The by-election results in September 1978 showed Labour actually doing better than it had four years earlier, in October 1974.

If Callaghan went, he might finish up with another small majority, but Thatcher certainly wouldn't get in. There was no way the Tories would get their hands on the oil. Every single Labour MP screamed for an election now. For six long years since the Arab–Israeli war and the Heath blackout, the Old Labour unions had been immensely patient and loyal. They had taken pay rises lower than inflation. There had been some strikes, though nothing that could not be handled, yet they were weary. It was time for a new start.

Callaghan went to the TUC Conference and, as has been seen many times on television, sang the old song about Maggie waiting at the church, and taunted her for her impatience. The following day he stunned the Cabinet, the country and every single MP by announcing that, like Napoleon, he was going to soldier on through the winter, give the Scots their referendum, and hang on to make certain of the oil.

It was a winter and two by-elections too far. It was one of the most disastrous political errors in history. The unions were furious and cancelled the wages policy agreement. Strikes in the coldest winter and deepest snow for thirty-two years crippled hospitals, cemeteries, railways and other essential services. As the economy got better, life for the punters got worse. To cap it all, the Scottish referendum didn't reach 40 per cent in favour, and Callaghan was stuck in the Ides of March, looking down the barrel of Mrs Thatcher's cannon. She had waited a long time for this. Immediately after the referendum failure, she delivered the *coup de grâce* on a motion of no confidence in the Government.

Everybody had had enough. The IRA warned the Irish Catholic MPs, Gerry Fitt and Frank Maguire, that they and their families would be murdered if they kept the Labour Government in office. They meant it too. Both of them had no option but to abstain (and actually flew over from Ireland to do so in public).

The Scots Nats decided to take away their support too. It was a divided split-decision vote, with the majority coming from a couple of MPs knowing they would lose their seats, and opting for a spring election rather than October, because it would be easier to get a teaching job in the spring than in the autumn.

The great vote of no confidence came on 28 March 1979.

Labour's luck ran out when Tom Swain, the MP for North-East Derbyshire, was killed in a car crash three weeks before, with not enough time to hold a by-election. Another MP, Sir Alfred Broughton, was gravely ill and his doctor forbade him to travel. He died four days after the vote.

Labour lost it by 310–311, after superhuman efforts by the Fixit Four and the Whip's Office right up to within ten minutes of the ten o'clock vote. Even so, afterwards the Scots Nats whip, Hamish Gray, admitted that he had voted against the Labour Government then instantly had a terrible pang of guilt, and had run across to the other Lobby to vote the other way to cancel his vote out. But he was beaten by the eight-minute rule, and locked out. The Scots Nats lost nine of their eleven seats.

Callaghan was out too. And the Tories would be in for the next eighteen years, with the oil being used for tax cuts while factories, pits, shipyards and union jobs died everywhere, not just in Scotland.

Just to show their power over Parliament, the IRA blew up Tory MP Airey Neave, Mrs Thatcher's right-hand man, in his car as he left the House of Commons car park, two days after the vote. The Labour bog trotters had lost to the Irish bog trotters. Peace in Ireland was another twenty years away.

And by then the North Sea oil would have produced a staggering £80,000 million for four future Tory Governments.

Old Labour had suffered severe self-inflicted wounds from which it never recovered.

Eleven

OLD LABOUR TURNS INTO
JUVENILE LABOUR

THE derogatory term 'Old Labour', used with much derision by today's younger mobile-phone, fax-it MPs, and Party members with pagers and e-mail, is a very unfair and sad tag for the evacuee kids of my generation, who rebuilt the country after the war. We were the true Old Labour.

The loony Labour Party, which came a generation later in the Eighties, were definitely not 'Old Labour'. They were the *nouveau riche* polytechnic juvenile Labour. They were a generation who inherited the massive majorities which their mums and dads had built up, and then casually dissipated them with all the abandonment of Regency bucks gambling and squandering the family fortune. The Eighties loonies, many of whom are now New Labour Government ministers, even Cabinet ministers, must shudder to recall how they took over big city councils, including London, and ran them like kids running amok in adventure playgrounds, vandalizing years of painstaking work by their parents, who had won them and kept control. Their juvenile irresponsibility was awesome, their arrogance and political suicide tendency unbelievable.

And the man who gave them the chance to sail the ship over the edge of the world was one of the best friends I ever had. His name is Tony Benn. Or the Right Honourable Anthony Wedgwood Benn, as he was called when he first got elected to

Parliament nearly fifty years ago at the age of twenty-five, as the Member for Bristol South-East.

Tony comes from a family which for five generations have had MPs in Parliament, including himself, his son and his dad. He was born and grew up a stone's throw from the House of Commons, on the site where the Labour Party Headquarters on Millbank now stands. As a toddler he would wander over to chat to neighbour Oswald Mosley in nearby Smith Square and walked to school at Westminster every day.

The last time I was with Tony Blair in Downing Street, in the Cabinet Room, I pointed out to him that Tony Benn had been sitting there when he was five years old to watch the Trooping the Colour, enjoying tea and biscuits with the first Labour Prime Minister, Ramsey Macdonald, back in 1930, before he met Gandhi when his father was Secretary of State for India, and before his father later became Viscount Stansgate, a hereditary peer.

Tony Benn even grew up living next door to Sidney and Beatrice Webb, who founded the Labour Party a century ago. Although Tony is only eight years older than me, his background and mine could not have been more different. Yet, just as the slums and shop-floor had put iron into my soul, so the British House of Lords had put a hatred of the establishment and a love of democracy into Tony's.

Four years after young Benn entered the House, with four kids to keep, his father died and Tony automatically inherited the peerage. Inside a day, despite Benn's long-stated announcement and adamant demands that he did not want the peerage and wished to stay an MP, his wages were stopped and he was prevented from entering the Commons to represent the people who had elected him.

For the next eight years, Benn fought a battle in Parliament for the right to keep his seat. He took on the highest law courts, and received very little help or support from the Labour Party National Executive Committee, or the Labour front bench at that time, despite commanding enormous support from the Party's rank and file. He even fought by-elections to try to get back in again but was still disqualified. The long campaign cost him all his savings and years in limbo. Just like I had suffered at the hands of the establishment in exposing the sleazy side of MPs for hire, and had been sent into limbo too.

In the Labour Government of 1974 Wilson made Benn Secretary of State for Industry. Tony knew everything about Parliament and government. I knew everything about industry, because I had worked in it for twenty years at both white- and blue-collar level. He rescued me from limbo by appointing me his PPS and for the next two years it was back on the roller-coaster for the most exhilarating time I ever spent in politics.

Tony was a brilliant strategist and his profound depth of knowledge put him light-years in front of his Cabinet colleagues. A democrat to the core, though not always with the best of judgement, he had pushed hard for a referendum on Britain's entry into the Common Market, as it was called then, because he and the left were totally against it, then promptly lost the vote when the big battalions of Fleet Street persuaded the voters to stay in, which locked us into the EC for ever.

Tony's weakness was his inordinate love of the working-class Party members, and they loved and adored him in return. He had the natural charm of a polite public schoolboy, any women in his company immediately fell in love with him, and he was a Pied Piper when it came to kids. His love for the 'Noble Savage' was never more evident than at miners' galas, trade union marches, demonstrations, or any platform from which he could preach the gospel of why power should belong to the people at the ballot box, and not the bankers, the Whitehall mandarins, the Queen, the Prime Minister, or any other appointee with patronage to give out. I once had to tell him on *Newsnight* that 'There are just as many shits in the working class as there are in the middle class', and I do not think he ever forgave me.

He was the Cabinet minister and I was his PPS, which stands for Personal Private Secretary, but was actually a 'minder', as the popular Arthur Daley TV series called it in the Seventies. A gofer. A bag-carrier, chauffeur, aide, working-class advisor, and even interpreter for the comics at Barnsley Miners' Institute, plus general networker, gossip-gatherer and grapevine-plucker of what was happening at the grass roots and in the smoke-filled rooms.

At the Department of Industry Tony had a brilliant idea. A cunning plan. Marvellously simple. British industry was dying on its feet, never having spent a penny on new tools and tackle since the highly profitable war. Its machinery was clapped out. The crafty Japs and Germans, not allowed to make weapons, were churning out washing-machines, televisions, motorbikes, etc., miles better than ours, while our industry still concentrated on making aircraft carriers and military helicopters.

Tony's plan was to run British industry like British agriculture. The Milk Marketing Board, and the Egg Marketing Board, etc., laid down the number of gallons of milk and tons of eggs to be produced, with big subsidies for farmers; why then couldn't we do the same for steel and cars and glass, instead of the perpetual booms and slumps? All it needed was 'planning agreements'.

Why not indeed? No farmer ever went bust. Our farms were the best in Europe; why couldn't our industry be the same? The unions agreed too, they loved the idea. Unfortunately, the other Cabinet ministers, especially the Treasury, were appalled. The last thing they wanted was to hand out even more subsidies. The engineering employers didn't agree either. Nor did the Prime Minister, the Stock Exchange, the Bank of England and all of Fleet Street, who saw this as more back-door socialism by a

Government hanging on by a fingernail, or the odd vote of a dying man on a stretcher.

So Benn became the Bogeyman. Like any tried and tested Hollywood movie script, in politics, too, there has to be a Bogeyman. A vampire. Or in a murder mystery the butler has to be the one who did it. Dammit, the public have been trained for years to boo and fear the Bogeyman. Without him there is no story. No headlines. No Quasimodo coming down from the bell-tower to frighten the front stalls and the maiden aunts in their nighties.

And if the Bogeyman is a beautifully spoken left-winger, betraying his establishment background, then the media are going to stab a stake right through his heart every time the sun comes up.

And the *Sun*, plus the *Mail* and the *Express* and practically all the other papers did. Every day, in every edition. No other politician since the war, not even Neil Kinnock, has been so personally abused as Tony Benn. Day after day journalists would stake out his house, following his kids to school, effing and blinding at them because they would not talk about their dad. They searched his dustbin every night, rented a flat opposite his house to take long-range photos, bugged his telephone and even dressed in white coats to impersonate junior doctors when he had to go in hospital, then tried to get photographs and interview the other patients and staff.

Tony remained his usual charming self, relying on television word of mouth and public appearances to get his message across. He was undoubtedly one of history's greatest orators and preachers, explaining the details of policy in simple language (some of which I wrote, changing 'investment and resources' to 'new tools and tackle') to bring standing ovations at Party Conferences and public halls all over Britain.

It was in a pub garden during the lunch-break of an enormous rally at the Sobell Hall in Islington just before the EC referendum that he casually dropped a bombshell. Tony came from a family of life-long teetotallers, who had seen the effects of the demon drink in the Victorian East End, and he himself drank nothing but several gallons of tea every day. But he never tried to impose his ban on anybody else, so we went to the pub.

We sat with his two Parliamentary advisors, Frances Morrell and Francis Cripps (grandson of the famous Stafford, who had had the Bristol seat before Tony), and who were known to one and all as Big Frankie and Little Frankie, because Mrs Morrell was a handsome, buxom political feminist, and Francis Cripps a much smaller, charming intellectual thinker.

Tony casually said, 'I wonder if old Harold Wilson is going to retire? Quit the Prime Minister's job? Only he has ordered every previous Prime Minister to have a chauffeur-driven car on the grounds of IRA security, whether they want one or not.'

A week later, after Wilson had won the referendum to stay in Europe, he got revenge on his chief troublemaker Benn by sacking him from his industry post and switching him to the relatively calmer waters of Energy to bring in the new North Sea oilfields, while keeping the miners happy, as Wilson put it.

I advised Tony to quit. Leave the Cabinet, go out into the country and campaign, I told him, and he would then walk the next leadership campaign, following an election we were undoubtedly going to lose. He spent a night with his family thinking it over. The next day, amazingly, the Labour MPs on the Industry Bill Committee actually went on strike and sent a message to the Prime Minister that they would not continue unless Benn was reinstated.

But Tony decided not to give up his Cabinet seat power, and to take the Energy job instead. It was a monumental political and career mistake. The first mistake in taking a path which would traumatically change Labour history.

Tony Benn's shrewd guess in the pub garden was absolutely

right. And nine months later Wilson did retire, to the enormous shock and surprise of the whole world, never mind Parliament. Although thirty-seven Labour MPs (including me) gave him a rotten leaving present by voting against a new round of cuts in Government spending. For which he promptly sacked me on his last day as Prime Minister, only to have Tony Benn reinstate me the day after Wilson had left.

But the stunned Labour MPs very quickly got over their shock. Here was a 'whole new ball game' as 1976 transatlantic slang put it. The Prime Minister's job was 'up for grabs', in Seventies soundbites, and the new Prime Minister would have a hundred paid jobs to give out to all the sycophants, coat-hangers, and others who would sell their votes for a junior minister's position.

Benn decided to run for Prime Minister. And I was to be in charge of his campaign. It would have been much easier if he had quit after the referendum. Staying on meant that every time he criticized the Government over its nuclear policy or spending, his opponents would simply demand to know why he had stayed in office in the Cabinet instead of quitting.

The timing was not good for Tony. If Wilson had stayed on until after the next election, it would have been better. In 1976 the Labour Government was losing councils and by-elections everywhere, and many MPs were furious with Benn for continually causing arguments, rows and splits, and encouraging demonstrations against Government policy.

'Who have we got on our side?' he asked me and Maggie at his house one night, together with Carol, his very attractive and intelligent wife (we had sent out for burgers because Tony only lived on sandwiches). 'You and me both,' I answered.

There were six candidates, all Cabinet ministers, and it looked as if Tony Benn would be bottom, with Michael Foot picking up all of the left-wing vote. But we stuck at it. Tony worked his charm on individual MPs, who were invited to meet him in his room (like all teetotallers he would pour out whisky or gin in half-pint tumblers as though it were beer), and he actually posted an election manifesto to every MP. It was the first time Labour MPs had ever seen a potential leader discuss policy instead of plots, and it was quite refreshing.

In the first ballot, Foot came top with 90 votes. Callaghan got 84, Jenkins 56, Benn a surprising 37, Healey 30 and Crosland 17. Benn had beaten both the Chancellor of the Exchequer and the Foreign Secretary and consequently was a natural to follow on after the elderly Michael Foot in leading the Party, when the next Prime Minister or Leader of the Opposition was chosen.

We were both very pleased at the 37, but it was only about 15 per cent of the total vote. 'Why didn't we get more?' asked Benn, puzzled. 'Because that's your maximum,' I told him bluntly. 'The simple fact is, Tony, that your policies scare MPs to death in marginal seats. The first thing MPs ask, when they have to vote for a leader, is "Can this man hold my seat?" and too many of them think you can't because too many of the *Sun* and *Mail* readers have now been persuaded that you are a revolutionary sent from Moscow. MPs have all got kids and mortgages. Just like any other worker, they don't want to be made redundant. They would sooner have a quiet life than political uproar.'

Which didn't go down very well with Tony. To him politics was a crusade, not a job. Pioneers who went into politics should not expect an easy ride or a job for life. It was only natural that they and their families should have to suffer for the cause, as he and his family had done. The concept of time-servers and governmental lackeys desperately seeking ministerial jobs was just not acceptable.

It was then that he made a decision which was to change the whole future of the Labour Party for the next twenty years, and hand it over to an army of young, quite literally daft, loony left, student Party activists, who couldn't run a proverbial whelk stall, never mind the country, or a big city like London or Liverpool.

'In that case we will change the system,' Tony said. 'Instead of the MPs choosing the Prime Minister, or the Party Leader, we will let the party constituencies and the unions do it. They and the MPs will each have a third of the votes.' But there was to be no such democratic nonsense as one member, one vote. The unions' third would be cast by the unions' leaders, and the constituency third by a handful of left-wing plotters (who were exactly the same plotters as those in the unions), giving them two votes each.

Now, he decided, all MPs would have to be 'reselected' in the middle of every Parliament. They would be faced with an impossible choice. An MP could either vote in Parliament as the Government whips told him. Or ignore the whips and vote instead as the loonies in the constituency party ordered (and face deselection if he didn't), or vote as the public wanted him to do, in which case he would not get nominated anyway. Either way the MP couldn't win. There was no way MPs would become anything but timid mice, desperate to keep their cheese and stay out of the mousetrap.

That's when I parted company with Tony and accepted a whip's job from the new Prime Minister, Jim Callaghan, to become a poacher turned gamekeeper.

Tony Benn was the darling of the Labour Party Conference and the new rules were duly endorsed by it after the National Executive Committee, led and dominated by Tony, drew them up.

The following October, with the fading Labour Government facing its winter of discontent, I went to the rostrum at the Labour Party Conference and begged the delegates not to support the 'mandatory' reselection of MPs, to allow at least those constituencies which were happy with their MP to keep him, without making him walk over the hot coals.

I pointed out that MPs got no redundancy money if they lost their seat. They got six months' wages instead. But only if they stood and fought the election. Any MP who got the sack would be compelled to run for the money, and it would split the Labour Party vote in half.

These sacked MPs could even form a new breakaway party! There are at least twenty-five Labour MPs now who are on the brink of doing that, I warned. Later, at the 1980 Blackpool Conference, I yelled from the rostrum, 'If Roy Jenkins wanted to form a party of twenty-five sacked MPs now, in this Parliament, they could be in business in six months, and they would be backed by the media.'

It caused an uproar. The entire 2,000 delegates and visitors yelled, booed and slow-handclapped me off the rostrum. Sam McClusky, the Seamen's Union Secretary who was chairing the session, advised me to 'go and join them', but later apologized privately for his remarks.

Actually, I was wrong. When the SDP broke away three months later, led by Roy Jenkins, there turned out to be twenty-seven Labour MPs not twenty-five, and one from the Tories too.

But prophets never have any honour. Least of all in politics. What's more, there was a nasty stink of greed, ambition and cynicism right through the younger delegates, which I had never seen in the Labour Party before or since.

In the late Seventies and early Eighties a new generation of Labour Party members had appeared. They were mainly from the polytechnics and universities and often sons and daughters of the old-time Party and trade union horny-handed sons of toil, who had sweated in the pits, the steelworks, shipyards and car factories of Britain.

Their mums and dads had made great sacrifices to send them to university, but a huge number of students had simply taken the soft option of a degree in social studies or local government and had swamped the town halls up and down the country. Often they'd be employed by one town hall while sitting on the council for the town next door, and running that one almost full-time.

It almost seemed as if this Seventies generation were bitter that they too had not had the opportunity of suffering real poverty and hardship to prove their machismo like we did, but had only been able to study it at university. They did not want to run the existing Party or Government machine. They simply wanted to prove their virility by smashing it and starting again.

They honestly thought that a 'few years' in Opposition (it turned out to be eighteen) to 'clear out the dead wood', as they called sitting MPs, would do the Party a world of good, (just as Mrs Thatcher thought closing half the factories in Britain would make Britain rich).

But above all they were careerists. They all wanted to become MPs and politicians themselves. They wanted to be instantly famous without the long grind of serving on local councils and going step by step up the ladder, wearily touring the country speaking in dreary, cold Labour halls, waiting for older MPs to retire or die. They wanted to do it now. On television. Turfing out sitting MPs *en masse* was the fastest way to climb the ladder, and sod the MPs' families or past loyal service.

'I'd sooner be in opposition than have a government like the last one,' they serenaded, safe in their town hall and teacher jobs where they would never be made redundant. So, instead of persuading the public to vote Labour, they spent months and months changing the rule-book to get themselves a good job.

Added to the donkey jacket social workers were the total nutters. These thought that while ever there was a Labour Government or even a large number of Labour MPs there could never be a revolution. They did not want capitalism to succeed or be propped up. If Labour ever produced full employment, then who would storm the barricades? Sacking all the existing MPs and replacing them by just fifty hardline Militant Tendency kamikazi pilots would be a good swap, they seriously suggested.

Tony Benn, perhaps inadvertently, and with the best of democratic intentions, had opened the door to a wind of change which

211

blew the Party back twenty years. After the May 1979 election the carpet-baggers flooded in and swept through local parties everywhere. None of them ever gave the last Labour Government any credit for keeping going night after night by carrying in the votes on stretchers. It was non-stop abuse, denigration and ridicule of all surviving Labour MPs. At the Party Conference some genius had the bright idea of seating all the sitting MPs together at the side of the hall on a raised platform of chairs where they could be pointed at, like prisoners in the dock, and vilified as traitors to the cause.

Tony Benn got his way at the October 1980 Conference. He persuaded it to hold another one-day conference three months later, on 31 January 1981, to draw up the new rules. His suggestion of the Party Leader being chosen by thirds, with the unions, the constituency parties and the MPs all having equal shares of the vote, was likely to be accepted.

Except, except, as usual, there was another almighty balls-up. At the last minute the division of the vote was changed by the left, aided by some dopey union leaders, to 40, 40, 30. Thus the MPs' votes for their own leader were reduced to just 30 per cent. One member, one vote was never even mentioned.

It was just what the 'Gang of Four' had been waiting for. Secretly, four ex-Labour Government Cabinet ministers, David Owen, Roy Jenkins, Shirley Williams and Bill Rodgers, had been plotting with several other MPs, as I told the 1980 Conference, to form a breakaway party. On the Saturday, when the delegates overwhelmingly supported the proposal on 40, 40, 30, David Owen, flushed and angry, had been booed off the platform and jeered out of the hall by the rabble-rousers and guillotine mob.

On Sunday, the next day, as planned, the four of them announced they would set up the SDP and break away from the Labour Party. By March they had seventeen Labour MPs backing them. Seventeen MPs who knew they had no chance of surviving reselection and were better off cutting and running to jump on another ship. It was carefully planned, with no mass exodus. One by one, spread over many weeks, single MPs would defect to make it look as if the Labour Party was slowly crumbling away.

The young Bennites, the Militant Tendency and Socialist Workers Party, and all the other ragbag crazy elements could not care less. They were not interested in winning a General Election. A safe seat for themselves would be quite satisfactory, thank you.

The new machinery invented by Tony Benn and the left had to have a try-out of course. Jim Callaghan deliberately stood down as Leader, before the rule-book could be changed, rather than face their scorn, and also to allow the sitting MPs to choose their own leader for the last time. At least twenty-seven of those MPs, knowing they were going to form a new party, to be called the SDP, the Social Democratic Party, deliberately voted for Michael Foot rather than Denis Healey, to keep the party they were quitting on the left, to make it easier for them to justify leaving, and to swing their Labour seat to SDP next time.

Such is the treachery of politics.

The new Leader, Michael Foot, an engaging old rebel and tremendous conference orator, had received votes from both left and right because it was thought his healing qualities and the great respect in which he was held might pull the Party together to make peace on all sides. Yet he had only beaten runner-up right-wing Denis Healey by ten votes in a 139–129 score. If the SDP had not voted, then Healey would have been Leader. The hard left promptly decided that Healey had to go, to show who was now running the Party, and prove conclusively that the rank-and-file mutiny was a success.

Tony Benn then committed his next grave error by deciding to cause an entirely unnecessary contest for the Deputy Leadership, a nothing job in terms of power, simply to show who was in command. I heard the rumour on an all-night sitting on 1

April, and sought out Benn in his office. At two in the morning I urged him not to stand and split the Party. Not only did he refuse, he went straight to the Press Association and announced it to all the morning papers, to guarantee even more disastrous headlines.

He had not even consulted the left-wing Tribune Group of Labour MPs to get their backing, and many of them were furious that their support had been taken for granted. But most of them were quite happy to put Benn into second place, all ready to take over from Foot if we lost the next election in 1983, as we surely would.

Except, except, as the plot thickens, a young, exceedingly bright Welsh orator called Neil Kinnock ran a spoiler through the winning plan. He could read the plot as well as anybody could and was no slouch himself when it came to plotting, especially to enhance his own career. Not yet forty, he had been in Parliament ten years and had had a meteoric rise on the left wing. A superb performer on a platform, with his wit and Welsh *hywel*, he had constantly refused to become a junior minister or accept any job in the previous Labour Government, and could hold up clean hands on all the unpopular decisions it had made, choosing to work his way up the left wing of the Party ladder instead.

His voting record was suitably rebellious. He had campaigned against the Common Market, against nuclear weapons, against Healey's cuts, and had actually forced through the referendum on devolution which had brought down the last Labour Government.

Neil had carefully cultivated all the unofficial London-based way-out fringes of the so-called 'Campaign for Labour Party Democracy' which believed in any form of perverted democracy except one member, one vote, and which ranged from the 'Rank and File Mobilizing Committee' to any local playgroup whose mothers happened to be 'against the bomb'. With all the usual mandatory attacks on the Royal Family's pay rise, etc. His attendance and voting record during the dark days of 1978 had fallen to five out of ten simply because he spent so much time touring the constituencies drawing up personal support by castigating his own government, which was surviving on stretcher votes.

Neil had virtually gone straight into Parliament at the age of twenty-eight, having lost none of his students' union fire. He was probably the most popular man in the Labour Party among the new young delegates, eager for revolution. His glamorous and friendly down-to-earth-wife, Glenys, was immensely popular too. At Labour Party Conferences Neil would star in the 'End of the Peers' show revue and bring the House down singing 'Old Man Callaghan' to the tune of 'Old Man River': 'He must know somethin', but he don't do nothin'.' The trendy London media loved him for attacking the Labour front-bench. He was a regular writer for the *Guardian*, appeared on every political TV chat show, and travelled tirelessly up and down the motorways at weekends, speaking at meetings and gathering acclamation everywhere. He was absolutely in tune with the new generation of buccaneers who wanted revolution and surgery, not healing and ointment.

Kinnock, now aged thirty-nine, knew that a Benn victory, with Healey sidelined, would be only one stop from making Benn the next Leader of the Party. He had to find some way of defeating Benn and keeping Healey in the job, while at the same time not alienating his own left-wing support.

As Benn had not bothered asking the Tribune Group of MPs for their support before announcing his candidature, Kinnock promptly announced that he would abstain on the vote, and recommended other Tribune MPs join him. Thirty-seven did. And I was one of them. Not to stop Benn, or to enhance Kinnock's career. But simply to try to keep Healey in the job as a bastion of sanity and prove to the voters that the juvenile Loonies had not entirely taken over the ship. It would have been disloyal to Tony Benn for me to actually vote for Healey, but it made temporary sense to keep the status quo. Meanwhile, Neil Kinnock wrote a

3,000-word article in *Tribune* castigating the whole idea of the unnecessary contest and conflict, which naturally infuriated Benn's supporters.

Once again, as unemployment soared, and Thatcher cut DSS benefits and changed the rules to cut old age pension increases, the Labour Party played on its fiddle as Rome burned. Thatcher was immensely unpopular and losing support in the opinion polls every day. But Labour was not cashing in on it. The new SDP, linking up with the Liberals, was.

Healey fought a persistent battle right through the summer, speaking at union conferences everywhere. With thirty-seven MPs threatening to abstain, it was obvious that Benn would pick up the constituency votes but that Healey might outweigh him in the union vote. In actual fact the stupid decision to plump for 40, 40, 30, instead of thirds, might cost Benn the ticket.

It did. On a secret ballot Healey received 50.4 per cent and Benn 49.6. The votes of just three more MPs would have swung it for him. I abstained and so did Joan Lestor, Neil Kinnock, Stan Orme, Jeff Rooker, John Evans, Martin O'Neill, Doug Hoyle, and Bob Kilroy-Silk, who later became a national TV star.

Kinnock was savagely abused verbally, and physically by the left hardliners who screamed that he had put his career in front of the left-wing ticket, let Healey in and betrayed Tony Benn. Later that week he was attacked in the Gents by a young delegate who karate-kicked him. Kinnock fought back and later told his wife in the bar that the Labour Shadow Minister for Education (as he then was) beat the shit out of the thug. Neil, an ex-rugby player, could have too.

At the Tribunal rally he was scathingly attacked by Margaret Beckett and heckled with cries of 'Traitor' and 'Judas'.

Benn never really recovered the stature and worship he had once enjoyed. Sadly, Tony lost his Bristol seat in the 1983 election less than two years later, following boundary changes, and would not have been eligible to run for Leader to succeed Foot anyway.

And by then Kinnock had it stitched up.

All younger generations are attracted to any organization which is banned. The idea of belonging to a secret mafia such as the Militant Tendency is automatically exciting and adds a bit of spice to students of boring Humanities or Philosophy. Shifting the power from Parliament to smoke-filled rooms above pubs and making sitting MPs tremble at the threat of dismissal by young socialist activists in T-shirts and jeans makes up for never having had the pride of sleeping three kids to a bed, or wearing clogs at the pit. Especially if the new Che Guevaras find themselves constantly interviewed on television on how they intend to smash the system. The more damage they did to the Labour Party, the more famous they became.

The adrenaline of chat-show revolution becomes addictive, and there were plenty of new young Labour councillors hooked on it. TV producers quickly caught on that minor councillor firebrands make better TV than cautious, defensive MPs.

For the first time in history, the hard left had a national platform on TV and in the national daily press. And did they enjoy it! Paper tigers like Tariq Ali, whose bushy moustache made him look for all the world like a kid's cartoon character carrying a big round bomb labelled 'BOMB' under his cloak, were given unlimited licence to attack Labour. With impeccable timing, the BBC announced the important event that Tariq had actually joined the Labour Party on the morning of the Hillhead by-election, which the SDP promptly won. Way-out parrots of fire like Red Ted Knight and Linda Bellos were welcomed as visiting royalty from Lambeth on to *Newsnight*, *Any Questions*, or by-election panels, every day. Providing of course they flew the red flag and yelled the slogans of revolution, terrifying Labour voters into thinking that Walworth Road, the Party Headquarters, was run from Moscow.

The Tory newspapers loved the hard left, as they loved Militant Tendency leaders in Liverpool. Any one of whom could be guaranteed to do the Tories' job for them by losing Labour votes whenever they opened their mouth on TV or made shock horror headlines in the *Sun*, the *Mail*, or the *Express*.

Every single one of them was talking a language of 'Smash, grab, fight, destroy'. They earned little money, had nothing to spend, and nothing to occupy their time except marching, and demonstrating for every crackpot cause, chanting 'Maggie, Maggie, Maggie Out, Out, Out', and carrying banners for *News at Ten*. In addition there were always a few elderly Fagins around, whose political careers had not glittered as well as they expected, to encourage and train the Artful Dodgers and naïve Olivers to do the dirty work. This regularly seemed to involve getting rid of the local Dad's Army councillors, who promptly joined the SDP and got elected for them instead.

The takeover of the hard left was remorseless. Arthur Lewis, sacked by his local party in Newham, denounced them as 'hundred per cent Trotskyist, Militant Tendency, Communist and IRA supporters'. As these idiots committed political arson, Shirley Williams won a by-election from the Tories at Crosby, near Liverpool, for the first SDP victory. Roy Jenkins, narrowly defeated in the safe Labour seat of Warrington, went on to win Glasgow Hillside. All the SDP defectors still in Parliament howled at the undemocratic block votes of the unions at the Labour Party Conference, but not one SDP defector, elected on Labour votes, ever offered to stand down and fight again as SDP.

Thatcher's cuts cost her votes right across the country, and in local elections the Tories were nearly wiped out. Long-standing, well-experienced Labour councillors were also wiped out, summarily ejected from their tenure by the new selection procedures and replaced by *nouveau* Marxists whose only experience of the working class was to sell them a paper as they poured out of the factory gates.

When the Labour Party regained the Greater London Council, within hours of the votes being counted its tried and tested Labour leaders were ejected and replaced by inexperienced new committee chairmen under their new leader, Ken Livingstone.

The new masters of the Greater London Council spent the ratepayers' money as though it came off a Monopoly board. The councillors would hand out cash to 'CND Mothers' or 'SEQUEL', a group which organized social nights for lesbians. On a budget of £800 million a year the GLC juveniles regularly overspent by £300 million, and simply stuck it on the rates they collected from every house and business. Any loony cause could get a grant. A whole new gay scene swept across London, mostly funded by councils in Brent, Haringey, Islington, Lambeth and other inner city areas who allocated spending on council house repairs as a very low priority, but poured funds into silly groups called 'CISSY', meaning 'Campaign to Impede Sex Stereotyping in the Young', or 'GASP', standing for 'Group Against Sexual Practice'. The Monster Raving Loonies really did rule some local Labour councils. Haringey actually wanted to put questionnaires in their employees' pay packets, asking 'Are you a homosexual?'

When former Labour Government Chief Whip Bob Mellish quit his seat to call a by-election after his working-class party in Bermondsey chose a gay rights campaigner, Peter Tatchell, to succeed him, it set the gay rights campaign back for ten years.

Tatchell lived in a council flat and shared the neighbourhood's poverty, vandalized misery, noise and graffiti with his neighbours (Cockneys who quickly asked what good would he be as an MP if he couldn't fix himself a better council flat than that) but was violently abused by the macho Millwall supporters, because he was a twenty-seven-year old Australian who spoke with a camp accent and carried a shoulder-bag. The Liberals won the seat and turned a 12,000 Labour majority into a 7,000 victory for them and have held it ever since – with an MP who supports gay rights but who is obviously not a loony. Meanwhile, as the AIDS fears grew, Labour's by-election winner at Fulham, Nick Raynsford, was actually castigated by the left for daring to put pictures of his wife and kids on his election address.

The GLC leader, Ken Livingstone, gloried in any daft action just as long as it made him famous. The more spectacular the own goal, the more often the TV producers sent for him. This local councillor received the same coverage as any pop star or Cabinet minister – but only if he stirred up mischief and mayhem. He would don a pantomime outfit to appear in *The Mikado*, to the delight of the media and Tory MPs, while the SDP were winning GLC seats in Croydon and St Pancras North, previously a rock-solid Labour council area which had a very large Irish population. None of which deterred Livingstone from building up contact with Sinn Fein and the IRA. Livingstone, as the leader of the largest council in Britain, actually refused to represent it at Prince Charles's and Lady Diana's wedding 'to show solidarity with the IRA hunger strikers'. He claimed that 'what Britain has done to Ireland is worse than what Hitler did to the Jews'.

Livingstone's sky-high business rates emptied London's offices as companies moved out of town. His master plan to bring in low fares for public transport was blocked by the courts simply because the GLC were too stupid to do their homework and wait to introduce it in the next financial year. The Council cut London Transport fares by 32 per cent, to great cheers from the passengers. Until a far-flung Tory district council in Bromley went to court saying it was unfair to make the Bromley ratepayers pay for it, when they hadn't even got a Tube station, and why should they subsidize cheap Tube fares for West End tourists anyway?

The courts agreed. Livingstone was told to pay back the £125 million the cheap fare policy had cost and to double the fares to find the money. It was another fine mess the juveniles had got Labour into.

If Mrs Thatcher had not stupidly abolished the GLC in 1994 from under him to gain short-term votes, Ken would have finished up as the political clown he was, instead of a cheeky, likeable rogue with a ready London wit on any phone-in or panel game. Thatcher shot her own fox. With the GLC gone, there was nobody else to blame for the mess London was in.

Some time later, Goldsmith's College of London University carried out an extensive research into the loony tunes and published a report titled *HIT AND MYTH. THE MEDIA TREATMENT OF LONDON COUNCILS*. It traced the stories backwards through the journalists who sold them or made them up, and every single one was pure fiction. They were all lies. Barefaced untruths worthy of Goebbels and Hitler.

The problem was that most of these highly damaging, vote-losing stories were not officially denied or rebutted. Some of the councillors just did not bother. Any publicity was better than no publicity. Livingstone admitted that GLC councillors would have hysterical laughter sessions at the outrageous allegations and even compete to see who could attract the daftest headline. But the tragedy was that the hard left who were being denigrated just did not care. The opinion polls showed Labour standing at just 23 per cent in December 1981. But votes did not matter. The revolution, when it came, would take care of it all.

The policy of Labour councils handing out grants to every daft social service pressure group actually increased the strength of the hard left in local parties, while the threat of reselection kept the MPs silent in Westminster. The common-sense wing of the Labour Party never got a look in.

Consequently, the common-sense Labour voters switched their support to the SDP and the Liberals. There were many inside stories among MPs at Westminster of vicious battles to oust sitting MPs in local constituencies. Some MPs simply quit politics for a quiet life, with their place taken by well-organized left-wing plotters. Inside stories of fiddled union branch 'percentage votes' for meetings which were never held, or results deliberately sent in late after the ballot deadline, or stacks of last-minute votes from new members, who could not even speak English, and whose votes were cast and counted for them, were rife.

Many sitting MPs, sickened with the new system, just walked away or looked for other jobs, while others bit their lip and suffered the abuse heaped on them for the sake of their kids and mortgages. Ironically, many of the newcomers, or the ones who came later in seats Labour should never have lost in 1992, are currently in Tony Blair's New Labour Government, holding down ministerial jobs and beavering away at the Despatch Box bringing in policies (common-sense policies) which they furiously derided on their 1980s upward mobility climb to Westminster.

In the February of 1983, on the Friday morning after Tatchell had lost the very safe seat of Southwark and Bermondsey by the biggest by-election swing in history, a group of loyalist Labour MPs met in the Tea Room and decided the situation could not go on. Andrew Bennett, Jeff Rooker, Dale Campbell Savours, Bob Kilroy-Silk, Austin Mitchell, Phillip Whitehead and myself decided we would demand a meeting with the Leader, Michael Foot, who had denounced Peter Tatchell then done nothing to stop his candidature and tell him he would have to go. Foot was a wonderful orator and probably the best-loved man in the Party, but his control over it had been not just abysmal, but disastrous. If Foot refused to stand down we would publicly call for him to quit, even though it would cause another ruckus. Dale Campbell Savours had done a straw poll which showed that 115 sensible middle-of-the-road Labour MPs thought Foot should move out.

As usual, the whips had their ear to the ground and got to Foot and Michael Cocks, the Chief Whip, first, and the coup was promptly stalled by an immediate announcement that the Party would instantly move the writ for another by-election at Darlington. It would be disastrous to call for the sacking of the Leader while a by-election was on, so the knives were put back in the drawer.

Darlington was a very marginal seat and every political commentator wrote that the new popular SDP would take it off Labour. But surprisingly, the whole of the North-East Labour parties rallied round and fought a magnificent battle, far away from London and Liverpool loonies, to hold it, with a 1 per cent swing to Labour. Which saved Foot to fight another day.

It was an astonishing and surprising result. Surprising to Mrs Thatcher too, because on her reckoning it was a seat the Conservatives should have won instead of coming third. Despite the total adulation of Mrs Thatcher by the British media after Britain had decisively won the Falklands War against Argentina (in football terms the equivalent of Arsenal beating Brentford), the Tories' share of the opinion polls was still barely 40 per cent.

Since the 1979 election 12,000 firms in Britain had gone bust. Unemployment had rocketed from one million to three. Mrs Thatcher's policies had devastated the North and the Midlands, even if not yet the South, and she was smart enough to know she could only win if she went early, while the glow of the Falklands victory was still warm, and while the SDP breakaways were splitting the anti-Tory vote two ways, as Labour loonies still ran the Labour Party.

It was a very shrewd political move, backed by a superbly organized campaign with unlimited cash to spend on poster and newspaper advertising and well-staged television performances. As usual, the Labour Party was in tatters, blood-stained, weary, divided and worn.

The Party Headquarters published a manifesto 15,000 words in length, which was quickly entitled 'the longest suicide note in history', detailing every dot and comma of every resolution passed by the ranters and block votes of the Party Conference. Which the Tories of course immediately costed, and quite rightly forecast its spending would bankrupt Britain in twelve months. They then bought thousands of copies to distribute all over the country.

The organization of the Labour campaign would have Hattersley, Foot, Healey, Kinnock and any other 'spokesman' pouring forth different individual policies, all at the same time, in the far corners of Britain, and all shown contradicting each other on TV news an hour later. Invariably the loudspeaker would not work, the Party members would have to push the van to make it start, some idiot would throw eggs or bananas, and an exhausted frontbench spokesman on his twenty-seventh public speech of the day would rise to the bait of a Union Jack flag-flyer and denounce all war battles, even though 'Our Boys' had just won one in the Falklands.

Just as former Prime Minister Jim Callaghan used the election to attack his own party's policy on defence and nuclear disarmament, Neil Kinnock attacked the 1982 sinking of the Argentinian cruiser the *General Belgrano*, forgetting that day was the anniversary of when the Argies had killed thirty-nine Welsh Guardsmen at Bluff Cove.

At the 1983 election the Labour MPs, led by ageing, daydreaming Scout leaders, and chased and harried by the packs of political untrained naïve militant students behind them, were slaughtered. Mrs Thatcher's majority of thirty was turned into a majority of 188 over Labour. Labour seats, some of which had been held for generations, and their candidates were machine-gunned down like British Tommies at the Somme.

The breakaway SDP won only six seats, but they split the regular Labour vote in half in a hundred more, allowing the Tories to win on the British first-past-the-post electoral system. Labour lost its deposit in 119 seats. Its 27 per cent of the vote was the lowest of any General Election it had ever fought in history.

The SDP and Liberals, banding together in an alliance, had totalled 7.8 million votes. Labour totalled 8.5. Yet with first-past-the-post, Labour had still managed to hold on to 209 seats while the Liberals and SDP had only twenty-three. If just 2 or 3 per cent more of the voters had turned against the Loony Labour Party, it would have been wiped off the face of the British political map for ever.

Instead, 'clearing out the dead wood,' as the ambitious young Benn-led careerists had decided to do, had opened the doors to 18 unbroken years of Conservative government. Even then, some of them were daft enough to think it had simply brought the revolution closer. Fortunately, none of them took notice of a twenty-nine-year-old lad called Tony Blair who had been selected for the safe seat in Sedgefield in Durham just days before the election, after losing his deposit and gaining only 3,800 votes in a by-election at Beaconsfield, Berkshire just a couple of months before.

Twelve

THE MINERS' STRIKE

THERE is no tougher, more dangerous, unhealthy and unhygienic job than coal mining. For colliers, life consists of six- or seven-hour shifts in a hot, terrifying black hole, a mile underground.

There is about as much space at the coal face as there is under your kitchen table. Imagine that space forming a tunnel a hundred yards long. The floor is an uneven bed of loose cobbles wrecking your hands and knees as you crawl, after first walking half a mile to get there, preceded by a mile-long bogey ride in pitch dark. There is no light except that on your heavy helmet, which makes your head sweat and jolts your neck every five minutes when it cracks against the low ceiling. The thick dust chokes your throat, ears and eyes and penetrates every pore.

As you crawl the hundred yards dodging the pit props holding up the low roof, there is a moving steel conveyor belt running alongside your knees. One slip and you will be on it. Or perhaps leave an arm or leg under it. Worst of all, at the other side of the belt is a terrifying revolving four-foot-diameter drum pounding into the coal face like a huge circular saw, tearing, gouging and ripping out tons of coal and toppling it on to the moving belt next to you.

If the belt stops for any reason, your pay drops. Tonnage is everything. Bent double like an animal trapped inside a burrow, it would be an achievement to survive. To actually do a hard physical job in those conditions, worse than any murderer or rapist in prison would have to endure, starting at six in the morning, or any other shift the pit chooses, right round the clock, is a hell of a life.

It is not for the squeamish. There are no toilets down a pit. If a miner 'takes short', he has to crawl a few yards away from his mates and use coal dust for toilet paper because there is no running water either. Like a cat, he squats over a shovel for a litter, then throws it into the out-by. Every day, as the cutter moves on, the props will be withdrawn and the roof allowed to fall in with a thundering crash to bury the detritus and discarded rubble. There is no smoking allowed and food and drink soon go bad because of the foul air.

It's a hard, cruel life which produces tough warriors and survivors. Few miners worry about having a day off if they have a good win on the horses, because they regard a day off as an extra day on their life. Which they will soon be coughing away at the age of fifty. By then their lungs will be lined with more black dust than the bricks of any 100-year-old Victorian slum.

Up until the early 1980s, school leavers in scattered mining villages could expect nothing but an eternity of shift work, relentless toil and early infirmity in a small village with no large shops, no cinema, restaurant or night-club, and only the leisure activities of beer and bingo and pigeon racing or bowls at the Miners' Institute.

How much pay would you expect for a job like that? Any bloke outside a pit area would regard that sort of toil as a task to undertake for about five years as a young man, then quit, having earned enough to buy a business out of a six-figure nest-egg to show for the hard labour.

A deliberate venture. A cool assessment of five years' loss of life for Easy Street on the rest of it.

Yet although miners worked for top wages, the pay was

nothing special. And they were not employed by some grasping, rascally Victorian sweat-shop employer either. They worked for you and me. The taxpayer. In a publicly owned, mechanized industry. But not one like the safe and everlasting Town Hall. Or a bobby's job retiring on a whacking pension at forty-five. Or even a stressed-out teacher at fifty.

Most miners did not even live into their sixties and seventies to draw their Coal Board pension. I was once invited to a 'Widows' Tea' by the miners at Shireoaks, in my constituency. There were 259 widows of miners from the village pit, ranging in age from twenty-three to seventy-eight. That was the price of coal, with as many men dying crushed to death in the mines every year as there were victims who died in the Hillsborough football disaster. The miners were mourned silently and alone.

I was proud to represent the coal-miners of Bassetlaw, which covers all three of the Notts and Derbyshire and South Yorkshire coalfields, for well over thirty years. In that time, in travels all over the world, I have never met such genuine, brave, unassuming, decent, loyal, uncomplaining men and women as the coal-mining families right across Britain.

Someday, in the next century, in the same way as our nation remembers its dead from the wars, it will also remember those who died at work, or from work. And if I ever win the Lottery I will build the memorial in Worksop, the main town in Bassetlaw, to commemorate those who shed their blood to provide Britain's heating, lighting and power-generation. The pits in my constituency, over the years, were Manton, Shireoaks, Steetley, Harworth, Bevercotes, Firbeck, Welbeck and Warsop. There were power stations too at West Burton, High Marnham and Cottam.

During the miners' strike of 1984, when the National Union of Mineworkers split, and brother literally fought brother, with those on strike picketing those who carried on working, Bassetlaw experienced the same sort of division as the nation saw in Northern Ireland. It was border country.

British coalfields are not spread evenly under the sod. As they were discovered and expanded in remote rural areas, a hundred years ago, they attracted immigrants from all over the rest of the nation, who, like all immigrants, were prepared to work at rotten jobs for lousy pay. And consequently had a vested interest in forming themselves into trade unions which, because of the distance and poor public transport, became far more federalist and tribal than any other union.

The pitworkers' tribes, living like Red Indians on reservations in houses owned by the boss, and trading at his store, married the sisters of their workmates. All went to the same school, all drank in the same Miners' Welfare, all looked after their old folk, all ran the local council and social clubs too. It was all for one and one for all in the best tribal tradition.

Everything in the village centred on the pit. Just as the Red Indians depended on the buffaloes for food, clothing, and even shelter in their buffalo-skin tents, so miners depended on the coal.

Take away the coal and their lives were finished. In other towns redundant men could move down the road a couple of miles and take their skills to another factory. When a pit shut, there was no other factory. Coal-mining skills, unlike engineering, are not transferable or of any use in any other industry.

Consequently, when miners went on strike, like the Redskins, they were fighting for their families, their homes, their traditions, their roots. They were national brave warriors who faced death every day in their jobs, and it was apparent that whoever took them on would have to butcher them to the last brave as the United States cavalry did to the Indians at the Battle of Wounded Knee in 1890. Which was, of course, deliberate revenge for the Red Indians' victory in 1876 when the mighty Sioux, led by

Sitting Bull, had massacred General Custer at Little Bighorn in Montana.

In exactly the same way, the Conservative Party in opposition from 1974 to 1979 planned revenge, and the total destruction of the British unions, if they ever got back to power. They sought vengeance because the previous Tory Government lost the February 1974 snap election called by Ted Heath, simply because it could not govern the unions, and more especially the miners.

Led then by a wily old fox called Joe Gormley, from Lancashire (gormless in Lancashire means stupid, Gormley is the exact opposite) and Laurence Daly from Scotland, the miners, at that time amongst the poorest-paid workers in the country, picked their moment to strike, like any good Indian, when coal stocks were low and winter was coming on. Heath had no option but to save electricity by putting Britain on a three-day working week (with cuts in pay) with staggered shifts and hours for everybody; even London's theatres had staggered starting times, to dodge the power cuts. Houses were in darkness every evening, with the power cuts for each post code announced in the local papers. There were no street lights and every day that winter there was an air of doom and gloom, like a curfew in Poland.

The crunch came for Heath when an unknown young brave called Arthur Scargill organized a mass flying picket of thousands of miners and their supporters, to stop essential coke supplies from leaving a depot at Saltley in Birmingham. The police could not control them and had to admit defeat. Scargill's previous strategy of flying pickets had also closed the docks at Ipswich inside an hour.

An embarrassed cavalry had to admit that if thousands of strong young men, whether they are football hooligans or striking trade unionists, hit the streets, mob-handed, then normal policing will fail. The pickets will win by sheer weight of numbers and mobility. The Tories, under Mrs Thatcher, realized that the Victorian days of reading the Riot Act and putting trade unionists in gaol under the Conspiracy and Protection of Property Act 1875, as they had for the 'Shrewsbury Two', were useless, if thousands of running men simply disappeared into the back-streets, like the Vietcong freedom fighters had disappeared into the jungle.

In their years of Opposition, Thatcher, Nicholas Ridley and other right-wing hardliners like Norman Tebbit, planned diligently how to smash the unions once and for all, if the Tories won the 1979 election.

It was simple. Once they had a majority, they would take away all the subsidies from public industries and sell off the nationalized giants of gas, railways, electricity, water, telephones, etc., etc. If that put two million extra workers on the dole, then it would teach them a lesson. The dole queue would keep down wage demands, strip unions of their members and their cash, and frighten the rank and file away from even considering industrial action.

Then they would bring in laws to bankrupt any union which went on strike, by allowing their employers or any other contractors who suffered a loss to sue for damages running into millions. If the unions refused to pay, then the courts would seize or sequester their funds.

Closed shops, with their compulsory union membership (designed to stop freeloaders from picking up pay rises and better conditions without paying union subs), would also be outlawed. All strikes would have to be preceded by a secret postal ballot sent to the workers' home (so as to influence the wife with letters from the boss, backed by massive biased press reporting). Flying pickets would be outlawed, and it would be a criminal offence for any union or person to picket at another workplace not connected with the industry, such as railways, power stations, depots, ports, etc. For any of these offences, union leaders would be personally fined (not imprisoned; the Tories did not want any martyrs).

All union leaders would have to stand for election every five years by secret ballot too. A measure heartedly cheered and approved by the House of Lords, some of whose members had never stood for any election to get their jobs.

There was going to be no workers' revolution while Mrs Thatcher was Prime Minister. The Iron Lady was going to annihilate the unions once and for all.

But not the miners. Not just yet. First of all, in 1981, she took on the steelworkers – hardworking lads, but notoriously loath to strike against their paternal industry – to warn any future dissidents. Despite Arthur Scargill leading the steel pickets, the Government won easily.

Mrs Thatcher used the other secret Tory weapon too. Money. All the workers in steel towns like Corby, which had no other industry, would be given good redundancy cash. Because of the EEC rules, any miner losing his job would pick up two or three years' wages in redundancy. It sounded wonderful, but without any other work anywhere, miners soon realized that it was simply DSS benefits in advance, because none of them would be able to sell their house and move, and, if they were over fifty, they would probably never work again.

She also stockpiled coal at the power stations. Just like the Government stockpile of butter mountains in the EEC food chain, which provided massive subsidies to farmers. Who, however, because they voted Tory, would continue to be heavily subsidized, and not turned out to grass like the rest of British industry.

Still, as the 1983 election approached, Mrs Thatcher waited. She had a little war to fight in the Falklands first, and she had to get the new laws through Parliament too. There was no rush. The breakaway twenty-seven ex-Labour MPs who formed the SDP had split the Opposition vote in half, and she knew she would walk the next election.

In the meantime, old Joe Gormley, the miners' leader, reached retiring age and went off to his luxury union house in Sunbury-on-Thames, with its swimming pool, at a nominal rent, plus two years' salary as golden handshake, and two-thirds salary as pension (the miners have always been very generous to their leaders).

Scargill had prepared the ground well. His junior job in the NUM gave him a ready platform for any dispute, and an articulate 'Gobshite', as they are called in Yorkshire, was always in demand for chat shows, interviews and rent-a-quote on any TV programme which needed a miner's helmet and a pit cage in the background.

He was cocky, confident, often humorous, and a good mimic, and he spoke a language the miners readily understood and identified with. And he was a lot younger than any other contender. A one-time leader of the handful of Communists in Barnsley, he had been a firebrand since he left school and started at Woolley Colliery.

When Gormley retired in March 1981, Scargill ran for the union election for top job and stormed around the pits everywhere, often speaking to rallies of anything from 500 to 1,000 people. Probably at least half of them were not miners, but Communists, Trotskyists, Socialist Workers Party and other ragbag Militant Tendencies, but they would cheer to the invited TV cameras, and the Thatcher-loving press would give him all the rope he needed to hang the Labour Party loyalists who had previously run the National Union of Mineworkers for eighty years. Scargill had but one message. That Mrs Thatcher was going to close all the pits. Well, everybody knew that. Two-thirds of them were losing money as British industry declined and Britain bought foreign steel, cars, fridges and washing machines.

For some reason I have never fathomed, any working-class crowd of men, worried about their jobs, will become mesmerized by the rantings and ravings of rabble-rousers on a public platform, just like the followers of Hitler and Mussolini did, and will trample over any wise old sage who advocates caution and stealth to succeed, instead of vandalism and riot.

Old-time British generals and sea captains had to flog and shoot their men to force them into battle. Working-class heroes who can stamp, spit and foam in front of a megaphone never seemed to have any difficulty. They simply played the Pied Piper. Especially if they were a new young voice promising their mob adventure and excitement, away from the usual dreary round of everyday drudgery.

Once elected in February 1981, Scargill immediately called for a strike ballot against the employers' pay rise offer of 9 per cent, which was quite generous in view of the amount of cash the industry was losing. To Scargill's surprise, he lost. The sensible blokes in the pits, who didn't bother attending hysterical rallies, voted to take the cash by 55 per cent to 45 per cent.

By now, his union office was decorated with enormous pictures of Scargill, posing like Lenin, making speeches to the adoring peasants from the back of a lorry. He was planning to sell the miners' national headquarters in London and move it to Sheffield, because he did not like living in the capital, even though the miners' union had bought a penthouse in the City, near St Paul's, for their officials to stay in, as well as having his own personal chauffeur and all the rest of the trappings of a Third World demagogue.

To restore his power over his still faithful followers who totalled a mighty, vociferous army in the NUM, but nowhere near the silent majority he needed under the new laws of balloting (which incidentally had always been the NUM rules), Scargill returned to his old bogey of pit closures.

His tactics were always the same. He would call a 'Delegate Conference' of pit officials numbering about 180 men, one from each pit, to take a vote, which he knew would go in his favour. Then he would claim he had a 'mandate'. But on the following national ballot of all the men to confirm it, he invariably lost. In May 1982 he did this on pit closures, and promptly lost again, this time by 61 per cent to 39 per cent. A massive slap in the face.

At every pit the union always had five or six virtually full-time union men, paid by the Coal Board, not the unions, to settle the daily rows about bonuses, absenteeism, discipline, etc. These cushy numbers were elected by the branch to spend their time sitting in the union office, and could usually be relied on at the conferences to support what the union leaders wanted. However, when it came to the rank and file votes, the secret ballot often went the opposite way.

Mrs Thatcher knew that in the Eighties miners were very different from their dads, who had brought the previous Tory Government down in 1974. They were better paid. They had mortgages, not shabby pit houses. Or were buying the council houses the Tory Government had sold them. They had cars, foreign holidays, could shop in the towns and cities, and drive to night-clubs, football or a seaside caravan, etc. They were just not interested in Scargill's socialism of fight, grab, smash and revolution.

Thatcher, Ridley, Tebbit, Nigel Lawson, Peter Walker and the Tory Government's lawyers waited patiently. Just like the American cavalry had waited fourteen years for revenge at Wounded Knee, Dakota, where the mounted troops used Gatling machine-guns against tomahawks. Thatcher's planning was meticulous. She was out to smash the unions and any revolutionaries from Belfast to Barnsley for ever.

Just before the 1983 election she brought in the 'Butcher', a man called Ian MacGregor. He was the Chairman of British Steel, who had wiped out thousands of jobs in steel towns and reduced production of steel to about a quarter of the tonnage it had been.

MacGregor had been born in Edinburgh, but spent most of his life in America building up a fearsome reputation as a union buster and strike breaker, using the American union laws, which had now been introduced into Britain. He took over an industry losing cash with a warning from his predecessor, Norman Siddall, that fifteen pits would have to close and 15,000 jobs be lost. The hopeless pits were pulling down the profitable ones and it had to stop. Even though for as long as anybody could remember, miners at profitable modern pits, as good socialists, had always been happy to take less wages and for their pit to subsidize another so that the losses and jobs could be shared out.

Some pit closures had to happen, and always had, as coal in a seam ran out, and it became cheaper to sink another shaft in the coalfield. But this time no new shafts would be sunk. The closures, too, had always been agreed with the men, with some taking their voluntary redundancy or moving on, while others, such as the electricians or fitters, kept their trade and moved to another profitable pit. It was a tried and tested procedure of agreement.

But this time MacGregor deliberately broke it. He closed down Cortonwood Colliery in Barnsley, Scargill's backyard, at short notice without consulting anybody. It was a deliberate throw-down-the-gauntlet challenge, and done right at the end of the winter in March 1984. The Government had purposely piled up 60 million tons of coal, well over a year's supply, and with the summer in front of them, when electricity demands were low, they fired the first shot.

A wise old Indian like Joe Gormley would have walked away from the ambush and laughed, then waited for General Winter, like the Russians did to Napoleon. But Scargill was stupid. Or scared. Or both.

He had had his backside burned by the two ballot defeats, when he had stormed the barricades with his henchmen, then been rejected by the rank and file. If he stalled through the summer, he might not get the vote he needed in October or November. In actual fact, he would have walked a ballot then, because by the winter MacGregor would have closed even more pits, and hardened all the miners' battalions against the Government.

MacGregor and Thatcher judged, quite correctly, that Scargill's pride and vanity and lust for publicity and glory would be uncontrollable. He would be unable to resist leading his men into a Charge of the Light Brigade against the Government cannons lined up to blast his unions, and the whole of the British union movement, into smithereens. For ever. And he did.

Scargill's problem was that the scattered coalfields across Scotland, Wales, Durham, Yorkshire and the Midlands varied widely in their history and the character of the men. The NUM had never been a real national union, but was a federation of different areas. Each had its own funds, and gala and local control, with the most resistance to Scargill or a strike coming from the newer pits in the Midlands, many of them sunk since the war.

The men there knew that, or thought that (later to be proved wrong in 1992) their pits would never close like the older ones in Scotland, Wales, Durham and South Yorkshire would. Many of the miners in Notts had indeed left their old pits and homes in Durham and Scotland and Wales in the Fifties and Sixties to move to the newer, more profitable pits down south. They had uprooted their wives and families, like the early immigrants, and were not keen to go into a long strike, which would be of no benefit to them personally.

They knew that at the end of the strike the redundant Yorkshire miners would be picking up £15,000 to £20,000 in cash to pay off the debts they had accumulated. While the Notts miners would have to return to work having to pay piled-up debts out of their weekly wages.

Scargill knew that on a national ballot Notts and the Midlands would vote heavily against. Nevertheless, if the overall vote was a majority, they too would support the union.

They never got the chance. The Cortonwood closure sparked off an instant mass protest as miners all over South Yorkshire downed tools. Just as Thatcher and MacGregor knew it would. Exactly as they had planned.

Mrs Thatcher had carefully waited and watched the 1983 General Election results in those Midlands moderate seats. They were a disaster for Labour. In Nottinghamshire, the nine Labour seats had been reduced to three. Last-minute boundary changes, stupidly delayed by Michael Foot, had led to organized chaos at the General Election.

In Sherwood, a constituency with no fewer than twelve pits, the Tories had actually won the seat by 600 votes. The Labour majority in Mansfield had fallen from 17,000 to 2,000, and mine in Bassetlaw was down from 6,000 to 3,000.

Two days after the Cortonwood announcement, hundreds of angry miners gathered outside the union headquarters in Barnsley demanding action. The new Yorkshire leader, Jack Taylor, announced immediate strike action by all Yorkshire's miners. There would be no ballot. Scargill proclaimed that the Government's plan to shut fifteen pits was a fraud. In actual fact, they were going to shut seventy, and put 70,000 miners on the dole, with another 200,000 connected job losses.

He was right. Although he didn't know it at the time, his wild guess proved correct a year later.

Scotland too demanded all-out strike, quickly followed by Wales and Kent. The National Executive of the NUM then voted twenty-two to three to call an all-out strike *without a ballot*. Their 'mandate' for doing so, they said, was the meeting of left-wing Scargill poodles at the Conference three years before. They decided that any coalfield which didn't agree would be 'picketed out'. They would rely on the miners' traditional first commandment, that 'Thou shalt not cross any picket line, where a fellow worker is in dispute with the boss'.

And never mind what the new Thatcher laws said about

union rules, ballots, funds, etc. The Government can bugger off. The revolution is on its way, brothers.

The mood of exhilaration, defiance and lust for war spread across the coalfields, like the jingoism and white feathers at the outbreak of the First World War. If the soft Southerners and faint-hearts of the Midlands had put Thatcher back in power following her victory in the Falklands War, she would now have some real men to fight right here in her own backyard. Men who would be fighting for their jobs, families, villages and future.

Scargill's forecast was then raised and he claimed the certain closure of 115 pits out of 179 (which happened later in 1992, but for different reasons) and forecast that in ten years, there would be virtually no pits left in the whole of Scotland, Durham, Wales and Lancashire.

By 14 March, two weeks after the showdown, 133 pits were out on strike. In the intervening two weeks, Scargill's close colleagues and union staff had shifted huge amounts of the union's cash into foreign banks or other accounts abroad.

The Coal Board, probably ordered to do so by the Government, immediately went to the High Court for an injunction under the new laws, to stop the Yorkshire miners picketing other coalfields. Which Mr Justice Nolan instantly granted.

Coincidentally, Tony Benn, who had lost his seat in the General Election of June 1983, was back in business in coalmining Chesterfield, winning a by-election on 1 March 1984, the day before the carefully staged Cortonwood announcement.

Naturally, he and all the Labour MPs had no option but to support the fight against the pit closures, but Neil Kinnock knew there were few votes in it for Labour elsewhere in the marginal seats of the Midlands, which had supported Thatcher.

The police were turned out in their massed ranks to ensure the 'law' was obeyed. Meanwhile, in many areas, local pits in Notts and Derbyshire held their own unofficial ballots, scrupulously conducted, to let the pits show their own feelings. Practically every single pit voted 'No', some by large majorities. The split in the union was now as deep as the North–South split in the American Civil War, and practically impossible to heal.

Thatcher and MacGregor knew that with the Notts and Midlands pits continuing to produce coal, plus the year's supply they had stockpiled at the power stations, much of it hidden from sight except by helicopter, where the pickets couldn't get at it, there would be no repetition of the 1974 Ted Heath disaster of power cuts in British homes and factories.

Here was the class war, long promised by the militants, and eagerly anticipated too by the right-wing free marketeers of the Tory Party and the newspaper barons who had regularly lost production (*The Times* later went on strike for nearly a year), due to stupid union intransigence and resistance to change. It was going to be the civil war of the century, this time fought out not in the trenches, or secret terrorist activity as in Northern Ireland, but up front on television screens every night on *The Nine O'Clock News* or *News at Ten*.

As the spring weather turned warmer, every morning at 4.00 a.m. busloads of Yorkshire pickets would leave for the Notts and other Midlands pits which had decided to carry on working. The miners' union, having shifted most of its assets abroad, decided it could not afford to pay any strike pay, but it would periodically hand out cardboard boxes of groceries to families, and any miner volunteering for picket duty at 4.00 a.m. would receive a cash allowance of £4 a day to help out. Very few could afford not to turn up.

There were also ugly rumours that pit officials who had always been paid for attending out-of-hours meetings would continue to receive that cash too.

In the first couple of weeks, the flying pickets met with considerable success. Hundreds of loyal Notts miners, dismayed at the selfish attitude of many of their younger, inexperienced mates, refused to cross the picket lines and went home. To their credit there were dozens of miners at every pit in Notts, Leicestershire, Derbyshire, etc., who refused to work throughout the strike and stayed out for the whole year, proudly carrying their pit banner through the streets at every demonstration. The miners in my constituency at Notts pits like Harworth, with its history of division, suffered even more than the 'all-out' pits in Yorkshire, with bitter arguments which split families and even husbands and wives for ever.

But the success of the flying pickets did not last long. This time, unlike at Saltley, the police were ready for them. Although the Home Office will proudly claim that Britain has never had a national police force or secret service, on this occasion a national police force went into action like a planned military operation. The telephones of every MP, union official, etc., were undoubtedly tapped. None of the miners on the buses knew which pit that day they would be picketing, but the coppers did.

The police, using their helicopters, would erect barricades on all the roads, sometimes ten miles from the pit village. They would even visit the village the day before and order the chip shop, pub, grocer's and anywhere else the miners could get food, to stay closed. They even made the council close all the public toilets too. They had no legal authority to do so, but did it none the less. Then when the incoming horde urinated in the streets they could be photographed to show what animals they were.

It did not stop the pickets. Men used to crawling underground did not flinch at walking ten miles in the fresh air. They enjoyed it. The public were not allowed near the pit. Even the MPs were barred in their own constituency.

It was a gross infringement of civil liberties and also a breach of Parliamentary privilege to stop an MP going about his duties. To prove the point, I hired a bus, filled it with striking miners and toured every pit in Bassetlaw on a Freedom Ride, just like the Blacks in their Soweto townships in South Africa were doing, to show the police state which Thatcher was now running. It made about ten seconds on *News at Ten*, and the top cops had to let me walk to the pit gates under escort, much to their embarrassment.

However, if the police could stop picketing, they could not stop marches and demonstrations elsewhere, although by now the new laws meant the organizer had to give seven days' notice and follow a backstreet route laid down by the police.

On 2 May, Notts miners still at work actually staged their own demonstration against Scargill, when 6,000 of them took part in a right-to-work march in Mansfield, Notts, just outside my constituency, carrying banners saying 'ADOLF SCARGILL', amidst mounting violence from their mates on strike. The striking miners, led by Scargill, then retaliated twenty-one days later by organizing an enormous response in Mansfield, when this time 20,000 strikers stormed the streets in a two-mile procession, with Scargill stupidly raising his arm like a Roman gladiator to welcome them, only to have every tabloid newspaper photographer in Britain take pictures standing under the platform, so that it looked like a Nazi salute.

The civil war was well under way and Thatcher rejoiced. The mutiny in Scargill's ranks was well under way too. There are many ways of fighting the bosses, just as the Vietcong showed their many ways of fighting the most powerful war machine in the world and beating the American troops in the jungle. It is not done by the trench warfare of the 1914–18 pickets, and digging in for a long siege with the troops eating cats and dogs. It is better done by surprise and stealth. The French lorry drivers never plan anything. They simply block the traffic and paralyse the docks and motorways for a couple of days and then force the bosses to sit down to talk.

Scargill could have done the same by using the coal lorries which delivered the miners' free home coal to blockade and paralyse the M25 round London or the M1 into it. But he would not listen to the advice. He wanted the parades, and televised glory of Hitler or Mussolini with cheering crowds to satisfy his ego.

Like a lot more loonies, he believed the best way to recruit revolutionaries was to make them starve first. 'Jelly babies', as the working miners were insultingly called, could all be turned into revolutionaries if they were compelled to go hungry for a month and then shown the enemy. A theory which Stalin and Lenin also enforced by ten years in the Gulag for those who disagreed with their leadership.

There were no lightning ambushes, no attempt to put the union's case in any way, other than by chanting slogans in the streets, and no gentle persuasion of even asking the jelly babies at least to have a whip round, to buy a bit of grub for their mates fighting for their jobs.

By now 40,000 miners out of 175,000 had crossed the picket lines and were still at work. The police, obviously working to a carefully planned national operation (despite the police authorities supposedly being paid for, and run on County Council boundaries) were often unnecessarily brutal and provocative. Especially those brought up north from London and the south of England. Local bobbies from mining areas were sympathetic and often shared their sandwiches with the strikers. They knew the devastating impact pit closures would have. Many of them had brothers and relatives who worked in the pit. The Southern police could not care less. They hated being drafted in as an occupying army.

As they lined up to hold back the pickets, they would regularly taunt the miners. Usually by boasting that the massive overtime payments they were on would pay to take their kids to DisneyWorld in Florida (where few families had ever been in 1984), whilst the miners' kids would be lucky to get a packet of Polos for Christmas. That was when the fists would fly.

The pickets would arrive early morning, dressed in jeans and trainers to face massed ranks of coppers in helmets and heavy boots, carrying riot shields and batons and holding on to Alsatians. The lunch-time newscasts always set the scene for the day, showing the miners charging the police first, then the police charging the miners, when often it had happened the other way round. In minutes, the police spokesman would be on TV holding out a handful of nuts and bolts, garden wall stones, broken bottles, etc., any of which could be picked up in the pit yard, alleging that his men had had to suffer hails of missiles.

Even worse than that were the injuries inflicted on the miners. The Coal Board, and the Government, made it clear that any miner arrested for picketing would be dismissed from his job. Which meant no redundancy cash when the strike was over. Rather than face arrest, hundreds of miners did not bother going to hospital for broken heads, arms, collar-bones, etc., until days after the riot, then had to say they fell off their bike.

I personally saw dozens of miners who showed me their skulls split open and needing several stitches in the back of their head. In the back. Always the back, inflicted by riot sticks as they were running away. Funnily enough, the camera crews never seemed to be able to run fast enough to keep up with the bobbies on horseback. And no miner dared show his wounds, because the pit would have sacked him.

All mining MPs made dozens of complaints about police brutality, even involving miners' wives, who regularly accompanied their husbands in marches and demonstrations. In those days there was no Independent Police Authority to investigate complaints as there is now. The police handled their own complaints procedure. After one thirty-five-year-old woman in Langold in my constituency made a complaint, supported by me, when she had been thrown bodily into the back of a police van, she was visited at home by a plain-clothes inspector, who casually pointed out that she had once been fined £5 for shoplifting when she was sixteen years old, in a town fifty miles away. And did her husband or her neighbours know? Well, they would soon, because sadly the police would have to reveal it if the complaint went ahead. The very respectable woman tearfully dropped the complaint.

Of the thirty-two complaints I made, not one was accepted. Neither were those of any other MP.

With the Notts pits open and turning out coal in the hottest summer for years, Scargill had to change tactics and go in for mass demonstrations in the big city streets and at other plants away from the pits.

He was still stuck in a time-warp of eleven years earlier, when he and the wiser miners of that time had brought down Ted Heath by picketing not just the pits, but the plants which supplied other essential raw materials to the power stations.

Nightly the 140,000 striking miners were losing the media battle. The tabloid press like the *Express*, *Mail* and *Sun*, all supporting Thatcher to the limit, were as usual carrying crazy, totally unconfirmed stories of miners throwing paint over cats, loosening lorry wheels, terrifying rural villages worse than Count Dracula and even setting fire to a working miner's house. (The charred ruins were shown with great gravity on ITN News and several months later it was revealed that the bloke had done it himself for the insurance when he could not keep up the mortgage.)

Any crime – vandalism, hooliganism, drunken punch-ups – could safely be attributed to striking miners to show the others at work, and those thinking of going back, how the loonies took control. If ever the miners were interviewed the same news bulletin would show a bunch of scruffy, inarticulate yobbos, all shouting at once and gesticulating at the camera, totally untrained in putting across their case.

None of the TV programmes showed the taunts of the working miners coming out kissing their wage packets to the pickets. Or the strikers' kids having to stand in separate queues to qualify for free school dinners.

At the time of the strike, I was writing a column twice a week for the *Daily Star*, now a bit of a joke paper, but in 1984 having a circulation of 1.6 million (then very close to the circulation of the *Daily Mail*) simply because it printed in Manchester and got the late-night football results and reports (which the London-based *Sun* did not). The *Daily Star* generally supported the underdog and the unemployed, unlike the Thatcher lapdog *Sun*.

At the end of the strike, the Granada TV programme *What the Papers Say* awarded me its prestigious 'Columnist of the Year' prize for the articles I wrote about the strike, and generously said I was the only newspaper writer ever to receive a fan letter from Arthur Scargill. Which made Norman Tebbit wince when he had to present the 'Oscar' to me at the Savoy.

Scargill sent his letter to me after the Mansfield rally. It read: 'Dear Joe, I read your excellent article in the *Daily Star*, which I think puts the miners' case very well indeed. Could I also take this opportunity of thanking you for the first-class stand you have taken on this issue and the marvellous way in which you presented the case against pit closures on television, radio, and in the media, many thanks.' 16.5.1984.

I'm afraid he did not get a very grateful reply.

I wrote back to him via my column and told him he was putting me and Neil Kinnock and the other Labour MPs in an impossible position. When the strike started, Labour was in front of the Tories in the opinion polls. Two months later, it was twelve points behind.

I told him that the Labour Party was pig in the middle (it loses votes if it attacks the police, and loses the support of the unions and the miners if it does not), that we could live with the abuse, but what we could not stand was the sight of miner attacking miner, even inside the same family. What he should do was make the pickets and protests peaceful, and sit down in the road like Gandhi did in India. Use passive resistance, not Al Capone tactics.

The pride of these men fighting for their jobs would not allow them to tell anybody but me, their local MP and mate, about their poverty. One guy showed me his toilet. It had no bowl. When it was blocked up he tried to do his own Dynarod clearance and broke it. The DSS refused to lend his wife the money to pay for a new one (he as a striker got no DSS assistance) even though there was a two-month baby in the house and the stench was awful. He could not afford disinfectant either, and kept it covered with a plastic carrier-bag. As usual, a whip-round brought in enough for a friendly plumber to fix it.

In Barnsley market local stalls were soon selling wedding rings for £5 each. Earlier this century, the pawnshop would have lent money on them. In 1984 there were no pawnshops.

When a policewoman was badly beaten up in Grimethorpe (a real village) near Barnsley, by strikers and their wives, the woman quite rightly received enormous sympathy. What was not said was that the riot was caused because some stupid top cop gave the order to arrest twenty-three natives of the village (including women) who had been picking up bits of coal from the pit tip, which had lain there untouched for eighty years, simply to cook their kids a meal on a hearth fire. And this was 1984 not 1884.

Not mentioned either was the usual song the Southern bobbies would chortle: 'You got to nick a picket or two, boys. You got to a nick a picket or two.' Ironically, it came from the musical *Oliver*, about hungry kids.

After three months with the police and the courts controlling the pits, Scargill was in need of a rallying point and a large-scale battle to put the fight back into his impatient troops. He badly needed another Saltley, whether it was against the new laws or not.

There was a huge coking plant at Orgreave, on the edge of Sheffield, about half a mile from where Maggie and I bought our first house. The massive steel plants thirty miles away in Scunthorpe were desperate for the coke, because the ASLEF train drivers had backed the miners and refused to pick up and deliver it. Convoys of lorries were brought in to ferry it on to the nearby M1 and M18 and if the miners could blockade the plant, they would have achieved a major victory over MacGregor and Thatcher.

For three days over the Spring Bank Holiday at the end of May, 5,000 miners fought with the police to hold back nearly forty lorries. Scargill went on TV urging miners and trade unionists to come to Orgreave in their thousands on Monday, 4 June. They did. This time 10,000 travelled from as far as Kent, Scotland and South Wales. When their buses were stopped in Sheffield city centre, they just got out and walked the three miles to the depot.

Scargill was taken to hospital that day claiming he had been hit by a police riot shield. Other witnesses from the police say he slipped and fell down a ditch. Garden walls were demolished in nearby houses and used as hand grenades to bombard the police. The bobbies fought back with police dogs in TV scenes looking like a medieval battle between peasants on foot and the baron's tax collectors on horseback. One of whom fell off the horse and broke his leg. Scrap cars were pushed out of a nearby yard and set on fire. The miners put up other barricades against the horses.

As you might expect, on the first day of the riot 104 police in protective combat riot gear were injured, but only twenty-seven strikers in jeans and trainers were treated in hospital.

On the second day, seventy-two bobbies in protective clothing suffered injuries and fifty-one, would you believe, of those in T-shirts were also hurt. Over that week more than 30,000 striking miners were at Orgreave, but they could not stop the coke getting through. It was a fight the Government dared not lose and they pulled every trick in the book to win it. The 'Enemy Within', as

Thatcher called them, as though they were Nazis not British workmen, had to be stopped.

It was reliably reported some months later that the Queen, sitting at home in Buckingham Palace watching *News at Ten*, had seen the battles on the TV screen and, horrified, had insisted that her Prime Minister, Mrs Thatcher, come to the phone in Downing Street immediately and tell her what on earth was happening. All Prime Ministers visit the Queen at least once a week for an hour-long chat, but nobody could ever remember a monarch directly demanding an explanation after watching a news bulletin.

At Orgreave that week 527 striking miners were arrested, handcuffed, fingerprinted and locked up for twenty-six hours in overcrowded cells which had earlier been labelled 'Reserved for the National Union of Mineworkers'. Some of them were imprisoned simply for shouting abuse, or setting foot inside a no-go area, like blacks in South Africa. The 15,000 police on duty at Orgreave earned £55 a shift (in 1984 money) and had to stay in army camps, forbidden to go into the village pub, and were as angry and fed up as the miners. Even the local vicar was prohibited by the police and the curfew law from crossing the Yorkshire–Notts border.

Thirteen months later, when the strike had been over for four months, the trial of all the men collapsed. After ten weeks of evidence against the strikers, the police withdrew all the charges. The trial cost over half a million pounds, and the defence lawyers called it 'the worse example of a mass frame-up this century'. In other separate trials against pickets, at other pits, the charges were dropped too. The miners' union lawyers were adamant that the instructions given out by top cops on how to incapacitate demonstrators on picket lines and cause serious injuries were illegal.

Arrests had been made for no other reason than to allow the police to obtain bail conditions, which prohibited the men from picketing for the duration of the strike.

Nevertheless, innocent or not, the Coal Board sacked 600 men and one woman (an office cleaner at Harworth colliery), which meant they would never work again, and would lose years of accumulated pension, cheap coal allowance, and thousands of pounds of redundancy pay. All because of stitched-up police allegations proved by the courts to be worthless. To my fury and disgust, all the strikers at Harworth colliery were allowed to return to work, except the woman who was fired. The Equal Opportunities Commission refused to take up the woman's case because they said they did not get involved in industrial disputes.

Scargill himself had been arrested, as everybody expected, at a convenient spot where cameras were ready when police officers barred his way. The arrest was made by Chief Superintendent John Nesbit, a personal friend of mine, who actually had enormous sympathy for the miners because he too had started life as a school leaver down the pit before joining the police force.

The NUM commemorated the event by having a banner made with John Nesbit (later to be directly involved in the Hillsborough football disaster and now Ground Safety Commander at the stadium) leading Scargill by the arm.

Miners at Kiverton Colliery, near Worksop, claim they got their revenge for Scargill's arrest later that winter when, in thick snow, they built a huge snowman at the pit gates with a carrot nose, coke eyes and a bobby's helmet, and taunted a high-ranking police officer, yelling, 'Yoo-Hoo, Captain Plod!' and baring their backsides. The furious top cop ordered his four-wheel-drive Land Rover to push it down, but then, as the vehicle revved, the exhaust blew out blue smoke and snowballs hit the roof, he realized they had built it over a traffic bollard.

Often the strikers would build up the same rapport with local coppers that all prisoners of war have with their captors. A month after Orgreave, the NUM decided to mount the biggest miners' march ever seen right through London. In Parliament, the day after Orgreave, both Mrs Thatcher and the Home Secretary, Leon Brittan, had furiously attacked the miners. Tory MPs right round the nation were ordered to make public speeches whipping up a law-and-order fury into a vigilante mood. Police chiefs, TV, radio and the whole of Fleet Street brayed like a lynch mob and demanded retribution.

However, they knew better than to try to stop the London march. There was still a great deal of public support and sympathy for the miners. Too many other workers, even in the South, were now losing their jobs and joining the dole queues.

As the coaches travelled down the motorways to the capital, the miners' buses and the bobbies' buses kept pace with each other side by side, with the coppers holding up £10 notes and waving to the shabby pickets. Every time they waved, the lads dropped their jeans and pressed their bare arse cheeks against the bus windows in return. The gamekeepers and poachers were settling into that wary respect the British ruling class and working class have for each other.

As the buses emptied, the miners struck up their usual song of 'Bring out your riot gear. Yorkshire's here. Yorkshire's here', to the tune of a beautiful old hymn. Then, as the coppers lined up on parade and winced, every single miner went 'Baa-baa' and whistled the 'Cuckoo Waltz' (the Laurel and Hardy signature tune) as the bobbies marched in step to the sergeant's command.

As they marched past inevitably there would be a miner in a Maggie Thatcher mask holding a telephone shrieking 'Is that you, MacGregor? Stop them, stop them!' When the police halted and stood to attention, there was always one scruffy, barefaced bloke wearing a plastic bobby's helmet who would march down the ranks inspecting their uniforms, with hands clasped behind his back, like the Duke of Edinburgh, nodding and saying, 'Look here, my good man, your boots are dirtier than mine.' The cops never said a word. They would arrest him later. They could not tie him to the mast and award fifty lashes, but that was the end of his redundancy pay.

As the enormous throng of macho marching men reached the GLC headquarters at County Hall on the South Bank opposite Parliament practically every single employee turned out to welcome these brave lads from the provinces who were putting up the biggest battle Mrs Thatcher had ever had to face. The staff of the GLC, including many *Guardian* 'Wimmin', packed the footbridge over the Jubilee Gardens in their very trendy bib-and-brace feminist overalls, to wave and cheer as the parade passed under and the brass bands oomphad 'Cwm Rhondda' to the cheering crowds above. Although there was a stunned silence from the politically correct *Guardian* Wimmin when instead of singing 'Bread of Heaven! Bread of Heaven!' the marchers looked up and roared, 'Get your tits out! Get your tits out! Get your tits out for the lads!'

Most of the coppers would be trying not to laugh. Until invariably a bossy ambitious officer would turn up and shout, 'Right! Clear this space!' He would decide that the tattoos, ribald jokes and street theatre were an abuse of law and order. Then the weary coppers had to link arms and stamp backwards. Then the horses arrived. Those at the back could not see why they were being crushed, so one single idiot threw a stone and the whole sickening saga started again.

If the politicians and the media and all the other bigshots had simply left the two working-class miners and coppers together they would have had a football out inside half an hour and have been playing a match of Northern miners versus Southern soft coppers. Just like the Germans and the Tommies did at Christmas in 1914, before Earl Haig and General Kitchener heard about it.

As the strike stretched into its sixth month, with the hottest summer seen for many years, the miners kept up their infallible humour, announcing that 735 pets had disappeared in Rotherham and been turned into Big Mac whippetburgers, Kentucky fried pigeon and sweet and sour moggie. They proudly claimed they were smoking hooverbag fags, but unfortunately the telegrams they had sent to the miners in West Virginia for the recipe for moonshine whiskey had not yet been answered. Fortunately, the lads said, with no night shift, no tired-out husbands, no money, no booze, and nothing else to stroke, the women in South Yorkshire, though poorly shod, had never been more content and well satisfied.

In reality things were looking grim.

One young woman I met, aged nineteen, six months' pregnant, had not put on a pound in weight. She had no baby clothes, and the electricity was due to be cut off. She was receiving no benefit from the DSS, even though she was not married to her boyfriend and should have been entitled to it in her own right.

If a husband deserts his wife, or goes to gaol for murder, then this country has never punished his family by stopping benefit. But with strikers, Mrs Thatcher refused to allow the DSS to pay out a penny. Even though the woman may have been pleading with her husband to go back to work. Government adjudicators ruled that the miners' union should be paying £15 per week strike pay (which it was not) and deducted £15 from wives' benefits too.

Government adjudicators made similar local decisions on benefits and allowances for dependants which varied widely right across the country. Men who quit the industry to take other jobs were often still classed as miners and refused help. Over one billion pounds was held back in benefit.

In many solid pit areas where the miners ran the local council, the local school governors and every other committee, they responded by taking control of the town and village. During the school holidays, the schools were kept open and the school-dinner kitchens used to hand out free cooked meals to kids and strikers' families alike.

Local businessmen rallied round and extended their loans to the lads. They knew that if the pit went then their businesses too would collapse. They also knew that miners always paid their debts. It was a matter of personal pride and honour to them and their family.

The Electricity Board and Gas and Water too were very wary at disconnecting supplies, for fear of more violence and riots. At the very mention of disconnections, the miners would erect barricades at the entrance to the village streets, and after six months' hardship their women were more angry and determined than their men. Every miners' march would have its contingent of wives and mothers, many of them pushing baby buggies and prams, fiercely proud that they would not surrender.

By September both sides realized that talks had to take place as the summer expired. The strike had already cost the country more than the Falklands War had, and lasted longer. There had been ten times as many arrests as in the Brixton riots. The hire purchase companies had started to reclaim cars, TVs, videos, etc., and mortgage arrears were running into several hundred pounds for each house.

Without Scargill and Thatcher undoubtedly the Coal Board, even under MacGregor, and the miners' unions could have done a deal and thrashed out how many uneconomic pits would have to close. Especially after the other pit union, NACODS (the National Association of Colliery Overmen, Deputies and Shot-firers), had come off the fence in September and overwhelmingly voted to support the strike.

NACODS were the foremen underground who were in control of pit safety as well as production and were greatly concerned that the pit floors and roofs were closing together down below and would not be safe to go back and work in. If they came out then the industry was finished.

But talks broke down. Thatcher demanded total capitulation

without any terms of negotiated surrender at all. She was determined to smash the union in the courts and bankrupt it out of business. Scargill too refused to give an inch on any single pit closure, so the talks collapsed and NACODS stayed at work.

Just before the Labour Party Conference at the end of September, the High Court served a writ on Scargill. Then, when Scargill publicly refused to accept it before cheering crowds at Blackpool, promptly fined the union £200,000 and sequestered the union's assets of £10.7 million in funds and property, even though somehow £2 million had been hidden abroad.

Three days later, when the *Sunday Times* revealed that Colonel Gadaffi, the Libyan leader and sworn enemy of Britain and Mrs Thatcher, had handed over large sums of ready cash to one of Scargill's aides, public sympathy began to fade.

As the November winter arrived, with miners' kids cold and with nothing to face but a bleak, miserable Christmas, more and more miners began to drift back to work and cross the picket lines. Some with tears in their eyes. Families were split in bitter feuds which were to last years. Long-standing solid marriages were broken.

In Scargill's home village of Worsborough, strikers brought down power lines and blacked out 2,000 houses. At pits everywhere, even in the heartlands, miners would sneak back to work in the dark winter mornings in buses specially provided by the Coal Board, who offered huge return-to-work bonuses and coal allowances, past howling pickets several hundreds strong.

By February the Coal Board claimed that over half the miners in the country were back at work, and two miners in South Wales were on trial for murder after dropping a rock from a bridge on to a Coal Board taxi carrying miners to their pit.

Like Napoleon's army trudging back through the frost and snow from Moscow, or the defeated Confederate soldiers of the South in the American Civil War, the number of 'boomerangs', as they were nicknamed (because they struck then went back), grew day by day. These men were not scabs who refused to support their mates. They had been out for ten months, but many of them could see no end to what they thought was Scargill's madness or Thatcher's vindictive desire for revenge. Yet they were still abused and denigrated by Scargill's bully-boys.

On 5 March 1985, one year after the strike started, the NUM national delegates voted by 198 to 191 officially to end the strike.

The finest trade union the world had ever seen had been smashed. The strikers went back all together with heads held high, marching in step behind their brass bands and banners, defiant as ever, singing their songs and chanting their slogans. Women, and pensioners who had long since retired to live broken lives, often in old-age pain, marched with them, pushing their kids' buggies and waving to the crowds lining their village streets, putting two fingers up to the cameras and smiling bobbies, with grown men trying not to shed tears, wondering if they would ever work again.

There was no amnesty for the 600 sacked miners. Immediately the pit managers took revenge, altering shift hours and union recognition and introducing a whole host of new rules and regulations for the others.

The Coal Board in Derbyshire, Yorkshire, Notts and many other areas then sold off hundreds of miners' rented houses to private landlords in auctions at the Kensington Hilton hotel in London. Buyers came from round the world to buy streets of houses for as little £1,500 per house, like blocks of property on a Monopoly board.

Inside a few years, as the older pensioner miners coughed their last, some of the rascally get-rich-quick new landlords filled the houses with runaways, fly-by-nights, problem families evicted for not paying the rent elsewhere, and hopeless DSS transit cases, bringing in all the problems of drugs, crime, vandalism and violence which had never existed in pit areas before.

Also, the High Court still had the union's money.

Six months later, at the 1985 Labour Party Conference, the Electricians' union leader, Eric Hammond, scathingly shouted from the platform that the miners, like the soldiers in the First World War, had been 'lions led by donkeys'. He was absolutely right.

A year later, the *Evening Standard* and the *Daily Mail* reported that Scargill was trying to buy a farmhouse near Barnsley for £125,000. Five years later an enquiry into the strike by Gavin Lightman QC revealed that Scargill had bought the property just six months after the strike ended, although he claimed that like other union employees he had received no wages during the whole twelve months. £125,000 in 1985 would be worth about £350,000 today. Hundreds of striking miners had lost their homes, or been put in severe difficulties, while their leader had been sitting on a pile of money.

Exactly five years after the strike ended, the *Daily Mirror* alleged that Scargill received £163,000 from Colonel Gadaffi in cash. The ITV programme on Central Television, *The Cook Report*, also screened a half-hour special making the same allegations, and that £1 million from the Russian miners had also gone missing. The *Daily Mirror* came out with the statement that the Russian money had been paid into an account in Dublin which only Scargill knew about.

Scargill never sued either newspaper or Central Television.

Many of his predictions did come true, and the pits did close as every informed politician and industry expert knew they would. Twelve months after the 1984 strike, seventy out of 179 pits closed. The following year a further fifty went, and by 1993 fewer than thirty pits out of 179 were still open.

The final butchery came not from Mrs Thatcher, but from Michael Heseltine, just seven months after the Conservatives won the 1992 election under the new Prime Minister, John Major. In October, Heseltine announced that of the fifty profitable pits still open, thirty-one would close in the next six months. Another 30,000 miners would lose their jobs and the 'knock-on' effects would cost another 70,000 jobs too. There was immediate fury, even among many Tory back-benchers.

This time the Notts miners and miners in other areas which had worked through the strike would also be badly affected. Their so-called profitable pits would go, not because of financial difficulties, but because the EC in Brussels had ruled that the British Coal-fired power stations were polluting half of Europe by spreading acid rain across its lakes and forests.

It was actually a problem which could easily have been solved. It had been known for years that the steam from the power stations built thirty years ago contained poisonous sulphur, but it was not difficult to modernize the power stations to 'desulphurize' the steam and make it acceptable. Not only would it renew the plant, it would also have created a great deal of engineering work in the depression which had hit Britain following Major's disastrous Black Wednesday a month before, when his financial policies forced the Tory Government to quit the European Exchange Rate Mechanism and devalue the pound.

But Heseltine and Major refused to spend the money. It was simpler to shut all our pits and convert the power stations to gas from the North Sea. Or buy the gas and nuclear electricity at ridiculously low prices from France, Russia or the new Eastern Europe.

This time the mining towns – all of them, striking or not – were doomed. The betrayal caused fury and anger among those pits which had worked and even voted Tory, and who had formed their own union, the UDM.

Immediately Scargill was back in business, demanding a strike. This time nobody took any notice of him. But the colliery bands turned out to lead 100,000 marchers through Hyde Park, and right across the nation, often many, many miles from pit areas, there was an enormous wave of sympathy for these dwindling tribes of much maligned men. Thousands of the marchers now were young families, who had taken on mortgages after being convinced that their pit had a future and that pit closures were a thing of the past. They felt bitter and cheated, and rightly so.

In marginal Tory seats, four years later, the Tory Government was slaughtered in the Midlands, as it had been in every by-election following the 1992–3 closures. Major's Government had promised all sorts of special help for new jobs in pit areas, but delivered nothing. In just over ten years, a hundred thriving mining towns and villages had turned into derelict ghost lands of boarded-up shops, empty pubs and crime-ridden streets with all the inner-city problems of drugs, domestic violence and crime, neglected by Government, ignored by the media, with none of the political kudos or clout of the Scots Nats or Welsh Nationals in demanding new factories or jobs.

The plight of the old mining communities of Britain was vividly and immortally captured in the film *Brassed Off*, a story of a pit area in Barnsley called Grimethorpe, where the pit closure brings not only despair and poverty, but the end of its prize-winning brass band, famed and fêted by music lovers round the world for the purity and quality of its music. The entire band were amateurs (who recently turned down a trip to Hollywood for the Oscar presentations, because they had already promised to do a charity concert on that date).

The story of the musicians and their final performance at the Albert Hall, dedicated to their dying conductor, played by Pete Postlethwaite, and the suicide of their prize trombonist, reduced to earning a few quid a week as a clown at children's parties, after a lifetime in the pit, ought to reduce even Norman Tebbit to tears. Now translated to the stage, and constantly touring British theatres, following adulatory reviews at the National Theatre in London, *Brassed Off* regularly ends with a standing ovation for its story, characters and music.

The film has been shown around the world, which means that Grimethorpe is included on the American tourist map showing visitors from the USA the locations over here of British cult films, such as *The Full Monty*, *Notting Hill*, and *Trainspotting* as well as Nora Batty's house in *Last of the Summer Wine*.

The last group of film buffs to visit Grimethorpe, from Tucson, Arizona, were disappointed to find the 'In Cod we Trust' chip shop now boarded up and closed, the pit head and all its buildings demolished. The Welfare Hall, where the band practised, is another empty, boarded-up eyesore. There is grass growing through the pavements of the streets, and Barnsley currently has the record for the worst health, highest rate of poverty and lowest income in the country. In the EC statistics for Europe, parts of it are as poor as Poland. When Mrs Thatcher took office there were 200 pits in Britain, now there are just fourteen.

It was a cold, brutal, unnecessary destruction of an industry with 300 years' reserves of coal under our soil, thrown away by the two unstoppable egos of Thatcher and Scargill.

It was the end of the British trades union braves too.

Thirteen

OLD LABOUR DIES AT THE CANAL

WITHIN one day of the most disastrous defeat in Labour's history, in June 1983, the left wing of the Party was hard at work plotting the new regime.

Tony Benn had lost his seat in Bristol and therefore was ineligible to stand for the Leadership. Without waiting or even having the courtesy to allow Michael Foot the dignity of standing down from the job, Clive Jenkins, the union leader of the ASTMS, and Moss Evans, the leader of the giant Transport and General Workers, promptly announced Foot's retirement for him without giving the grand old man a chance to wave goodbye. Then they openly fronted a Welsh Taffia, as it was called, to campaign for Neil Kinnock as the new Messiah.

The fact that the two previous Leaders of the Labour Party, Foot and Callaghan, had also represented Welsh seats and been spectacularly unsuccessful, was not a factor at all.

Naturally the Tory press campaigned for Kinnock too. They would have campaigned for Ken Livingstone if he had been nominated. The press barons always gave massive coverage to any way-out Labour left-winger, and always had, on the basis that left-wingers terrified the housewives of Reading and Portsmouth and other seats in the South which any party had to gain to win an election. They were absolutely right in their thinking.

Roy Hattersley, a long-serving ex-Cabinet minister, also stood as Leader for the common-sense wing of the Party on a 'Solidarity' platform, named after the Polish shipyard workers under Lech Walesa, who had broken away from their hardline Communist government and burst into worldwide popularity for their stance.

The Kinnock campaign bandwagoned into a flying start. Because of the Welsh and left connections Foot did not complain at the shabby way he was treated. The unions gave their members no chance of saying who they wanted to nominate, and other candidates like Healey and Peter Shore were left behind at the starting gate. Kinnock promised he would maintain the Holy Grail of reselection, the block vote and the Conference choosing the Leader, and he was home and dry weeks before the ballot in Brighton three months later.

Particularly after he survived a car smash on the M4, when his car overturned, and every paper carried pictures of him standing unscathed by the side of it. 'Somebody up there likes me,' he joked, and with his natural charisma and appeal to the young at heart, stood with his hands on hips like a character from *Brideshead Revisited*, laughing at the policeman who pulled him from the wreckage. The bobby kept calling Neil 'Sir', which amused Kinnock, so Neil asked him his name too. 'Oliver,' the bobby answered. Neil laughed out loud and said, 'That's another fine mess you've got me into,' just as the camera flashed, and Labour went up 5 per cent in the opinion poll. Neil then lost his voice from too much public speaking, and for once in his life had to keep quiet, then, on the eve of the Conference vote at Brighton, slipped and fell into the sea (naturally his wife Glenys, who managed to skip out of the incoming tide, thought it was hilarious). The morning papers said he was not 'home and dry' yet, and altogether his campaign brought in the best image of a young trendy couple in charge, which Labour had not had since 1966.

Kinnock could do no wrong, and backed up by solid Number Two Hattersley with his wide experience of government, the duo were promptly named the 'dream ticket', with the pair of them dancing together like Morecambe and Wise on the end-of-the-pier cabaret, cavorting with one hand behind their neck and singing 'Bring me Sunshine, Bring me Tears'. And tears is what the pair of them got, after Neil pulled in 70 per cent of the total vote to Hattersley's 30 per cent.

Roy Hattersley, who I campaigned for, was nine years older than Kinnock and had held down Government ministers' or Opposition front-bench jobs at Defence, Employment, Environment and the Home Office, knowing how to pull levers and avoid trip-wires. Now he was patronizingly accepted by the left-wing majority as a useful addition to keep the new SDP Party at bay.

It looked as if everything might be coming up roses at long last for Labour, but, as everybody knew, the loonies had not changed their socks, and were still out there in limbo at loggerheads with logic and genuine democracy.

They did not waste any time in returning to the dreary left-wing conference jargon and all the rest of the boring rubbish which turned the viewers at home off all politics for another five years. Delegate after delegate in scruffy jeans, and shabby T-shirts, with lank, greasy hair and unhealthy skin (and that was only the women) stormed the barricades for 'TIGMOO', which stood for 'THIS GREAT MOVEMENT OF OURS'. Every single one of them was convinced that all it needed for Labour to win back a hundred seats next time was for the army to go on the doorstep selling *Class War Cry* like the Salvation Army did, and then voters would return in droves from the nice clean SDP and Liberals, once they heard the old-time tambourines and religious fervour.

In no time at all, the hard left was demanding that Kinnock and the front bench should push forward, and campaign even harder, on every daft policy which had handed over Labour votes to David Owen or Mrs Thatcher by the truckload.

Five months to the day after the dream ticket was selected, Mrs Thatcher set the Valley of Death trap for Arthur Scargill to charge his Light Brigade into, and Kinnock was 'kebabbed', to use his well-known phrase, and roasted by the pair of them. From day one of the miners' strike, both Kinnock and Hattersley were on the spit. Hattersley had no qualms. He had not been selected on a revolutionary ticket and wanted to disown the strike straight away and tell the men to go back to work. Neil Kinnock could not do that. If he had, then he would have been opposed at the next Conference and ousted.

By whom? By Tony Benn, who by then had won the first by-election in the new Parliament, and romped home at Chesterfield the day before the pit closure at Cortonwood which triggered off the strike was announced.

Labour MPs from mining areas like mine were furious when Neil refused to use any of the Opposition 'supply' days allocated to the Labour Party in Parliament to protest about police brutality, or the miners' wives and children's benefits being reduced by £15 a week, even though we were supported by ex-Cabinet ministers like Merlyn Rees and other ex-law officers. I moved the motion in the PLP that we should debate it on the floor of the House and Neil replied, 'You are asking me to be a leader who leads with his chin. It would be a futile gesture.'

Neil was beginning to learn what all leaders learn. It's one thing buttering up the mob to get the job, it's something totally different buttering up the floating voters to get to Downing Street. Without Kinnock's backing, the Speaker refused all back-bench MPs' applications for emergency debates, and the longest and most severe civil disruptions and public hardships went for months without any Parliamentary debate at all.

Which of course gave the media open season to carry on its out-and-out war against Labour, the unions and the nutters. Kinnock's diplomatic silence did not do him any good at all. He was taunted daily by the Tories on the Government benches, and in the year of the miners' strike, his personal rating in the opinion polls fell from 47 per cent to 31 per cent. At the Durham miners' gala in June, with over 100,000 loyal miners supporters giving standing ovations to Dennis Skinner and Arthur Scargill, some of the brass bands deliberately started to play loudly to drown out Kinnock's speech. By the end of it three-quarters of the crowd had walked away and left.

Pushed into debating the issue in the House by the Government, Kinnock made a fence-sitting speech on coal statistics and was kebabbed on his fence by a furious Thatcher on a law and order issue.

Yet still, at the end of the strike, Labour had a lead in the opinion polls by 39 per cent to the Tories' 33 per cent, with the SDP/Liberal Alliance on 27 per cent.

Even then the new Leader's real problem was the local loony councils which were alienating all sympathy with their nonsense spending and massive perpetual increases in local rates. For as long as any political expert could remember, as sure as night follows day, local councils had always been a different colour to the national government. If it was a Labour government in Westminster, then the councils would be Conservative, and vice versa. Whenever a government had to take an unpopular measure, its supporters would stay at home for the local elections, and the opposition turn out in strength. Nineteen eighty-three was no exception.

The Tory councillors were slowly being wiped off the face of the political map. Whatever Mrs Thatcher handed to the voters in income tax cuts, Labour councils would take back in rate increases. In her first budget after the 1983 election Mrs Thatcher, to mighty cheers from Tories everywhere, brought in rate-capping. In future every local council would be allocated a fixed amount they could spend, and if they borrowed any extra cash after that, the local councillors would be surcharged and have to pay for it personally.

Secretly, every sensible Labour MP silently cheered Mrs Thatcher's new law and hoped it would stop the tide of the crazy polytechnic indoctrination of a party which dumbed down in dirty donkey jackets, spouting unintelligible gibberish which the genuine working class ran a mile to avoid. The gravy train of unlimited town hall jobs for friends of the cliques, factions, demo marchers and militants was going to be derailed.

As could be expected, it was meat and drink to the Militants of Lambeth, Liverpool, and all the other fringe revolutionaries who could fight, smash, grab, control and occupy every town hall if they had enough money to spend.

The Militant Tendency revolutionaries were actually very different to the intellectual soft left polytechnic warriors. They were mainly working-class for a start, occupying working-class council seats in low-income cities such as Bradford, often not in a majority, but superbly organized, with a hard-core centralized army accepting a disciplined regime. They were anti-black, anti-gay, anti-women, anti-intellectual, solidly working-class and basically not far from the national socialism of Stalin or Hitler (although they would never admit it), demanding that a high proportion of their members' income, even from the benefits of the unemployed, should be paid to Central Office. They led a spartan life-style and were unscrupulous how and where they raised their funds, blatantly latching on to the front of any unemployed parade or strikers' march or even charity with their own anonymous collecting buckets.

These were the spartans of the left who would take on Thatcher because they had no mortgages to lose if they were surcharged, and anybody at the London County Council, like Ken Livingstone, who did not, was a Southern softie (except of course for Lambeth with its proud history of riots and burning cars).

The Militant Tendency told Thatcher to go to hell. Especially in Liverpool.

Twenty years after the Beatles, swinging Liverpool (apart from its football) was dead on its feet. Facing the wrong way from Europe to attract the new terminals and shipping it needed, with its factories closing faster than pubs on Good Friday, its brassy second-generation Irish were no longer the fascinating leaders of Sixties fashion, music, sport, politics, TV and music-hall wit.

Back in the Sixties more people had heard of the River Mersey in Liverpool than of the Hudson River in New York. For the first time ever, southerners stopped taking the mickey out of northern accents and Maggie May doing the knees-up on Lime Street and Bold Street, and tuned into *Z Cars* with relish.

But in the early Eighties TV viewers were watching *Boys from the Blackstuff*, about the despair of Merseyside's building workers, and *Yosser*, the deranged unemployed navvie who would say 'Give us a job', then head-butt the foreman who refused, with all the grace of a goal-scoring leader from Liverpool – Toshack, Hately or Keegan. Or the insult of a comedy programme called *Bread*, which showed every Scouser as a scrounging layabout fiddling his DSS benefit, but for some unfathomable reason was loved in Liverpool, even though it did the city devastating damage amongst any potential employers even considering building a new factory there.

The Militant Tendency stormed into power in Liverpool in May 1983. By 1985 they had turned the Town Hall over to the hardline Liverpool unions and handed out hundreds of new Council jobs to their own supporters. The Militant leaders Derek Hatton and Tony Mulhearn were working-class, witty firebrands straight out of any Northern soap opera, who like Arthur Scargill, or Neil Kinnock, could mount a platform and establish an immediate rapport with the hard-up, disaffected crowd with a couple of merry quips and soundbite sarcasm.

They were a TV producer's dream, and Mrs Thatcher's too.

When Thatcher decided to freeze their cash they simply ignored her. The Militant organization even managed to get three of their members selected for safe seats in Parliament. Pat Wall was elected in Bradford North, Dave Nellist in Coventry South East, and Terry Fields in Liverpool Broadgreen. The 'soft left', as Kinnock's supporters were called, were no real threat to him, because they had all campaigned to put Neil into the Leader's job.

However, the hard Militant revolutionary left, from Scargill to the poor, white, male, unemployed political tough nuts, who had nothing to lose and no career ambitions, were a different 'enemy within' the Labour Party itself, even though the Party rule-book specifically stated that no members could, in effect, operate 'a party within a party'.

In 1985 Neil Kinnock was in a trap, much of his own making. He could not afford to alienate the soft left who had put him there, yet he had to pull back the council-house and blue-collar votes Labour had lost in marginal seats in the Midlands and South.

In the middle of the miners' strike, the IRA had planted a bomb in the Grand Hotel in Brighton timed to explode under Mrs Thatcher's bedroom when she retired for the night. Fortunately, she went to the bathroom after midnight and when the bomb went off, she survived. But five others, including one MP and the wife of another, were killed, and thirty-one leading figures in the Tory Party and their wives were severely injured. It was a terrorist outrage which shocked Britain and brought the Tories huge waves of sympathy.

As usual the loonies cracked offensive jokes along the lines of 'What do you reckon to the Brighton bomb killing the Tories? Well, it's a start isn't it?'

By the summer of 1985, Kinnock, now in mid-Parliament, and realizing Labour was unelectable, had to take drastic steps to change the Party's image without upsetting too many members by changing its policies. He and Glenys had a very acceptable image of nice, friendly genuine people, who really did care about other people too, in complete contrast to the hardline Thatcherism of the dole queue and Government cuts in everything from education to the Health Service, simply to find the cash for tax cuts for the rich. The miners' strike was causing serious economic fears about Britain's stability, and in the middle of it in January 1985, the pound actually fell to $1.10, the lowest in history. Mrs Thatcher's own Conservative MPs in Parliament were growing rebellious and regularly refusing to support her policies.

With the Militants spreading their wings, Kinnock tried to change the voting system by which MPs were reselected to one member, one vote, to keep out the hard left in Parliament, but was roundly defeated by the ambitious delegates who were relishing the power they had over their existing MPs and their own ambitious chance of grabbing a seat too.

A drastic change of image from loonies to nice guys and families was essential. It was then that Neil asked an unknown television producer called Peter Mandelson to change the unacceptable face of Labour, and become the Party's first Director of Campaigns and Communications in September 1985. One moderate member of the National Executive Committee described Mandelson as 'tough, confident, and nasty. Just what the sensible wing of the Party needs.'

Mandelson invented the Red Rose symbol for Labour (not entirely original because other socialist parties in Europe also used it), but for once it did look as if the Labour Party was trying to court the voters instead of smashing them into submission with taxes, marches and slogans.

Naturally, Tory wits said the Red Rose would be lovely if it wasn't for all the pricks and thorns underneath. At which Labour wits resuscitated the old adage that the Tory Party emblem should be a condom, because it stands up well to inflation but halts all production, and while it lulls the women voters into a false sense of security, it eventually turns out to be nothing but a cover for a bunch of dickheads. As for the Liberals, a banana emblem is ideal, because they all start off green and straight, then quickly turn yellow and bent.

But more than a rose was required to prove that the Trotskyites and anarchists had not taken over. Kinnock needed to prove that he was in command, and a month after Mandelson's appointment chose to do so at the 1985 Bournemouth Conference. Six months after the miners' strike ended, he performed the biggest U-turn seen in 50 years of Labour history and launched a highly charged emotional attack on the Labour council in Liverpool who had led the city to bankruptcy in their militant fight against the Government's rate-capping.

Labour councils in Lambeth, Liverpool, Sheffield and many cities had declared that they would not carry out the Government's new rate-capping legislation. They would simply carry on spending and let the Tory Government pick up the debts. One by one they backed down as it became apparent that the Government would implement the law, and individually surcharge and bankrupt each councillor. Eventually in Lambeth thirty-six councillors were surcharged and disqualified.

In Liverpool, where the Council said it would not cut back, it appeared to have the support of the voters, and 50,000 protesters marched through the streets with another 25,000 going on a one-day strike as well. On 14 June, despite warnings, the Council levied a rate rise of 9 per cent and on 8 September, all forty-nine councillors who voted for it were surcharged £106,000 for the delay in waiting until June to set the rate charge. On 25 September the Council employees rejected an all-out strike and the councillors were then forced to make immediate cuts and redundancies to balance the books, or pay the deficit themselves. It was a stupid, irresponsible political gesture and protest simply to defend their own suicidal glory. A week later Hatton and his friends sat at the Bournemouth Conference preening themselves at their TV infamy.

It was then that Kinnock, with the camera on him, watching every word and inflection, struck at the wreckers who had taken over many Labour councils. He yelled from the rostrum: 'I'll tell you what happens with impossible promises! You start with far-fetched resolutions. They are then pickled into a rigid dogma. A code. And you go through the years sticking to that! Outdated, misplaced, irrelevant to the real needs, and you end up with the grotesque chaos of a Labour council hiring taxis to scuttle round a city handing out redundancy notices to its own workers.'

As Liverpool had done.

It was an astonishing attack by a Labour Leader on his own Labour councils and Militant members whether in the cities or unions. Derek Hatton and Liverpool Labour MP Eric Heffer, a previous Party Chairman, were on their feet yelling back in fury and then Heffer marched petulantly out of the hall in high dudgeon, followed by TV cameras.

Kinnock went on to a cacophony of boos and cheers. 'I am telling you, no matter how entertaining and fulfilling it is to short-term egos, you can't play politics with people's jobs or with their services or homes! Comrades,' he boomed, 'it seems to me that some of our number are like latter-day public schoolboys. It seems it matters not whether you won or lost, but how you played the game. We cannot take that inspiration from Rudyard Kipling. Those game players get isolated, hammered, blocked off. They then try to blame other workers, and people of the city, for not showing sufficient revolutionary consciousness. Always some-body else! Then they claim a rampant victory. Whose victory? Not victory for the people. We all see the casualties. They are not found amongst the leaders and enthusiasts. They are found among the people whose jobs are destroyed, and living standards pushed down to deeper depths of insecurity and misery!'

His coruscating attack on his own Conference put him firmly lined up at long last with the sensible minority in the Party, with him calling the hard left 'purist and barren, mistaking barking for biting'. It was an astonishing assault on the hard left, who had given him so much support in the leadership contest exactly two years before, and sent an electric shock throughout Britain, never mind the Labour Party. Kinnock had been planning his 'realignment' for some months and his timing of the attack was superb.

A massive majority of the constituency delegates and MPs and sensible unions gave him an uproarious standing ovation and prolonged cheers. It was the speech from a Leader for which the honest, long-standing, rank-and-file members of the Party had been pining for years. He was a hero once more, looking in command, and determined to purge the good old Labour Party of its infiltrators, Moscow carpet-baggers and Kremlin fellow-travellers.

None cheered louder than the Labour MP for Knowsley, just outside Liverpool, a guy called Robert Kilroy-Silk. Kilroy came from a working-class Birmingham background, but had climbed out of it to become a lecturer at the Department of Political Theory at Liverpool University. A cheerful, witty, handsome man, he was an engaging companion and a good friend, even if he did pinch my jokes for the articles he wrote for *Chat* women's magazine. He had had a bellyful of the Militants in his constituency who had made his life hell since he got the seat.

In his cocky way, he had been daft enough to do an interview for *Newsnight* on the train down to London, after winning the seat in February 1974, and when the interviewers asked him how long he thought it would take him to become Prime Minister, he said, quite seriously, 'About fifteen years.' The other new MPs never let him forget it, and every time he stood up in the Chamber Dennis Skinner, or the Tories, would cry 'Only eleven more years and thirty days left, Bob! Better get a move on.'

Kilroy was being challenged for reselection by Tony Mulhearn, Hatton's sidekick, and Bob was demanding a full enquiry by the Party's National Executive Committee into Mulhearn's activities. Following Kinnock's speech, Kilroy and I were at a dinner hosted by the *Daily Star*, when he came back from the Gents rubbing his knuckles. One of the Liverpool Militants had pursued him into the lav and threatened how they were going to take revenge on him. He pushed Kilroy over the wash-basin, so Kilroy hit him with a left and unfortunately the guy went backwards through a window. Kilroy pulled him out by the throat and hit him again. When he came back to the dinner and told me, I had great delight in tipping off the *Star*'s conference journalists and putting it right on the front pages next to Kinnock's speech. Things were looking up.

The purge was on. In the following twelve months, 112 Militant members were expelled, and another 130 dealt with on disciplinary enquiries.

Despite their hatred of the establishment, many of them appealed to the courts (all on legal aid) against their expulsion, and were supported by the very same judges whom the Militants hated so much. The obliging judges ruled that the Labour Party membership card was in fact a 'binding contract', and the Party rule-book was 'simply a guide for friends', which could not overrule the 'law of tort', whatever that might mean.

All it did was to delay their expulsion until after the next Conference when the rules could be legally changed. Which was about what could be expected from the good old Labour Party.

Meanwhile, back at the town halls and county halls, Red Ken Livingstone was still filling the front pages of the *Sun*. Mrs Thatcher, in one of the daftest decisions ever made by any politician, decided to pull back some of her dwindling support by abolishing the whole Greater London Council. Here was a council systematically destroying any support for Labour, yet she abolished it. Even some of her own supporters protested at the shooting of their fox.

The Council promptly spent another £14 million on an advertising campaign in the cinemas and other papers protesting against its abolition, while Labour MPs in Parliament dutifully voted against the Abolition Bill, while silently praying that the Conservative Government would not back down. Livingstone's campaign against abolition consisted mainly of adverts and cinema slogans with Barbara Windsor, London's favourite Cockney, travelling on a bus shouting a daft slogan, 'Say No to No Say', which was plastered everywhere, followed by another message which read, '74 per cent say no'. To which another Cockney wag went round adding underneath, 'The other 26 per cent got pregnant.'

Even then Mrs Thatcher had difficulty in getting rid of County Hall, because the unelected House of Lords decided that as the GLC had been elected by the voters in 1985, Parliament did not have the right to abolish it. It would have to wait until the next county elections and could hang on in there until then, even though she could stop all its Government funds.

Kinnock's tough line and image change continued. The freckle-faced Welsh boyo, back-slapping and calling all women 'dear' or 'darling' as he kissed them, was revamped into a sober, well-dressed, statesmanlike leader (even though he did lose it once when clever yobbos humiliated him in a Chinese restaurant near his home. He just took them outside and stood them up against the wall and they ran off terrified). The common-sense wing of the unions backed him entirely. The unions had seen their membership dive as unemployment soared to well over three million in the 'official figures', which had been re-estimated thirty-two times by the Tories and were probably about four million in reality.

With fewer members, the full-time jobs of the union organizers were going down the drain too. It concentrated their minds wonderfully well. Party employees who wrote articles mildly condemning Labour's new outlook were sacked on the same day. Kinnock publicly called Livingstone 'a prat' and refused to talk to him directly. He said on television, 'I don't know why they behave like this. I think I would have to employ a psychiatrist to determine their motivations.'

I could have told him in one word. Vanity. The nutcases were drug addicts hooked on the sound of their own voice and needing a daily fix of the narcotic of publicity. And if it meant paying the price of feeding TV news and the morning papers with stories of mayhem, panic, chaos, and to use Kinnock's phrase, 'playing politics with people's lives and jobs', they could not kick the habit. Whether it was Hatton, Scargill or Livingstone, they rode on macho waves of 'Here we go' adulation and did not give a toss who won the election, so long as they went down in the history of the revolution. Whether it was cameras on the streets of Belfast, or the Greenham Common Women's Peace Camp, or the homeless kids beginning to sleep in doorways, it was all part of the glorious turmoil of upheaval.

Thatcher disbanded the GLC, and Derek Hatton (with his DEG 5 Y number plate, spelling 'Degsy' as all Dereks are nicknamed in Liverpool) was booted out too, together with the Lambeth councillors who refused to set a rate.

Despite Kinnock's attempts to save Kilroy-Silk from the mob, he quit as an MP and opted for a job in television (helped and advised by his next-door neighbour in Maidenhead, Terry Wogan), presenting a morning chat show. By this time Kinnock himself was breaking every rule in the new book. Instead of letting the loonies and Militants choose the candidates for by-elections and suffering another Peter Tatchell fiasco, the Party bosses at the NEC imposed a trusted local man, George Howarth, on Kilroy-Silk's consituency. He held the seat.

Meanwhile, as the 1987 election drew near, Thatcher's Chancellor, Nigel Lawson, was deliberately rigging the economy and keeping interest rates low to trigger off the biggest boom in house prices Britain had ever seen. His earlier tax cuts, paid for by savagely cutting local council grants and the Health Service, and selling off the nationalized gas, electricity and telephone industries, gave him the cash for a giveaway budget, and Thatcher ran early before the bubble burst.

Poverty in the North and Midlands was soaring, bringing crime and law and order problems throughout the country. The Conservative Party never worried about it. They simply said, if you want the alternative of a Labour Government with its flying pickets, then have it. So the public voted for the devil they knew best.

Labour, steered by Peter Mandelson, launched the best election campaign ever. This time, the Party's leading spokesmen and the cameras were in the right place at the right time, and Labour followed the Tories' device of promoting a Presidential-style election which had been so successful for Mrs Thatcher in 1979 and 1983.

Colin Welland and Hugh Hudson of the award-winning film *Chariots of Fire* were brought in to produce an astonishing party political broadcast simply called 'Kinnock', which received much acclaim. It was repeated later that week by popular demand. It showed Neil Kinnock and Glenys in casual clothes walking and relaxing on the hills and in the valleys of Wales, just chatting about kids and schools and hospitals, and the famous speech at Bournemouth, with no slogans or hard-sell, and the voters loved it.

Without doubt, Kinnock was by then the most popular Leader in Labour's history. He had swept out the stables and his good-bloke, friendly *bonhomie*, trusting nature and ready wit, like John Prescott's later, made him a great Labour Party and working-class party manager.

But the traditional North–South divide right across the British Isles, and the breakaway SDP splitting the traditional Labour vote, plus the fact that the Tory Party had a lead of 186 seats over Labour, could not do anything other than add up to another mammoth win for Mrs Thatcher.

Labour won only twenty-seven seats more than they started with and even lost six in the South. The Liberals gained just two and the SDP splitters one. The Tories still had a lead of 144 over Labour and it looked as if Mrs Thatcher and the Conservatives would rule for ever.

Particularly in London, where Livingstone and the inner city loony and polytechnic bolsheviks had actually lost five seats, including Fulham which the Party had won at a by-election. The Conservatives did not win one seat in the North and Midlands inner cities of Manchester, Liverpool, Newcastle, Bradford, Leicester or Stoke, and Ken Livingstone, having been selected for the safe high-poverty seat of Brent, had one of the worst swings against Labour in the country, only holding on to the very safe seat by a majority of 1,653.

Thatcher's tax cuts and fool's gold of soaring house prices convincing even council tenants who bought their homes that overnight they had made many thousands of pounds profit, even though the only way to cash it in was to go and live in a tent, worked perfectly. Labour's question, 'if things are getting better all the time, why is she having a June election after just four years instead of having it in October, when things will be better still?', was totally ignored and unanswered by the Tories and their media friends. Thatcher's slogan was simply, 'Don't let Labour ruin it', and the voters in the South who had never experienced factory closures did not. The old adage that the North lives on its skills and the South lives on its wits remained perfectly true. It was only the skills which had become obsolete.

The disappointing result was a savage shock to Labour, not least to all the newly selected soft left candidates who were looking forward to being MPs, even if the Party was still in opposition. They now had another four years to wait for a second chance. They were growing older and wiser, with families to keep, and beginning to heed the new Kinnock's advice that the Party could no longer continue down the road to glorious failure and the purity of powerlessness, constant diets of resolutions, condemning and deploring, or opposing the common-sense issues which decide elections. That included the issue of nuclear disarmament, which had undoubtedly cost Labour hundreds of thousands of votes when cautious elderly Labour voters who remembered the war opted for the SDP and Plymouth MP David Owen's defence policy instead.

The Party I had grown up in had changed irrevocably. The old-time working-class sons of toil had been driven out of the constituency parties and deselected or simply bored to death by constant ranting. They just were not made welcome any more. Whenever the local party workers wanted to talk about kids, jobs, buses, rents, bins, hospitals, pensions and all the other essentials of life, the poly lecturers in soft jobs would swamp them with 'the mandatory reference back to remit the composite on the unparalleled achievement of the Nicaraguan revolution, and extension of agricultural workers' cooperatives, and for any cessation of funding to the Contra forces, by the USA, plus twinning agreements to develop awareness of refugee programmes and foreign debts'. Phew.

After the election, I worked out that only forty-two of the 229 Labour MPs had ever earned a living at a manual job, and that was stretching it a bit, by counting one bloke who had worked his passage from being a grave-digger to a Redcoat at Butlin's. Our endangered species included ten miners, twenty lads who knew one end of a lathe from the other (including me), a couple each from the railways and docks, plus the odd bus, crane and lorry driver, and three straight out of the dole queue.

No wonder the turnout in solid Labour areas from the unemployed, poorly, sick and lame, pensioners, blue-collar shift clockers-in and the rest was getting lower and lower. Mr Mandelson's ideas were working and were fine for pulling in the intellectual *Guardian* reader social worker, teacher, town hall vote, but to the council tenants the Party simply talked gibberish, while the Tories sold them their houses at a third of their value, and cut taxes as well.

All the remaining 600 MPs, who were estate agents, stockbrokers, lecturers, farmers, ex-wing commanders, and white collars from the Town Hall and Health Authority refuges, were instant experts on TV when it came to pronouncing on why British workers no longer made good cars, or television, or ships, and why all our spare cash had to go on butter mountains and wine lakes in Europe, or nuclear weapons. But who was there to speak up for *Coronation Street* and *EastEnders*? Or even for the readers of the *Daily Star* (which I was writing for at the time)?

What the Party needed was a 'Working Class Group'. I told Mr Mandelson this and sent him 113 examples from the Labour manifesto of words, phrases, soundbites and A-level jargon which no tabloid newspaper would dream of using to pass on its message. The poor old 'Keepers of the Cloth Cap' had long been outvoted in the Party and reduced to standing there holding the cap out with one hand, while playing a mouth organ with the other. We had lost 'em, and lost 'em for good if we did not start and communicate.

I managed to convince a few trades union MPs in the bar that this was not a publicity stunt and we should form a club to show the readers of the *Sun* and the *Mirror* that the Labour Party did not now consist of 289,614 members who were social workers, teachers or Town Hall workers, together with twenty-seven former public schoolboys and girls who had become MPs, but that forty-two of us were still hanging on in there proud of our grass roots and class roots.

We knew we would get ragged-trouser, *beaujolais nouveau* jokes, but the criterion for membership would be that MPs would have had to have left school at fifteen, or as soon as they were old enough to start earning money, and gone straight into full-time manual work. Drop-outs who left at fifteen, and then went back to school later, because they did not like honest toil, and remained students until they were thrown out again into the world at thirty-two, would not be admitted.

We invited Mr Mandelson's staff to meet us so that we could tell them, as I had successfully told Tony Benn ten years before, that people who leave school at fifteen are not daft. They can understand any message, however complicated, if only it is written in their language, as Rupert Murdoch proved so often in the *Sun*. So why did the Labour Party not speak the same language?

Unfortunately, as so often happens in the bars of Parliament, prowling journalists got hold of the letter we sent out to the forty-two genuine members, and 285 MPs applied to join. Including a large number of Tories, who were adamant that they too fulfilled the criterion. At the first meeting we had to throw out Nicholas Soames, Winston Churchill's grandson, for gate-crashing. We told him he may have wangled an invitation to Prince Andrew's stag night, and swapped gags there with Billy Connolly, but it cut no clog leather with us. Soames claimed that his father had decided he was too thick to do a proper job and when Eton made him leave at eighteen he had worked in a garage before his dad got him an official commission in the 11th Hussars, the 'Cherry Pickers', as they are called.

Tim Sainsbury of the famous Sainsbury's supermarket chain, and a multi-multi-multi-millionaire, demanded to join because he said his dad sat him in front of a bacon-slicer at fifteen and made him work it to learn the business from the bottom. We threw him out too and decided that the next meeting we held would be in the weeks of the Derby, Ascot, Henley Regatta, the Lords Test and the Oxford and Cambridge match at Twickenham to protect the purists.

The tabloids, television and radio loved the idea. But to the trendy London-based commentators cloth caps and Northern accents were just too hilarious not to ridicule. So after a couple of meetings we decided to abandon it.

We did however go out with one final flourish. We told the press that we had given one last piece of advice to our working-class members. It was that when the Footsie (the Financial Times Share Index) touched 2,300, then SELL!

It was superb advice too. Three months later, in October 1987, the Stock Exchange crashed by 25 per cent, wiping £50 billion off share values in a landslide even bigger than 1929, and it just showed that the common-sense workers could beat the City experts any day.

The crash was very good news for Labour too. Inside a year, it brought the soaring house prices tumbling down when Nigel Lawson's phoney interest rates had to be raised and all those new, lower-income Conservative voters found that the mortgage they had rushed into had now left them with a debt considerably more than their house was worth. 'Negative equity' became a buzz word that the working class could quickly understand. As the recession now began to bite in the South and in the affluent areas of the Midlands, support for the Conservatives dropped like a stone.

The new militant MPs, far from being revolutionaries and storming the barricades, simply turned up in black leather jackets and ginger beards and contented themselves with making speeches advising the unions and the students to take to the streets.

Neil Kinnock kept up his ruthless purge and openly told his Labour MPs that any of them who joined the hard left newly formed Campaign Group in Parliament could say goodbye to any future promotion prospects and would not even sit on the front bench in opposition. Twenty-odd ambitious MPs immediately quit the group the following day and were appointed to the front bench quickly after! Some are still on it.

Several other new boys, who avidly climbed into bed with the loonies, to turf out sitting MPs, promptly jumped out again now they were in Parliament themselves and put their own promotion prospects first. It was the smartest career move some of them ever made. Kinnock's luck began to change. The SDP alliance with the Liberals broke up due to the arrogance of David Owen and his SDP band of three. Owen insisted that the SDP would continue to support nuclear weapons while the Liberals voted overwhelmingly not to. Owen then formed a 'breakaway' SDP of his own. The Conservatives actually held the very safe seat of Richmond in Yorkshire by only a whisker simply because the SDP and the Liberals stupidly both stood against each other and split the Opposition vote. A young unknown Tory called William Hague managed to hang on to it.

At the 1988 Conference the hard left opposed both Kinnock and Hattersley for the Leadership and put up Tony Benn and Eric Heffer to stand against them. Both polled ridiculous scores, with Benn receiving just 11 per cent of the poll and Heffer less than 2 per cent. Even his own Liverpool constituencies did not support him. But still the Labour support was patchy. The safe Glasgow seat of Govan went to the Scottish National Party with a swing of 33 per cent, simply because the local Labour party were once again allowed to field their own choice of candidate.

In the late Eighties, technology was moving fast, with the rapid spread of computerization which was to prove a godsend to the Labour Party. For years the hard left had managed to manipulate the so-called secret ballots for choosing MPs and councillors simply by controlling the membership lists of local parties. Secretarial records were a joke. Often the lists were written on the back of old envelopes, letters were never sent out, subscriptions not collected, organizations disbanded and re-formed under another name, and meetings, times and places moved to another venue, with only the dedicated hard left delegates being told.

Long lists of new members would be handed in, often people who could not read or write English, and whose names had been forged without their permission. Those who controlled the books controlled the Party. Mandelson and Kinnock and new Party Secretary Larry Whitty introduced a computerized membership scheme with subs paid directly to Head Office, and stopped the nonsense of the hard left keeping new members out by simply not collecting their subs or refusing their applications.

The Party's fund-raising was modernized and the ludicrous machinery of the Party Conferences (which lost the Party a million votes every time they were televised with their incomprehensible rituals and jargon) was drastically overhauled into some semblance of debate as opposed to combat.

It was the same advanced technology which brought Kinnock his biggest bonus when the recently elected Russian Communist leader, Mikhail Gorbachev, realized that without the latest microchip technology, the Russian economy would not only be unable to keep pace with the latest American weaponry and the future star wars, but would eventually turn Russia and all its satellites into Third World countries. When Gorbachev started dismantling his medium- and short-range nuclear missiles, and then his chemical weapons too, the row about whether or not Britain should have its own nuclear weapons, which had cost Labour hundreds of thousands of votes at every election, was no longer a winner for the Tories.

In August 1989, the cruise missiles at Greenham Common, which had led to protests by over 250,000 people in London just five years before, with 300 arrests outside the House of Commons, began to be loaded in to aeroplanes and sent back to America. In November that year the Berlin Wall came down, and as the Conservative and SDP fortunes slumped, it looked as if the Labour Party was back in business. That summer Labour defeated the Tory Government in a nationwide vote for the Euro elections. It was the Party's first national victory over the Conservatives for fifteen years.

Meanwhile, Mrs Thatcher, as all leaders eventually do, scored yet again the biggest own goal ever seen in politics. She introduced the poll tax.

Sick to death of seeing the Tories wiped out at local elections, she had the unbelievably daft idea that every household, whether it was a six-bedroomed mansion or a tiny cottage, should pay exactly the same local rates. The only way to make the British people turn out for local elections and really care about what their local council are doing is to make every house in the same local authority pay the same amount of tax, she said.

The last time England had a poll tax was in the Peasants' Revolt of 1381. Any sensible politician or voter in the real world really did begin to think that Mrs Thatcher had gone crazy. The Tory Party was now in a turmoil as bad as the Labour Party had ever been. Ten years as Prime Minister and she was now facing an economic crisis, with Chancellor Lawson resigning just weeks after the Tory Party Conference in October and little-known John Major moving on to become the Chancellor.

In a laughable but deadly serious challenge to her leadership, a little-known back-bencher, Sir Anthony Meyer, said he would stand against her as a 'stalking horse' to make her fight for her Prime Minister's job. With the Labour Party rolling in the aisles of Parliament at the comedy taking place in the Tory Party instead of their own, Meyer picked up only thirty-eight votes but another thirty-odd abstained.

It was a warning of mutiny in the Tory ranks which Labour should have been wary of, not delighted in. The comparative peace in the Labour Party took a buffeting as once more the hard left and the ruffians took to the streets against Thatcher's Poll Tax. This time they had a great deal of sympathy from long-suffering working-class Tory voters who had lost their jobs, or at least their overtime, seen the value of their little cottage first soar then crash, and were now faced with an unbelievable new tax in which they would pay exactly the same council tax as the Lord of the Manor up the road in his thirty-room mansion.

In March 1990, just before the poll tax was due to start, Labour overturned a 14,000 Tory majority to win the seat of Mid Staffordshire, where the local Tory MP had committed suicide following the property crash. Many other Tory MPs felt like doing the same when the poll tax came in ten days later. Meanwhile the loonies were back in business, thanks to Thatcher's stupidity. A huge wave of violent demonstrations swept Britain, with the usual arrests, mounted police charges, paint-throwing and all the bully-boy tactics on television which had cost Labour so many law and order votes in the miners' strike. Even football hooligans, angry at another daft Thatcher plan to make all fans produce identity cards at the turnstiles, were chanting, 'We're not paying the poll tax.' Secretly Labour were worried for another reason. Thousands of lower-paid workers, and those registered as unemployed, but actually working on the black economy, were deliberately taking their names off the voters' register, to hide from the Town Hall lists, and to dodge paying the tax.

The Tories did not mind. In marginal London constituencies, they worked out, the hideaways would cost Labour at least six seats they might win (which is what actually happened). As usual the Tory newspapers, the *Sun*, *Mail*, *Express* and *Times*, highlighted every Militant to worsen Labour's position. Especially when Glasgow Militant supporter Tommy Sheridan was actually elected from his prison cell. In Scotland, where the poll tax had been introduced a year earlier than in England and Wales, the Scottish Militants actually had four councillors elected in Glasgow. One more than the Scots Nats and Liberals combined.

Once again, Labour's Achilles' heel was showing blisters. Every experienced Labour MP in Parliament was now warning supporters to soft-pedal. The opinion polls were showing a Labour lead, with the General Election only eighteen months away. It was obvious that the best vote-winner Labour had was not Neil Kinnock, but Mrs Thatcher. She was loathed, not just by her own MPs, but by loyal Tory voters across Britain. On every doorstep the voters said they would never vote Tory again while she was Prime Minister. It was obvious therefore that Labour's strategy should have been to prop her up, to carefully nurse her in office until the next election, but as usual the hot-heads, even in Parliament, charged at her instead.

It was non-stop attack on her with furious debates and arguments every day. Throughout 1990 she launched attack after attack on the European Community and its monetary policies, undermining her own new Chancellor, John Major, and her Foreign Secretary, Sir Geoffrey Howe. Until eventually on 13 November, Geoffrey Howe resigned and made his farewell with a stiletto-wielding speech from the back benches on television, standing just a few feet away from Mrs Thatcher, and allowing Michael Heseltine to fling down the gauntlet for another Leadership contest.

All the sycophantic lackeys in her Cabinet ditched her in hours even as she won the vote by 204 to Heseltine's 152, just four votes short of the overall majority she needed under the Tory system of choosing their Leader with only MPs having a vote. Two days later, knowing that those who had voted for her would now scuttle away, her Cabinet colleagues told her to go too. She quit, leaving Downing Street in tears in her Prime Ministerial car to drive to the Palace and hand in her resignation to the Queen.

It was a big blow to Labour too. The Tory MPs, surprisingly following Shakespeare's advice that he who wields the dagger never wears the crown, promptly turned their backs on Heseltine and went instead for the honest-looking new recruit with a clean record, John Major. A man who had entered Parliament only eleven years before, on the same day that Thatcher became Prime Minister herself. He immediately scrapped the poll tax and put Heseltine (who had come second) in charge of bringing in a new structured council tax, with each house listed in one of eight bands based on its estimated current value.

It worked. Then, as it often does in politics, the wheel of fortune went spinning around once more. Six weeks after Major was elected, the Gulf War broke out. A nice little scuffle, with the Iraqis routed, cheered up the Tory voters. Six months later, President Gorbachev was booted out in Russia and the new Prime Minister Major could fly to Washington, Moscow and Peking to look like a world statesman. The Tory Party began to climb back in the polls, and with the Tory papers responding by waging vicious personal attacks on Kinnock and the Militants, while constantly showing a smiling, grey-haired, genial Major sitting at the top tables of Europe thrashing out the Maastricht Treaty, their vote began to stand up.

None the less Labour carried on doing well, winning by-elections in Newport and Langbaurgh after the Tory Chancellor had to raise VAT to 17½ per cent to make up for the poll tax losses. Kinnock continued with the purge of Militants and in a key by-election in Walton, Liverpool, after left-wing MP Eric Heffer had died, official Labour, with Peter Kilfoyle as candidate, openly took on Militant Labour and won hands down, with the hard left polling 2,600 votes to Peter Kilfoyle's 21,317 and the Tories getting 1,155. Which was almost as bad a result for the Tories as for the SDP in a previous by-election on Merseyside, when they actually managed to poll fewer votes than Screaming Lord Sutch and the Monster Raving Loony Party.

Kinnock ruthlessly booted out the Militant MPs Dave Nellist in Coventry and Terry Fields in Liverpool for their constant attacks on official Labour policy, particularly when Terry Fields received enormous media publicity after he was jailed for sixty days for refusing to pay his Poll Tax. Then he suspended another sixty members in Liverpool who had campaigned against Kilfoyle.

Tory Chairman Chris Patten, aided and abetted by the 'capitalist running dogs of Fleet Street', as Militants not inaccurately called them, wrote daily, well-publicized letters to Kinnock mentioning the names of twenty-five fellow-travellers in the ranks of Labour MPs. But the Labour Party Conference majority of 8–1 in favour of the explusions showed that Labour was at last wanting to win the next election and keep its opinion poll lead.

Old Labour, or perhaps it is better to call it Last Century Labour, died at exactly 9 p.m. on Wednesday, 1 April 1992, just eight days before General Election Day, and amazingly, just 100 yards from the canal in Attercliffe where this book began.

Sheffield had carried on spending, regardless of Mrs Thatcher's economic sanctions, or high interest rates, and took the view that if five miles of steelworks had gone bust and been bulldozed and another ten square miles of slum terraced houses had been flattened along the canal on Attercliffe Road, then something had to be put back into the empty space, preferably big buildings to create jobs.

So the Council, led first by David Blunkett, then Clive Betts, now a Cabinet minister and Labour whip respectively, set to work and agreed to the building of the biggest hypermarket in Europe at the edge of the M1, called Meadowhall, which regularly attracts 80,000 visitors every Saturday. Plus a brand-new 37,000-seater stadium, which every year hosts one of the only two Rolling Stones or Tina Turner concerts in Britain. Plus an indoor 12,000-seater Arena to stage Pavarotti performances, or *Les Misérables*, or Disney ice shows, plus Olympic swimming pools, a future city airport and a supertram to carry in the crowds, plus acres of cinemas, burger bars, night-clubs, restaurants, a 'Centretainment' and a retail park to create hundreds of new jobs on the derelict land. Unfortunately, it damned near bankrupted the city to pay for it all. To say nothing of a few years later handing over an impregnable Labour majority to the Liberals, who had simply done nothing but stay silent, then knock on every door blaming every voter's domestic problem on the fact that Labour had no money to solve it because it had all been spent on supertrams and pleasure.

However, Sheffield was an ideal venue for the greatest election rally ever held in the history of the Labour Party. Neil Kinnock's Campaign Committee decided that the days of Labour's cloth cap image were over. This 1992 election would not be fought with a shoe-string amateur campaign outflanked by Tory glossy press advertising. This time it would be Labour who had the glitz and glamour. David Owen and the SDP were dead and Labour was going to regain its natural cautious, sober, working-class support.

The revolutionaries, the picket lines, the loonies and nutters were gone. Out. Finished. Now the media was the message. Kinnock would not be exhausted by interminable public meetings, shouting hoarsely down a loudspeaker. This time the word of mouth would be straight to television on 150 small soundbites in 150 different studios, not long, passionate speeches on far-flung platforms.

The economy was getting worse, with 1,200 businesses a week going bust. Unemployment, even after fiddling the figures downwards thirty-two times, was still 2.6 million. The new shine was beginning to wear off Major. At worst, the opinion polls, usually highly accurate in British elections, said that Labour would be the biggest party in a hung Parliament.

As the campaign went on, often in torrential rain, Labour got better, with Major abandoning his usual orchestrated speeches and actually adopting an Old Labour style, using a loudhailer while standing on a soap-box in shopping centres.

On 1 April, just a week before voting, a Mori poll in *The Times* gave Labour its biggest lead so far, of seven points over the Conservatives. It was the third poll that week to put Labour in a good lead. The figures of Labour 42 per cent, Conservatives 35 and Liberal Democrats 19, added up to a winning ticket. The Tories were facing defeat. The Stock Exchange and City markets took fright as Labour staged an American-style indoor razzama-tazz glamour show in front of 10,000 supporters, arriving from a 100-mile radius in 250 coaches off the nearby M1.

On a giant screen in the Sheffield Arena, there were music

videos, strobe disco lights, laser beams, fireworks, streamers, with pop group Simply Red and Mick Hucknall pounding out 'Something's got me started'. The violinist Nigel Kennedy and others were proudly reassuring in their support for Labour. Live performers included the opera singer Elizabeth Brice, singing 'Summertime', a pipe band, gospel singers, local school kids belting out 'Any Dream Will Do', plus messages from every stalwart in the Party, including Barbara Castle, plus Roy Hattersley (he even booked a box for his old mother), and John Smith to warm up for Kinnock before he arrived by helicopter.

It was billed as the biggest political rally seen in Britain since the war, at a cost of £150,000, and better than any American Democratic or Republican rally I have ever seen. It was organized by Jim Parrish and Charles Clarke, now the MP for Norwich. It was superb, the most professional presentation ever staged in any General Election. At long, long last, Labour was in the public relations business and actually selling itself as a high-class political organization which could run the country, while Major was standing in the rain on his soap-box.

Because of the weather, Kinnock's helicopter arrived early. The rest of the Shadow Cabinet were waiting at the entrance to the Arena to accompany him down the broad centre aisle and up the wide stairs to the platform. His entrance on the stage, on his own at first, to make a major speech for television, was planned for exactly nine o'clock so that the BBC News could take it live straight from Sheffield.

His early arrival meant he had to fill in the time by walking around the tiered sides of the Arena, backed by the throng of Shadow Cabinet MPs and Party leaders, with the music pounding as he was grabbed, hugged and kissed by women Party members and men fighting to shake his hand. It was genuine adulation for a very popular, genuine guy who had turned the Party round, and for the first time in eighteen years, had made the Party look like winners.

The applause, roars, cheers and tears from 10,000 fans standing on their seats in a stirring, emotional welcome home boyo, from the die-hard grass roots of northern Old Labour, ran through the Arena like old-time religion. It was the almost forgotten joy of the spine-tingling, goose-pimpled hysteria of a thousand brass band marches and banners flying high. It was passionate politics at its best from a generation who really cared for society, and would fight to the death for it.

But then Neil blew it.

As he reached the top of the steps, alone on the stage, he turned round to face the cheering fans, punched the air with a clenched fist, let out a war whoop of sheer delight and with a little skip yelled, 'Well all right!', as though he had scored at Wembley, or carried a try at Cardiff Arms Park.

And that was the first thing the sober viewers at home saw on the News. It was a genuine, sincere display of pleasure, but to all those at home it looked like triumphalism. It looked like the old cocky Kinnock celebrating victory seven days before the votes were in the bag.

Neil went on to make a speech of hot blood and fire, outlining the misery to working people and the struggling middle class of thirteen years of Tory rule. Up to that stage, it had been a campaign of TV clips of Kinnock with laughing kids or welcoming friendly pensioners, all carefully controlled in a new, for Labour, Presidential style and referred to by one cameraman as 'sanitized pap'.

After the Arena celebration, Matthew Parris, a former Conservative MP, wrote in *The Times* that the image choked the intellect and there was something disgusting about the occasion. To this day, nobody at Millbank, the Labour Party Headquarters, will ever admit to having had anything to do with the event.

Matters were not helped by the ancient Labour Party open-topped battle bus that the press were transported in from the East Midlands airport getting stuck in the mud of the car park, which had not yet been surfaced, and had been churned up by the 250 supporters' buses. It couldn't be pushed loose and it would have been much quicker to travel back to London in a car via the M1 instead of flying. Another coach took an hour to arrive and then promptly broke down on the M1, with the weary hacks arriving at London airport at 5.00 a.m., to start another campaign day.

All of it Labour's fault of, course, including the weather, and all ripe for savaging that the laser beams and choirs were just a fig leaf for the same old loonies who could not run a parish raffle without it being a cock-up.

Worse was to come. The threatened Labour lead and victory unleashed the most ferocious vindictive personal attack on a politician ever seen in an election campaign. The *Sun*, *Daily Mail* and *Daily Express* blitzed Neil Kinnock the man. When they were not brutally denigrating him they were driving home the message that he had changed his mind on so many issues, including defence and public expenditure, that he would certainly change it again and impose big tax increases once he was elected. On polling day, the desperate *Sun* splashed its 3.6 million copies on the front page with an old joke, even then, of 'If Kinnock wins today, will the last person to leave Britain turn out the lights', along with all its usual crude cartoons and abuse.

Also on polling day, the BBC organized its most sophisticated exit poll ever. Instead of just asking the voters who they had plumped for as they left the polling staion, they carefully selected 14,000 target voters in strategic seats, and asked them to mark a duplicate ballot paper in secret and place it in a BBC ballot box too. On that the BBC predicted the Tories would be twenty-five seats short of a majority. Then, when the results came in, the BBC changed its forecast. Then changed it again and again. For the first time in history, the polls had got it wrong. They had been listening to liars. All those floating voters who had said they would gladly pay a bit more tax for better schools and hospitals, even a lot of them who actually worked in health and education, had lied and reluctantly voted Tory instead. Pop star Mick Jagger summed it up accurately when they asked him afterwards which way he had voted and he said, 'I have to admit that in my heart and in my head I am Labour, but my wallet tells me I have to vote Conservative.'

Half an hour after midnight, the Tories had gained an overall majority when the Conservatives showed they were still holding seats like Basildon in Essex, which always swung with the Government party.

A day later, it was the *Sun* screaming again on its front page, 'It Was the *Sun* Wot Won It'. Major had held on despite losing 40 seats and still had an overall majority of twenty-one, cut down from an original overall majority of 100 which Mrs Thatcher had enjoyed.

The gloom and despair in the grief-stricken Labour Party were traumatic. Many of the Party and some of its MPs (especially those on the front bench expecting ministers' jobs) were openly loudly castigating the loonies and their actions of the past twelve years for the defeat. Although it would be asking too much for them to admit their own part in previous humiliations.

The old-style Labour policies of tax and take, to spend and give away elsewhere, were finished. The old-style back-of-an-envelope wheeling and dealing of votes had to end too. And new faces at the top were needed.

Kinnock offered his resignation immediately and blamed himself for the defeat but no politician on earth could have won votes with the personal battering he had taken. Seven years later, on a BBC programme in June 1999, by which time he was a European Commissioner in Brussels, holding a top job in the organization he had fought so passionately against twenty years earlier on his upward climb, he talked frankly of the mistakes he made, which left the voters thinking he was immature and frivolous. Neil admitted that the voters just could not see him as Prime Minister. 'It's in the biochemistry,' he said. 'It's a pity, but it's a fact of life.' He recalled that his appearance on a pop video with Tracey Ullman and his willingness to go on television singing and dancing with his wife had accumulated into a lack of earnestness. Of how he had physically hit people after they had struck him, and how it all added up to an impression of immaturity, whereas a degree of formality and detachment might not win votes, but does not offend minds.

Neil was absolutely right. Those of us who campaigned for Hattersley and for Blair, instead of Kinnock and John Prescott, knew it at the time, but then we also knew the Labour Party always loved a loser more than a winner, because so many of its members were losers in life too.

Until Tony Blair and Gordon Brown showed them how to win. But that's another story.

Fourteen

THE DOG AND THE LAMP-POST

EVERY young journalist on national newspapers is taught that the relationship between them and the politicians should be the same as the dog and the lamp-post. Which does not surprise politicians. They are taught at their dad's knee that newspapers are no use to anybody because they are too thin to hold chip-shop vinegar, and too thick to use as toilet paper.

Contrary to the legends of class warfare, most trades union members in Britain had never been on strike in their life. Ninety per cent of the companies which went bust in the depression had never had a strike in their history. But in three industries in particular, the unions possessed wildcat, disruptive strength. In the docks, the ship had to catch the tide. If it did not the cargo might go rotten, it would cause long delays and break contracts at the other end of the trip, and dockers, especially in London and Liverpool, were experts at demanding more money for any spurious reason as the high tide drew near. Car workers who stopped the conveyor belt turning out two cars a minute could cost a company massive amounts of money in lost production. In the newspaper print rooms, the unions of NGA and SOGAT, the National Graphical Association and the Society of Graphical Allied Trades, could halt the production of a newspaper for hours with any trivial excuse, and literally hold the newspaper owners to ransom. News does not keep. Day-old newspapers are worthless, even for fish and chips and khazi walls.

In these industries, the bosses were grabbed by the throat and made to pay up every day by unofficial shop stewards, whose 'bruvvers' on the job were earning at least twice the national average wage, often for a four-day week.

The overmanning in a Fleet Street print room was a joke. Old guys aged seventy-four would sit at the side of the machinery, doing absolutely nothing but read the paper, because the union insisted on keeping the same number of jobs on the plant, as it had since 1902. Every printer knew that it was absolutely essential that the next morning's copies were loaded on to the 10.45 evening train from King's Cross and to head north to link up with the national distribution network. Miss the train and the paper was trash.

Theft was common as the small vans left Fleet Street for the short journey to King's Cross with hundreds of copies 'falling off the back of the van', to be picked up for free by organized street-corner news stands all over the West End, some of whose owners also owned villas in Spain on the proceeds. 'Old Spanish Customs' prevailed, of handouts in cash with casual workers signing their name for it as 'Mickey Mouse', to dodge the taxman, often getting £100 a day for a Saturday shift back in the Seventies.

Jobs in the industry, as in the docks, had been handed down from father to son for generations, leading to an incestuous workforce where Artful Dodger traditions were a family culture. It was very, very rare to see a black docker or printworker, even in the Eighties. All the unions would pass resolutions against apartheid in South Africa while their members practised it avidly at work, and when Enoch Powell made his infamous 'rivers of blood' speech in 1968, London dockers actually marched to Parliament to support him.

There was not a lot the newspaper owners could do to stop it. In 1968 a cocky upstart Australian called Rupert Murdoch bought the *News of the World*, Britain's biggest-selling newspaper, and the *Sun*, later expanding his empire to America. He was astonished to find that in Texas it took four men to work a printing press, five in Chicago, six in New York and Sydney (they had tough unions too), and an unbelievable eighteen in London.

His beloved soaraway *Sun* could not soar much farther north than the Midlands either, because he had no printing capacity in Manchester and consequently could not deliver the evening football results and match reports into northern editions of the *Sun*.

Victor Matthews, who had bought the *Express* newspapers, had spare printing machinery in Manchester used only for the *Sunday Express*, and launched the *Daily Star*, which could carry the late news stories. I wrote a twice-weekly column for it, and in 1981 suggested to Lloyd Turner, the Australian editor, that we should run a free bingo and adopt a northern Labour line to counteract the *Sun*'s Thatcher worship and southern bias. He did. And the circulation of the *Star* soared to 1.7 million to equal the circulation of the *Daily Mail* at the time. Bingo eventually cost Fleet Street £27 million in prize money, which, as I told Tony Benn, represented the greatest redistribution of wealth from Fleet Street proprietors to Coronation Street pensioners that the country had ever seen.

Very quickly the *Sun* and the *Mirror* had to introduce bingo too, until eventually, of course, the newspaper competitions cancelled each other out and new reader circulation dried up, but the *Daily Star* had broken the myth that it was for ever impossible to launch a new national daily paper which could survive.

It kept its circulation until 1987 when Jeffrey Archer was awarded £500,000 damages from the paper following a sensational libel trial.

Lloyd Turner, the editor, was stunned at the jury's verdict and was then sacked three weeks later by the new owner, Lord Stevens. As the editor, Lloyd had vigorously fought Archer's claims, even sending his reporters to interview Monica Coghlan several times and go-between Michael Stacpoole too, but Stacpoole then went to live abroad out of reach of a subpoena and the *Star*'s defence collapsed.

Lloyd Turner never recovered from the defeat and died of a stroke in 1997. After the trial Lord Stevens sent the *Daily Star* downmarket chasing the *Daily Sport* and now its circulation is a third of what it was then.

Years later in December 1999 just after Jeffrey Archer won the Tory Party nomination for the Mayor of London contest, potential witnesses at the 1987 libel trial revealed a different story from the one told in court twelve years earlier, but by then Lloyd Turner was dead and jobs and careers at the paper had long gone.

The bias against Labour in the early Eighties and the adulation of Mrs Thatcher was hysterical, and often as censored as anything put out by *Pravda* on behalf of the Soviet Union.

In the middle of the Falklands War, when Mrs Thatcher would stand at the Despatch Box and rant and rave about 'Our Boys' fighting for Britain, whipping up furious flag-waving patriotism, I wrote a piece in the *Daily Star* asking why we had never seen a picture of Mrs Thatcher herself in uniform. After all, she was older than the Queen and there were plenty of pictures of the Queen in battle-dress. Yet never a shot of Mrs Thatcher, the Prime Minister, wearing it. She was eighteen years old in October 1943, two years before the war ended, and wartime regulations said that women aged eighteen to thirty had to register for 'military or other purposes', assigned by Bevin's Ministry of Labour and National Service.

All the records show that Mrs Thatcher had been a student at Oxford. How had the young eighteen-year-old Margaret Hilda managed it? I had to do my national service later, why hadn't she? At the height of the Falklands War it was a pretty inflammatory statement, and enough to make old soldiers splutter and demand a firing squad. Yet amazingly, not one other national newspaper carried it. Nor did any TV channel or radio station. How curious. How biased.

By the early Eighties practically every national paper in London was in financial trouble. In the late Seventies the printworkers actually went on strike for a year at *The Times* and *Sunday Times*, after Murdoch had bought them. Journalists would arrive at work, prepare a paper, then nothing would appear. In frustration, the whole of Britain's national newspapers took it out on all trade unions, and the Labour Party, simply because they could not put their own house in order.

But in the mid-Eighties the new microchip computer technology emerged. Suddenly newspaper production did not need print rooms and printers. All it needed was journalists and button-pressers. And perhaps lorries too, so that they would not be tied to the trains and their rail unions, who would support the printworkers in any dispute.

Murdoch laid secret plans to shift all his newspaper production to a new plant in Wapping, a mile down the road in an old Dockland warehouse area. But he wanted a new plant, new employees and a new union with no demarcation lines or closed shop practices to run it.

He got it with the help of the electricians' union leader, Eric Hammond, the guy who just a few months before at the Labour Party Conference had referred to the striking miners as 'lions led by donkeys'. Eric Hammond and the EEPTU, his union, were fed up with the iron grip of the printers' unions on the industry, and saw the new computer technology as a natural creator of jobs for electricians, not printers. Like the miners a year before who saw their industry collapse, the printworkers now saw their own fortress crumbling. Later the duplicitous electricians' unions were hauled up before the TUC and threatened with expulsion for 'poaching' other union jobs, but eventually survived.

Six months after the miners' strike ended in 1985, another fortress at Wapping emerged in solid, windowless concrete blocks, with electricians shipped in daily from Southampton to install and run the new computers. Murdoch kept the negotiations on closing the Fleet Street plant going with the print unions right up until Friday, 24 January 1986, but two days after the journalists had voted to move to the new plant, the print unions foolishly called a strike like the miners had, and refused to go.

Now Murdoch did not need them. What's more, they had played into his hands. Now they were on strike, he could sack the lot of them under Thatcher's new laws, and did not even have to bother paying them redundancy pay or unfair dismissal either.

On Saturday night, 25 January 1986 Murdoch printed four million copies of the *News of the World* and the *Sunday Times* and sent them out on TNT lorries (a company in which he owned a large stake), bypassing the trains and railway unions, and distributed his papers all round the nation.

The print unions' 5,200 sacked members began picketing every night. Especially on Saturday nights, when the big distribution of the Sunday morning papers took place. Murdoch took the unions to court and the court decided that £17 million of SOGAT's assets should be seized. The NGA were fined £25,000 for defying a court injunction.

Yet surprisingly, all over the country, other members of the same print industry unions refused to cooperate with their London colleagues in blocking the distribution of Murdoch's newspaper, and even refused to help them financially, because of the London unions' long arrogance and abuse of the system, which had got all printworkers a bad name in the book, magazine and other associated industries.

The dispute was, in effect, not unlike the miners' strike of a year before, with the sensible guys refusing to follow the hotheads. One Saturday night in May 1986, over 250 pickets and police were injured in the weekly demonstrations and brawls at the Wapping exits. To try to halt the picketing, Murdoch offered redundancy payments totalling £50 million to the sacked 5,200, but again stupidly they refused. Labour councils everywhere banned Murdoch's paper from their libraries and the leaders of the Labour Party in Parliament refused to talk to him or his journalists. (He got his revenge later.)

Murdoch's rivals carefully watched what he had done and planned to follow him and attack their own unions too, while at the same time cynically trying to pick up any lost circulation he might have suffered. Murdoch's new managing director, Bill O'Neill, said, 'The print unions played poker with us and they lost.'

One year after Murdoch had moved to Wapping, and with the strikers getting desperate, the 'Alamo', as the miners always called the last battle in any dispute, was drawing near. The pickets had not managed to stop the paper going out. This time the Metropolitan Police had learned lessons from the miners' strike. Traffic lights from the plant would be synchronized, so that the heavy lorries could hit the street at speed and scatter the pickets, and the Metropolitan Police on their own ground had huge strength in numbers.

On Saturday, 24 January 1987, six months before the General Election, the police estimated that 12,000 trades union members marched to Wapping on the first anniversary, but that at least 5,000 were not print union workers. The marchers included many Labour MPs and would-be MPs (some of them Labour Government Ministers today). A union airship balloon, urging Londoners to boycott Murdoch newspapers, flew above the parade. A jazz band led the anniversary march from the back of a lorry which provided the platform and loudspeaker for the usual ranters and ravers to harangue the mob, including of course Arthur Scargill, who received an enormous welcome, because the workers and the Labour Party at that time loved nothing better than a loser.

Hundreds of rent-a-mob hooligans came from that afternoon's football Spion Kops carrying their lager in cans, which they first drank, then urinated in, before hurling them at the police or anybody else on the other side of the road. The London bobbies had not come in riot gear just to parade in it. One of their mates, PC Blakelock, had been killed and hacked to death with machetes by similar rioters in Tottenham on the Broadwater Farm council estate recently and the cops were in no mood for diplomatic discussions.

The lager men ripped up every paving-stone opposite the plant, and as the trucks left, bombarded the vehicles and the cops with the smashed concrete slabs. Like mounted cavalry the police brought up their horses, as they had done at Orgreave, and charged the crowd into scattering in one direction, where the back-up police snatch squads on foot were waiting with batons ready. Not one of them displayed his police identification number.

The rioters tied wire across the road to bring down the horses, tipped over the lorry the jazz band had arrived on, then spilled the petrol on to the tarmac and tried to ignite it with lighted flares. Inside minutes, the police produced a JCB tractor to haul it clear, as smoke grenades were hurled at them.

The rioters alleged that the police carried red paint sprays to identify those who were at the front of the attack. The best story of the Saturday night did not appear in the Sunday papers, nor on TV, which had neglected to cover it, but by Monday it was very big news, with statements by the Home Secretary and questions in Parliament.

The police alleged that the rioters had brought spears, hammers, sharpened stakes, ball-bearings, fireworks and petrol bombs with them. That they tried to set on fire the lorry which carried the band. That the majority of marchers had not taken part in the battle, and that the rioters came from the Stalinist Communist groups, together with the Trotskyists, Anarchists and Militant Tendency.

However, twenty legal observers who had gone along to the demonstration, including some barristers, blamed the police for scores of injuries to non-violent demonstrators by their methods.

It was just five months before the General Election of June 1987, and the 131st demonstration outside Wapping. Over the year 1,394 people were arrested and 1,250 of them convicted by the courts. Over that period the police claimed that forty policemen had been injured, together with eleven police horses.

Once again, the workers, not united, had been defeated. The official inquiry into the riot in 1990 admitted that the police command structure had been dramatically improved since the miners' strike ended in 1985, and the days of the flying pickets winning disputes were over.

Murdoch finally gave the strikers a handout, and they received about a third of what they would have got if they had not gone on strike in the first place, to give him the opening he badly needed.

After the strike the value of his plant in Wapping rocketed by over 300 per cent, as the rest of the old Fleet Street followed his example and moved out from highly valuable real estate sites in central London to other industrial sites along the river.

He had reduced his printworkers from 2,000 to 570. The 1,400 packers in the publishing room had been replaced by 112. His UK profits shot up by 85 per cent and the City of London and Mrs Thatcher's Government marvelled and exulted at his success. Several months later, in the June 1987 election, British national newspapers once more annihilated the Labour Party, Neil Kinnock, the unions and anybody else in a red rosette in another massive outpouring of anti-Labour hysteria.

For the unions and the Labour Party, it was just one more bitter pill to bite on.

As the new technology swept round the world creating the second or maybe the third industrial revolution after steam and electricity, the newspaper proprietors and barons found it was a double-edged weapon.

While the computers saved them a fortune in wages and manpower, they brought in a speed of communication which meant that the message of news, and brand-new information, went flat and boring in about ten minutes, anywhere round the globe. Nothing stayed new for very long and every story was as stale as old shellfish inside a couple of hours. Newspapers printing at 9.00 p.m., to deliver at 9.00 a.m., could not hope to compete with television or radio or even faxes, mobile phones and pagers. Their messages and versions of events twelve hours late were not as attractive or easily saleable.

Hard-up families could manage without a daily paper. Especially when free sheets were allowed to print all the week's TV programmes seven days in advance.

However, the papers did have one big advantage. Radio and television were bound by broadcasting standards of impartiality and decency. Many of them had to have their licences and franchises approved and reviewed by Parliament. These were awarded with stringent assurances of impartiality and decency, and could be, and sometimes were, taken away if there were too many complaints, or if the panel simply thought the standards were too low.

Newspapers had no such restrictions. The ancient 'freedom of the press' attitude, with the very feeble self-regulating Press Council run at that time by newspaper editors from the industry itself, gave newspapers total freedom to print whatever they chose. Which meant there were no restrictions on gossip, scandal, invasion of privacy, investigation, exposure, revelation of anybody's secrets, anywhere at any time, whether it was true or not.

They began to live by the old adage that 'Nothing excites the peasants more than a peep into the King's bedroom'.

Absolutely right too. And if the peep, then the outrage, had a loud Australian raspberry in response to the protest, everybody would want to read the story. It used to be whispered that the *Sun* once circulated a memo to all its journalists saying, 'What makes a great front page is some item or picture which makes their average reader say "Gee Whiz"', which a wag had crossed out and written 'Far Kinnell' instead. He was right.

News, the only news, which now mattered was dirty deeds of the famous. The papers would also in future decide the definition of dirt, and of fame too. Like medieval barons, they would point to culprits of their own choosing and without warning, trial, right of reply, evidence, rules or any pleas of mitigation allowed, put the victim into the stocks for a public flogging without any concern as to whether the 'revelation' would destroy their careers, marriages, reputation or health, or bring enormous grief to their families.

Royalty, rape victims, politicians, sportsmen, show business personalities, opera stars would all be stripped of their talent, achievements and dignity in what the papers called 'THE PUBLIC INTEREST'. Which meant of course that if the story interested the public and enhanced the profits of the media moguls, then it was justified. What the editors never managed to explain successfully was that if it was so essential for the public to know about the story, then why did the paper always try so hard to keep it exclusive to its own front page, instead of spreading it far and wide to all the other papers, or giving it to the police first?

Anyway, from now on the BBC and ITV could have the news first, and the tabloids would settle for the 'sleaze', as it was now called.

The exposure of what the rich and famous got up to would be banner-headlined front-page 'news', and if they were not rich and famous, then holding a 'public position' would do. Even if it was only a bonking traffic warden and the vicar's wife. They too would be publicly birched, with all the consequent headlines, pictures, cartoons, neighbours' quotes and interviews to highlight their shameful behaviour, just as they would have been in the witchcraft days of seventeenth-century Salem, Massachusetts.

Meanwhile, the tits would be on Page Three, in colour as usual.

The days of blackmailers being sent to gaol for threatening to bare the sins of the famous were now over. All peeping toms and extortionists had to do was to sell the secret to the daily and Sunday tabloids instead. But if they were wise they would get an agent to negotiate the price for them. Otherwise the paper might simply listen to the revelation, then throw the informer out of the office in mock disgust, and print the secrets for nothing by exposing what this blackmailing scoundrel had tried to demand ransom for revealing.

Dossiers and files were assiduously built up holding all the tales, secrets and family history which any average household keeps in its cupboard. Skeletons were eagerly researched and bought. And if the family of a Cabinet minister kept quiet about the ancestor who had been put into a lunatic asylum a hundred years ago because he killed the maid by hitting her over the head with a po, they could live in dread that sooner or later a tabloid would 'find a peg to hang it on' in the public interest. And why not, the hacks would plead in all innocence. It's a bloody good story.

Like the KGB in Russia, and the Stasi in East Germany before the Berlin Wall came down, the top tabloids had potential purveyors of 'Far Kinnell' stories on retainers.

The top tabloids even stitch up small-town local weekly papers on a contract, to give first choice of any local shock outrage to them, so they can print it on the day the weekly comes out, and 'spoil it' for any other competitor.

For fifty years in Washington, the head of the FBI, J. Edgar Hoover, reigned supreme and had Presidents as powerful as Jack Kennedy in total fear, because he had files on them all. He knew, from an army of informers, where the bones were buried, giving him the same sort of power that Stalin had, without even bothering to build a gulag.

In the new industry circulation depended on regular revelations about the private lives of the famous appearing every week. These well-known names were not just fair game, but prize foxes and deer, to be hunted, harried, driven underground or bitten to death by the riders and hounds who made their own rules, and did not believe in mercy.

In a short time, MPs such as Keith Hampson, Alan Amos, Ron Brown, Allan Roberts, Cecil Parkinson, Jimmy Dunne, Clare Short, Harvey Proctor, George Galloway, Keith Best, John Browne, even Paddy Ashdown were cruelly hounded for their entirely legal sexual affairs or long-forgotten history or any other behaviour, or simply for being in the wrong place at the wrong time, which would hardly have raised a tut-tut if they had not been MPs.

Royalty suffered too. The new editor of the *Sun*, Kelvin Mackenzie, splashed a picture on the front page of Princess Diana in a bikini, heavily pregnant, despite protests from the Queen's Press Officer, and then ran a front-page editorial claiming that the *Sun* respected the Royal Family's right to privacy, but the pictures were carefree, innocent and delightful. We think she looks terrific, the *Sun* said.

What the Princess thought did not matter.

Funnily enough, when the *Sunday Mirror* a few years later bought and printed pictures of Princess Di exercising in a private gym, and used a hidden camera for bendover shots, the *Sun* screamed that it was 'the act of a peeping tom. Disgusting treatment. Spying on someone's private moments is like stealing their soul'.

Exactly. And if a pervert in the street went into a ladies' lavatory and started taking pictures, he would very quickly be up before the bench, with the papers exposing his dirty deeds. Except of course that in this case the photographers were doing it 'in the public interest'.

There were extensive demands from back-benchers in all parties in Parliament that the Government should take action to curb the shameless excesses which the ferocious competition between the tabloids for circulation and profit out of the new technology was driving the industry into. The serious press deplored the invasion into the private life of any well-known face, from Buckingham Dallas to soap opera. But a grateful Mrs Thatcher was not going to alienate the best union-basher and election propagandist she had ever had. She believed in the free market for a free press no matter whose freedom it destroyed.

Yet even she could not control the back-benchers' Private Members' Bills drawn by ballot. In November 1988, seventeen months after the General Election and less than three years after the move to Wapping, Labour back-bencher Tony Worthington won the draw and announced he would bring in a bill to force newspapers to give a 'Right of Reply' to any victim they had personally pilloried. It would be not just 'in the public interest' but also in the interest of natural justice that any person accused of any misdemeanour was entitled to defend himself.

On its second reading, on a Friday afternoon, the bill received a majority of 100–26. Friday afternoon turnouts are notoriously low, with most MPs having to dash north to their constituency surgeries and party meetings, but it was a significant start.

Despite being filibustered in committee, the bill came back for its final stages and it was obvious from Tony's reception on TV and radio programmes that there was nationwide support for it.

For years in France, Germany, Belgium, Greece, Finland, Norway, Sweden, Canada and some states of the USA, press victims had been entitled to the right of reply. The fact that the legislation existed meant that Germany's biggest paper, *Bild*, with a circulation of five million a day, needed to print only fifteen replies a year, which showed that the system worked. It could in Britain too, where the only grievance procedure was a complaint to the Press Council. Who insisted that if they investigated it, the complainer had to sign a form giving away any right to go to court afterwards, plus his right to be represented by a lawyer, or appear before the Council in person. Although the papers could do both. Just like any medieval baron who also chose the judges and paid for the court.

But, but, but. In April 1989, just one week before the bill got to its final stages, Mrs Prime Minister had had to tell Parliament that the Government had endorsed the EC directive which enshrines in EC legislation the principle of a 'right to reply'. The Home Office Minister, David Renton, insisted that this only covered broadcasting, not newspapers, but he was prepared to announce that in the good old fudge-fudge, British way, the Government would set up a committee led by Sir David Calcutt QC to examine the whole dirty business. Sir David was an expert on the subject and Master of Magdalene College, Cambridge.

Which got the Government off the hook without an embarrassing vote against it from some of its own MPs in Parliament.

Despite the promise, the *Sun* paid for pictures, taken a thousand yards away with a telephoto lens, of Prince Charles 'holding Lady Penny Romsey in a warm lingering embrace at a hideaway villa in Majorca', and then got a rare slap on the wrist from the Press Council for not printing that the lady's distress was due to the fact that her four-year-old daughter had been diagnosed as having cancer.

Prince Charles's relationship with Camilla Parker-Bowles and the incredible Camillagate telephone tapping of their private conversations produced a wave of revulsion right across the country and in Parliament too. Not at their explicit chat, but at the way private conversations could now be tapped into using equipment bought at any shop on Tottenham Court Road, and then published by irresponsible newspapers for high profits.

Sir David Calcutt duly presented his report to the House in June 1990, by which time Mrs Thatcher was once again in deep, deep trouble, this time with her own Party over the poll tax cock-up, and the loss of several key by-elections.

Sir David's committee conceded there was anger and dismay, nay, fury about the way the tabloids were dragging Britain's beloved press freedom, which it had enjoyed since the days of Oliver Cromwell, through the gutter, but it thought the villains 'should be given one final chance' to put their house in order, otherwise legislation would have to be introduced to make them do so.

He recommended a small new Press Complaints Commission should be set up, 'whose members should not represent any particular interest' (ha ha, some hopes), even though his committee was 'persuaded that it would be possible to operate a satisfactory statutory tort of infringement or privacy without harm to serious investigative journalism'.

Which led the Home Office Minister in charge of press freedom, Mr David Mellor QC, to utter the famous words that the media were now drinking in the 'Last Chance Saloon'.

Had they got news for him.

There was no way a beleaguered Mrs T. was going to debate checks and balances on the printed word. She had not even dared to put VAT on newspapers, despite their enormous profits, and her Chancellor was so hard up for cash that he had to put it on gas and electricity for old age pensioners.

Four months later, Thatcher was elbowed out and Major had taken over.

As Kelvin Mackenzie proudly and correctly boasted on his front page, 'It Was The *Sun* Wot Won It'. And, like all mercenaries in war, they would now demand their price for the victory.

Mr Major, surprisingly, looked at first as if he meant business. He promptly set up a new Whitehall department called the

Department of Heritage (now called Culture, Media and Sport by New Labour) which would look after all the arts, media, sport, National Lottery, leisure, and connected purposes.

It would be run by, and tailored for, new Cabinet minister and the Prime Minister's personal friend, the Right Hon. David Mellor QC, the very man who had warned the barons that they were 'drinking in the Last Chance Saloon', and who once again told them that if they did not mend their ways, they were for the Calcutt.

Naturally the papers jibed that his Department would be the Department of Free Tickets and Fun for all MPs, pretending the press never get a freebie for anything. The jibe was a mistake. It simply made the Select Committee for that Department all the more determined to show it had teeth, and they quickly set up an inquiry into 'Privacy and Press Intrusion'. With very good reason too, because just four months after the *Sun* won the Election, new supremo David Mellor was entrapped in a honey-pot of bugged telephones, bought bedroom pictures and an affair with a young actress.

The Sunday tabloid, the *People*, ran the exclusive story by persuading or paying the landlord of the flat to bug his own phone (therefore the papers were not breaking the law), and take pictures of her room with its mattress on the floor, after he had recognized the Cabinet minister. The actress later sold the story and all the details to the press, and David Mellor was kebabbed by the tabloids, scarcely before he had stepped into the arena. Ultimately, he had to resign when the *Sun* bought the actress's story, printed every detail (including some she admitted later she had made up), and made the Rt Hon. QC a laughing stock.

After that nobody could stop the editors' blood lust. The Chancellor of the Exchequer, Norman Lamont, was hounded out of office when he moved into Eleven Downing Street, and a firm of estate agents inadvertently let off the basement flat of his Notting Hill home to a woman running a 'sex therapy' business.

The media instantly named her 'Miss Whiplash', then accused Lamont of using public funds to get her evicted, then of not paying his hotel bill at the Tory Party Conference. They finally used the new technology to reveal he had been overdrawn on his credit card limit twenty-two times (even buying booze with it in a red-light area) and no wonder the country was in a financial mess if Lamont was running it. Even though he did keep having to run out of crisis meetings in Europe to explain why he had been buying wine in Paddington.

From then on Mr Major, an honest guy, took fright. Newspapers paraded the lurid details of how twenty years before, as a young single man, he had had an affair with a woman much older than himself. Then came pictures of his teenage son (now a happily married man) skylarking in a red dress at a private party.

They gleefully revealed that twenty-five years ago, a Tory woman Cabinet minister had her first child months before she married its father. Then, in the next couple of years, they added the scalps of Steven Norris, Tim Yeo, Alan Duncan, Gary Waller, David Ashby, Dennis Skinner and suicide death Stephen Milligan to their trophies, even using entrapment and bugs to try to persuade MPs to accept cash for putting down questions. Which two stupid Tory MPs fell for, out of the twenty who were offered it.

The regular weekly headlines meant that politicians had now better tread in fear of their masters or pay with their hide.

And the Calcutt threats were as dead as David Mellor's career.

Fortunately, the long tradition of the independence of Parliament's Select Committees, consisting of about twelve or thirteen experienced back-benchers sitting around a horse-shoe-style table and cross-examining witnesses at length, still exists and is a much cherished, highly respected method of democracy at work.

All MPs are very good at asking questions and at knowing when these are being dodged too, and Select Committees have special powers to send for people and papers. It would be a contempt of Parliament for anyone to refuse to appear, and very few ignore the warning. Experienced MPs, believe it or not, listen closely to what their voters complain about in the pub, and relish the chance to put the same questions to the top brass who spend their life surrounded by sycophants and unquestioning yes men. The Select Committees are totally independent of any Government direction or influence.

So, in the autumn of 1992, following the Mellor exposure, the all-party Select Committee on National Heritage which covered the press decided to investigate the serious concern about privacy and media intrusion. I sat on it as an ex-Fleet Street columnist. It was chaired by Gerald Kaufman MP, a former *Daily Mirror* executive and head of Prime Minister Harold Wilson's Press Department. Other members with long-standing experience of Parliament or the media, even of their lash, included former Cabinet minister Paul Channon, Alan Howarth, John Gorst, Toby Jessel, John Maxton, John Sykes, Gyles Brandreth, Brian Davies, Jim Callaghan (Heywood and Middleton) and Dr John Blackburn.

The first problem the Committee had was to try to define 'privacy'. And who better to do that than the top lawyers of the Bar Council, who were against a privacy law because they said 'privacy' could not be defined in court to satisfy lawyers.

Our Committee asked to interview Sir Desmond Browne QC, Mr James Michael, a senior lecturer in law from University College, and good old Arthur Davidson QC, my mate and former MP for Accrington, who by now had risen to become the Chairman of the Fleet Street Lawyers' Society, and the legal director of the Mirror Group of newspapers.

By sheer coincidence, the *Sun* carried a front-page story the previous day about a poor bloke who took a bath in his own house and by mistake, in the steam, and because he had not been wearing his glasses, picked up what he thought was a tube of anal cream and used it. Unfortunately it was not anal cream, but Superglue, and he glued his buttocks together instead. Absolutely hilarious. But had the *Sun* the legal right to destroy the man's privacy and make him a laughing stock, M'Lud?

He was not a famous person. Now he would not be able to go into the pub any more or go to work for the next twenty years without crude jokes and a dozen nicknames. Now he was destined to be a permanent figure of fun and ridicule for the rest of his life, simply because of a bathroom accident.

Sir Desmond had not read the front-page story. But it seems it had emerged because the man's wife had told her next-door neighbour. 'Oh well, that puts it in the public domain,' said the lawyers. Which means that any freelance journalist can sell the bathroom secret to a paper who can then syndicate it around the world (and did). So it is up yours, Mr Stickybum.

Just like the Victorians used to laugh and jeer at the Elephant Man and avidly pay to see freak shows of the disabled, or the lions in Regent's Park Zoo, press victims are now legitimate exhibits for cruel ridicule. Although the lawyers did admit there ought to be a law against 'surreptitious surveillance' by long-range cameras on to private property and that they had been advocating such a law since 1981.

The Committee went on to study and hear weeks of evidence from over fifty organizations ranging from the Press Association to Women Against Rape, the Press Complaints Commission, the Association of British Editors, several newspapers, ITN, the BBC, police experts on bugging and long-range photography, and even, in private, Mr Charles Anson, the Press Secretary to the Queen. When he asked to give his evidence in private it infuriated the tabloids, because they would not be able to print any juicy details of the Palace he might reveal (including details of bribes offered to maids who worked at the Palace looking after the royal bedrooms). It is an outrage, the press yelled. An abuse of democracy and press freedom, said the *Sun*, who once broke an embargo on the Queen's Christmas Speech by publishing it three days early, and infuriating the rest of the papers.

Some of the evidence the Committee heard was very moving. Especially from the widows of servicemen killed by the IRA, whose privacy and grief had been totally wrecked by photographers climbing trees at the funeral, camping on their doorstep, interviewing the relations, demanding old family pictures, phoning them at all hours of the night, frightening pregnant relatives, invading local pubs offering money for stories, all at a time of horrendous shocking death, and asking the women to pose for photographs and 'try to look like a grieving widow three days after her husband has died', then persecuting the kids to pose because 'Daddy would have liked it'.

Jill Saward, the daughter of a vicar, who was brutally raped by men who broke into an Ealing vicarage at Christmas-time told us how the police had revealed the details to the media within nine hours of the crime, with one tabloid printing her photograph with a black line simply blocking out her eyes. Even though the law stated quite clearly that it is illegal to identify rape victims. The *News of the World* carried cartoons of the crime, she claimed, and photographers hired a room in the pub across the road to take long-range pictures.

Another witness had been falsely accused by the press of taking letters from Princess Anne when she worked for her, and had been besieged in her house for days. The Police Scientific Development branch told us how easy it would be to take long-range pictures of the Duchess of York sunbathing topless beside a private bathing pool in France.

The highlight of the inquiry came when the committee sent for Mr Kelvin Mackenzie, the editor of the *Sun*, and its other leading executives, to examine the written evidence they had submitted. Murdoch had made Mackenzie editor in 1982 at the age of thirty-six when he got rid of the previous editor, Larry

Lamb, who had failed to latch on to the obvious fact that bingo was going to be a circulation soaraway, if the *Sun* did not introduce it quickly to catch up on the *Star* and the *Mirror*.

Kelvin Mackenzie was, and is, undoubtedly the sharpest news-sniffer, copy-taster and presenter the British press has ever had. He had the knack of switching on a laser beam which could cut to the heart of a story in seconds, explaining what it was all about (or what he wanted the reader to think it was all about) in three lines, adding a few puns, cartoons, wisecracks and even camp Frankie Howerd shrill, shocked innuendoes to liven up and slant any message his master wanted to sell. He had a boredom threshold even lower than that of the average Essex-man, lager-swigging, belching, spitting and farting readers the paper specialized in at that time, and produced a highly profitable money-making machine for Rupert Murdoch's other activities. If there was one man whose views totally reflected the Thatcher years of Southern bias, jingoism, loadsamoney Harry Enfield, dogs' bollocks, xenophobia, gay-bashing, hating loony lefties, social security scroungers, beggars, dossers, squatters, demonstrators, students, gaolbirds and the IRA, it was Kelvin. And if anything he hated politicians (except for Mrs Thatcher) more than any of them.

Which all made for a 'bloody good read'.

His most famous headlines were 'FREDDIE STARR ATE MY HAMSTER', 'STICK IT UP YOUR JUNTA' and 'GOTCHA' after the sinking of the *Belgrano*, with the death of hundreds of Argentinian servicemen as she sailed away from the battle zone.

The *Sun* printers had even gone on strike themselves during the miners' strike because of the gross personal abuse of Scargill and the paper calling the miners the scum of the earth.

Then, after alleging that Elton John had consorted with rent boys, it cost the *Sun* £1.5 million in libel damages and costs, but

316

nothing stopped the daily headlines of shock-horror nudge-and-wink strewth.

Consequently, the public area of committee room fifteen was packed with journalists from every aspect of the print and electronic media, and TV cameras. Making one of his rare public appearances, Mackenzie had come to perform for his adoring public (and they had better be adoring because most of them might want to work for him one day), and perform he did.

With an air of injured innocence, he immediately accused the Committee of MPs of being 'hostile' to the press and biased. Astonishingly, after the way the News International papers had battered Neil Kinnock, the Labour Party, the unions and any red rosette for the past twenty years, here was the Roman Emperor crying foul at the slaves on the cross.

'If the next Defender of the Faith [Prince Charles] is going to be somebody who cuckolds somebody else's wife, I can quite easily justify publishing tape-recordings of tapped private conversations,' he said, for all the world like a Witchfinder General. 'If it's all right to read about it in Timbuktu, then it's all right to read it here,' Mackenzie proclaimed.

Like all bosses who ever appear before Select Committees, he was not used to being interrupted when he pontificated at length, and became very angry when we tried to 'edit' his replies. Play the game, chaps, he protested. I want to respond and you keep banging in.

Why had the *Sun* bugged every mobile phone around their office two months earlier, then reported all the conversations? It was in the public interest to show how scanners work, Kelvin said. We did not do it to infringe their privacy. We did not print their names. We did it to show that if you go to Tandy's and pay £100 you can do this sort of thing.

Mackenzie went on to tell the Committee that Lindi St Clair, the woman known, or not known to some of you, as Miss

Whiplash, had made a whole series of allegations about people in public life, and named them – and extraordinary names too, I might add. We could say it is in the public interest, and then what would happen is that all you gentlemen would troop down to the Strand (to the Law Courts), pick up huge amounts of tax-free wonga, and say thank you very much.

Mr Mackenzie defended the Ealing rape case as a story which had 'touched the hearts of the nation very much'. The *Sun*'s headline of 'Our John has gone potty and glued up his botty' had been immortal, he argued. He would not disagree that the grief of widows should be protected, but who a Cabinet minister is having an affair with, and how many times a night, and does he wear a Chelsea kit, is a matter of taste and judgement. Who is going to decide on that?

Well, not the victim, that's for sure.

Mr Mackenzie did regret what the *Sun* had printed about the Hillsborough disaster (when ninety-five football fans were crushed to death and the paper accused drunken Liverpool supporters of punching, kicking and urinating on police officers, firemen, and ambulance crews as they tried to revive the victims). Unfortunately, he had believed what a Tory MP had told the paper, and the police had not denied it.

It had to be said that Kelvin Mackenzie took on his political critics and turned in an astonishing bravura performance. The sycophantic audience of scribbling journalists loved it and said so in their papers and television and radio reports the day after. He got rave reviews. Unfortunately, as Oscar Wilde did a hundred years before, he played to the gallery and not the jury, and lost the verdict.

Every single MP on the Committee of six Labour and five Tories shook their heads in the private closed session afterwards, and even the grateful Tories who had heaved a sigh of astonished relief at winning the 1992 election (Wot the *Sun* had Won for them), voted thumbs up for legislation to protect media victims.

The Select Committee demanded an Ombudsman who could listen to appeals against the self-regulation verdicts of the Press Complaints Commission. The Commission rules were, and still are, simply a Highway Code for editors. Unfortunately, if newspapers do knock somebody down and seriously injure them, there is no fine, no insurance payout, no loss of licence, and the offender is not even named and shamed by the inquiry, or sacked or suspended like any red-card footballer. The editor is totally free to go away and do it again the very next day after printing a small apology at the bottom of page nine.

We said a Privacy Bill should be introduced to make it illegal to take photographs on private property, or bug telephones, or publish intimate pictures without consent, to buy or sell tapes or pictures without consent, and to bring back the Victorian law of 'besetting' premises to control door-stepping, stalking, and harassment by freelancers. Although the Committee did make it very clear they were unanimous about the protection of the 'public interest', and that politicians who chose to enter the arena, together with other TV stars, etc., should not expect to escape public scrutiny, and should be exposed if they said one thing and did another.

But like any other accused, they too should have an automatic right of reply to defend themselves. We said there should be no restrictions either on press investigations of any action which might involve a criminal offence.

And what happened?

Nothing happened. A terrified Conservative Government, way behind in the opinion polls, meekly replied to the recommendations of the Committee by saying – that while they agreed with the recommendations for an Ombudsman, the Government at this stage thought it better to ask the Press Council to put its own house in order once again with another last chance, and to try harder to improve its own self-regulation with a new code of practice.

A few months later, Kelvin Mackenzie surprisingly moved on from his job as editor of the *Sun* Wot Won It, and by January 1994, the paper stopped supporting the Tories, with a headline saying 'What Fools We Were'. By 1997 it was advising its readers to vote Labour because it knew the Tories could not win and the paper could not bear to back a loser.

After Labour won the election in 1997, the tabloids blithely carried on as normal, assassinating, or severely wounding, politicians such as Foreign Secretary Robin Cook over his divorce, Ron Davies, Harriet Harman, Peter Mandelson, Geoffrey Robinson, and sportsmen Glen Hoddle and Will Carling. None of whom escaped either execution or prolonged torture on the rack for staying silent about their alleged sins, none of which was a crime. Although they were of 'public interest' and sold newspapers.

In May 1999 the *Sun* was again castigated by the rest of the daily papers for paying an alleged £100,000 for a topless photograph of Sophie Rhys-Jones, who was due to marry the Queen's son, Prince Edward, at Westminster Abbey a few days later. The paper casually apologized and paid Sophie Rhys-Jones £75,000 in compensation.

Which is more than the directors of Newcastle United got, or Lawrence Dallaglio, the England rugby captain, received, when *News of the World* reporters obtained secret tape-recordings of private conversations by impersonating foreign businessmen and sports sponsors. Their job and business prospects were severely damaged by 'off the record' late-night chats in bars and bedrooms. In that month too, the son of Camilla Parker-Bowles, Prince Charles's friend, was 'exposed' for taking cocaine in Cannes, and Lenny Henry accused of having a secret girlfriend which, despite his strenuous denials, caused a lot of grief to his wife, Dawn French.

As expected, the Press Complaints Commission called the publication of Sophie Rhys-Jones's topless photo 'a grave error' and said 'such a mistake must never happen again'. Ha. Ha. Ha.

On 9 June 1999, George Galloway, MP for Glasgow Kelvin, raised the issue in an adjournment debate in Parliament. Mr Galloway is no stranger to the tabloids, or to the libel courts where he is not without success. He is also a newspaper columnist. He gave full details of the *News of the World*'s 'entrapment' tactics in several other cases and asked how the Press Complaints Commission could be independent when the editor of the *News of the World* sat on it.

But the Labour Government's response, as could be expected, was that the Government was committed to the current self-regulatory system.

A system which plainly does not work except in favour of the newspapers who run it. Not one word of George Galloway's debate appeared in the tabloid newspapers.

The simple fact is that no change can get through Parliament without the consent of the Government at a very high level. And at that level the only thing which concerns the Cabinet is the next General Election, and how soon it will be here.

Tabloid papers can and do have a great influence on those five million voters who take no interest in politics from one election to the next, and simply vote on impulse depending on whether they think the Party Leader is a goodie or a baddie, or a wise man or a fool. Or even if they think he will win, because everybody likes to back the winner.

In which case Mr Murdoch had better support Tony Blair at the next election in 2001, because the Tories have no chance of turning over Labour's majority of 186 seats.

But, but, but. Mr Murdoch's dilemma is that he does not want the EC currency, the euro, to be introduced in Britain. The Labour Party, however, does, and the Tory party does not. So does he back the losers, the Tories? Or back the winners, Labour?

Any kid at school knows that if you take a pound coin around Europe and change it into francs at the French border and then guilders in Holland, etc., etc., right across Europe, then you will end up with less than 60p. The money-changers will have taken the rest.

Global operators in TV, news, films and sport like Mr Murdoch can often make more money by switching their product from one currency and country to another than they can by manufacturing the goods in the first place. So obviously they do not want a single currency where the French, British, Italians or anybody else can instantly measure how much they are paying for the programme.

The technology too is making it harder and harder for the dog to pee on the moving lamp-post. Worldwide websites can now break the news first. Independents can produce virtual journalism too, without having to bother about libel or advertising. Before long victims will be sending their own version of events around the world to take revenge, and give their side of the story.

A simple little change to amend the law of copyright would make two-thirds of the problem disappear (and so would a large proportion of tabloid profits). Currently, the law says that the copyright of a photograph belongs to the person who took the picture. He can sell it, publish it, use it, in any way he chooses. He can do the same with tape-recordings too, whether taken with consent or not.

But why should that be so? Anybody taking pictures or making recordings of Andrew Lloyd Webber's *Phantom of the Opera* would be hauled up before the magistrates for attempting to sell them.

Why then should a person's face or voice not be his own copyright and intellectual property? There would of course be no law against taking photographs or making recordings. The breaking of the law would only occur if they were sold on, or published for gain, without that person's permission.

Why should Cherie Blair not have the right to stop a picture of her in her bathing costume, on a hotel beach, from being sold around the world and splashed all over the pages of morning newspapers? Would any mother of four children welcome that intrusion?

Sportsmen, politicians, show business personalities would not object to the law. They love publicity. And there could be an exemption clause for pictures and tapes taken of a person at work doing their job.

But the profit motive for intrusion would cease. The profit motive which killed Princess Diana trying to escape the chasing photographers and the profit motive which has destroyed the lives, families and career of so many victims who had committed no crime except that of creating gossip.

Will any government put such a law on the statute book?

No. Not while it ever has to face elections and a hostile press. But the European Union might, and one day probably will, and legislate that privacy is a basic human right, just as much as free speech and sexual or racial equality.

Fifteen

ALL POLITICAL CAREERS END IN TEARS

A T least, that is what Enoch Powell should have said when he sounded his prophet's warning many years ago. But Enoch wasn't a tabloid journalist. So he simply said that all political careers end in failure. And they do. Even the highest Cabinet minister or Prime Minister ultimately gets voted out, driven out or reshuffled, and ends up like Mrs Thatcher, sacked by her own Party, leaving for Buckingham Palace in her limousine with tears streaming down her cheeks. But more often than not it is the media that kills them with deaths by a thousand soundbites.

In March 1999 it happened to me when the Sunday papers were tipped off that police had raided a Thai massage parlour in Northampton three months earlier, and found me in it.

Why did I go there? Who knows? I don't. Maybe it was mischievous devilment at the age of sixty-five. Maybe, like those old guys in the long-running TV programme *Last of the Summer Wine*, it was one last adventure before old age finally took over.

I had been happily married for forty years, and still am. But I can tell all those blokes who haven't yet reached sixty-five, that all of us are still eighteen in the head from time to time. There is a self-destruct button just waiting to be pressed, and sometimes the temptation to press it is irresistible. Guys who have been adventurers, warriors, chance-takers and macho combatants living on adrenaline and the tang of the arena, will forever think they can drink all night, still run a marathon in the morning, and win the Lottery in the afternoon. Like kids scrumping apples, even if their mother has a bowl of beautiful fruit on the table at home, some of us are hooked on risk.

The list is endless. Bill Clinton, Hugh Grant, George Michael, Ron Davies, David Mellor, all the way back to Jeremy Thorpe, John Profumo and Prime Minister Gladstone. None could resist pressing the button. Even footballers do the daftest things when TV cameras are on them, ranging from Eric Cantona jumping into the crowd to attack a fan, to David Beckham giving a sly kick to an Argentinian, which was caught on screen and probably lost England the World Cup.

In November 1998 I completed thirty years in Parliament. The Government Chief whip, Ann Taylor, asked me to move the Queen's Speech at the opening of the new session on Tuesday the 24th. It is just about the highest honour a back-bencher can achieve. The Prime Minister writes the Queen's Speech for her of course, then after she has read it from the throne, the Cabinet and Opposition and back-benchers troop back to the Commons to debate it. But before Tony Blair, William Hague and Paddy Ashdown start to lead the main debate, a long-serving old stalwart back-bencher, plus one of the newest younger MPs, are awarded the honour of moving and seconding the proceedings, to a packed house and television.

This introduction is expected to be a fairly relaxed overture by an old pro who has seen it all before and inevitably has been in the House since all the current Party Leaders were lads, laced with a few jokes, anecdotes and fatherly advice. It can be an absolute disaster (and sometimes has been in the past) but if the mood is set right and the crack crackles then it is a joy. For me, with fingers crossed, it went very well. Linda Clarke QC, a talented newcomer and barrister from Edinburgh Pentlands, seconded it with superb aplomb and Tony Blair passed back from the front bench a personal handwritten note which I will always cherish.

My daughter Lucy, a journalist in Barnsley and Doncaster, had just won the 'Yorkshire News Reporter of the Year' competition for gaining the first exclusive interview with William Hague's mother (Lucy said she would not write anything rotten because her dad was an MP too and she knew how much it hurt) and William Hague was kind enough to mention it.

In my speech I spoke about the old-timers left in the new Labour Party now, with me, Dennis Skinner and Tony Benn, all having three constituencies butting on to each other, being like Compo, Foggy and Clegg in *Last of the Summer Wine*, reliving old battles and getting into scrapes. And how thirty years on Labour was still battling to abolish the House of Lords, introduce a minimum wage, and sort out the 'Common Market'. So 'What's New, Pussycat?', as Tom Jones was singing in 1968. And still is.

Altogether a great, memorable day to preserve on a family video.

All public performers or arena gladiators know that the narcotic of triumphant adrenaline continues for a day or two afterwards and the feeling of walking on air, even for a battle-scarred old veteran, is exhilarating.

Two days later I was driving home up the M1 at three o'clock on Thursday afternoon when on a crazy impulse I turned off to go for a massage in Northampton. Unfortunately, and unknown to me, the premises next door to a chip shop in a shopping parade had been the source of complaints from neighbouring shops, who objected to its presence and demanded its closure, along with a similar establishment a hundred yards or so down the road. Northampton is a pleasant, law-abiding middle-class town and the citizens were insisting on police action to remove the place.

Ten minutes after I went into the private room and was ready for the massage all hell let loose, to coin a cliché. The staff were screaming, doors slamming, and somebody was pounding on the

10 DOWNING STREET
LONDON SW1A 2AA

THE PRIME MINISTER

27th Nov.

Dear Joe,

well done on
the P.S. — it was a
brilliant speech and had the
whole House behind you.

Thank you!

your ever

Tony

door of the room I was in, smashing it down with a sledgehammer. In the few minutes it took to break through I got dressed and honestly thought it was a raid by a rival gang to rob the place or wreck it. About four or five men burst in, one using a hand-held camcorder. None of them was very tall, and all were wearing jeans, casual jackets or sweaters.

They were amicable and friendly and immediately introduced themselves as police officers. 'Don't worry, mate,' one chatted, 'we're not interested in any customers. You are not committing any offence. We are looking for illegal immigrants and drugs. But we need your name and address in case there is a row about the damage and if we have to contact you to prove we didn't use any excessive force, except on the door.'

It looked as if I was the only customer in the place at the time, so I readily agreed to cooperate. But having had long experience of knowing how any single thing involving an MP has a way of ending up in the papers, I gave my other Christian name, and said J. William Ashton, and my London address at the Barbican together with its telephone number, which was in the London phone book.

And why not? It's my name and it's where I live most of the week. Nobody asked for my occupation but the polite detective said he had to have some ID and I didn't have any on me. However, there was some in my car. We walked back to where it was parked and I then showed him my diary with the Barbican address and phone number on the front page, together with my Switch bank card with my name and initials on it, and he was satisfied. He admired my car which I had bought just two weeks before and obviously noted the number.

'You probably won't hear anything more about it,' he said as he left, and then I drove away, but knowing I had made one daft mistake. When the bobby asked me for my date of birth I realized that not only had I celebrated thirty years in Parliament I had also reached the age of sixty-five at the same time and I was going to look a bloody laughing stock as an old age pensioner, so I foolishly knocked six months off.

I didn't tell a soul about the incident. It was no use spoiling Christmas, and two months later when it got towards the end of January it was time to heave a sigh of relief. Until Tuesday, 26 January when the postman knocked on my Barbican door with a recorded delivery from the detective constable asking me to travel up to Northampton to meet him, because my car was registered in Sheffield and it didn't add up with an address in London. It was pretty obvious then that if the police had contacted the car dealer I had bought it from they could soon have traced that I was an MP.

Once again it was imperative to consult with my lifelong friend and saviour, Arthur Davidson QC, who met me inside the hour. Arthur, as a barrister, wasn't allowed to approach the police directly, but made a quick phone call to Ian Burton, of Burton Copeland, one of the top solicitors at Lincoln's Inn. He is a lawyer renowned for his expertise on media affairs, who had handled problems for some of the most publicized names in London. I told Ian and Arthur that no sexual activity had taken place, that it had never been offered, nor had I paid for it.

Ian contacted the Northampton police and got them to agree to send someone to London rather than have me visit Northampton and face the possibility of prying eyes. On 9 February a Northampton police inspector travelled to Ian's office and told us that his principal purpose was to identify me. He laughed and seemed to agree that it was a classic case of Sod's Law that I happened to be in that place at that time.

We all then shook hands and parted amicably and I got the feeling that all of us thought it would be the last of it. However, Ian Burton warned me that in any situation it is impossible to stop gossip. There will always be someone somewhere who finds it an unbearable burden to keep a piece of gossip to himself, but the papers would be very foolish to print any defamatory story without evidence and proof.

Several weeks before the meeting with Ian Burton and the police inspector I had been in long discussions with another group of London lawyers regarding televised football and the millions of pounds poured into the game, particularly from BSkyB to the Premier League. Since 1990 I had also been an unpaid Director of the Premier League club Sheffield Wednesday, and Chairman of the Parliamentary All-Party Football Group, which had over 150 MPs and Lords among its members.

The previous September, when Parliament was in recess, Rupert Murdoch, whose company owned BSkyB, had made a bid worth £650 million to buy Manchester United FC, the biggest and richest football club in the world. Manchester United was four times bigger than the average Premier League club and with its wealth was virtually unbeatable.

Football had become extensively televised by satellite seven years earlier. The millions injected by BSkyB had actually helped the sport immensely by paying for new stadiums following the Hillsborough disaster and by bringing the games to fans in pubs who never before could afford to travel to pay to see the big matches. The game was moving into worldwide global satellite entertainment with a turnover of multi-million dollars but none of the global competitions could ever be a success without Manchester United in the tournament. Whoever owned the club would hold all the stakes on both sides of the television bargaining table.

Rupert Murdoch was determined to buy Manchester United, but he also owned the biggest football television station in Britain, BSkyB. He would in effect become both the biggest buyer and the biggest seller in the business and selling to himself. To MPs, there was no way this could be classed as fair trading. Our Parliamentary Group, with MPs from all parties right across the country, objected strongly. How could this be 'in the public interest'? Surely the bid should be examined by the Monopolies and Mergers Commission before the deal was allowed to go through?

The buy-out aroused enormous controversy, with practically the whole football community against it, including clubs, fans, other newspapers not owned by Murdoch, and all politicians too. Our Football Group of MPs played it absolutely fairly and invited both Manchester United and the executives of BSkyB to Parliament to hear their side of the case. We even invited BSkyB to hold a football forum at the Labour Party Conference for a question and answer session with the delegates and fans. As Chairman I saw to it that the 'right of reply' was extended fairly and squarely to both sides.

Peter Mandelson, who had built bridges with the *Sun* and Murdoch during the 1997 election campaign, had become the newly appointed Secretary of State for Trade and Industry in September and he had the power to give the bid the go-ahead or to refer it to the Monopolies and Mergers Commission for approval. Murdoch had been delighted when years earlier Mrs Thatcher had turned down Parliamentary demands that his attempt to buy *The Times* and the *Sunday Times* should be examined by the Commission, and he had been warmly supportive of her ever after.

This time, however, Peter Mandelson took stock and realized that football had millions of voters, and while it is easy for any government to outvote 150 MPs from the Opposition Party, it is a different matter when most of the opposition comes from its own MPs. He had no option, no doubt backed by Tony Blair, but to put the bid up for examination by the Commission, and allow any objectors to make their case. Which our group did, with our detailed written submission of evidence followed by a lengthy cross-examination of myself, Deputy Chair Joan Walley, MP for Port Vale, and our expert researcher Phil French, from the Football Trust. We got the impression from the Commission that it was very favourably received and I went back and spread the news to the MPs and all the football directors I knew up and down the country that Murdoch would lose.

At the beginning of the year Peter Mandelson was involved in an uproar with all the newspapers. First with an allegation of homosexuality on the BBC's *Newsnight* then, with further stories that he had borrowed over £370,000 from Treasury Minister Geoffrey Robinson, before the election, to buy a house in Notting Hill. Although why that should be a sacking offence nobody could fathom out, except that it got a lot of bad publicity. Peter quit his ministerial job. So too did Geoffrey Robinson, also by sheer coincidence a major shareholder and director of Premier League club Coventry City, and astonishingly, in six months of football and tabloid turmoil, the England team manager, Glen Hoddle, was ousted for three stupid sentences about the disabled in a taped telephone conversation with a *Times* reporter. The Football Association Chief Executive, Graham Kelly, was forced out, together with the FA Chairman and Keith Wiseman, after hysterical headlines for some minor infringement of wheeling and dealing to get England an extra vote to stage the World Cup. Meanwhile the Premier League chief, Peter Leaver QC, also had to quit over another proposed BSkyB TV deal.

All of this, no doubt whatsoever, was an amazing run of football coincidence as the Commission studied its evidence.

Back at the Ashton home at the end of February, while I was in London, the family had a visit from a local *Sun* reporter and photographer who had read that our cat did tricks. Such as peeing against an electricity socket by the side of the kitchen fire and sending sparks shooting across the hearth. Could they take pictures inside the house, please, and even if they were not printed they would send a set as a souvenir. Anybody could be forgiven for thinking that the cat was a setup, I said to my cat-loving wife when I arrived home later.

Friday, 12 March was the deadline day for the Monopolies and Mergers Commission to hand its BSkyB report to the new Secretary of State for Trade and Industry, Stephen Byers MP, who had taken over from Peter Mandelson. On Sky News that morning it was strongly featured as 'Decision Day' when the future of televised football would be decided. Yet strangely enough, it wasn't mentioned at all on BBC Breakfast News. The BBC was right. There was no news. The report had to go to the Minister and no doubt the Cabinet for them to study it for a month before an official announcement was made.

Somebody had got it wrong somewhere.

Saturday, 13 March was Maggie's birthday. I had gone to the barber's at ten o'clock in the morning when the phone rang at home and a voice saying the caller was from a national Sunday paper asked for me, and then, when my daughter said I was out, said, 'We have heard the *News of the World* is running a story tomorrow that your dad has been caught by the police in a brothel.'

It was as brutal and full in the face as that. No attempt to wait until I returned half an hour later to take the call personally. No attempt to soften the blow in any way. Not even the decency to allow me to contact my family, or tell my agent, Sally Jackson, first. They blasted the accusation in the cruellest fashion and caused serious distress, shock and mental torment to my wife, daughter and colleagues in the Bassetlaw constituency Labour party.

No politician expects any sympathy from marauding journalists but even their families don't get any either. It is a fallacy to think that victims are warned in advance and advised to leave town and hide, so that the paper can preserve the exclusivity of its story. The news hits the family home with all the impact of a Wild West outlaw raid.

Inside an hour our house was surrounded back and front by carloads of news hounds and cameramen. A white Transit van with an aerial was parked permanently at the back next to the telegraph pole, and the procession of journalists walked down the path, ringing the bell, banging on the door, shouting through the letter-box and pushing notes through it every ten minutes. The phone rang non-stop, even with the answerphone on, with a bombardment of calls. We couldn't switch it off because we knew my agent and other Party workers who were also being bombarded would be trying to contact me.

My wife Maggie and daughter Lucy were shell-shocked and stunned and in a highly distressed state as I quietly explained the true story of what had happened.

Saturday is an impossible day to contact friends and colleagues. Even if you have their home private number, they have gone shopping, or are not in, for some other reason, and all office numbers are useless. Naturally the newsdesks of the papers had telephoned the Labour Party standby press officer, who contacted the Chief Whip, etc., etc., but in the chaos of door-banging, bell-ringing and having virtually to sit on the stairs away from windows and long-range cameras, it was quite literally a fox hunt.

Even more so when I drove to my brother-in-law's council maisonette to take him two tickets for the match at Hillsborough that afternoon because it was pretty obvious that if I went to the game there would be more cameras on me than on the players. Fortunately our garage at the back has an electronic door which can be operated with a remote control from inside the car, so I could drive straight out, chased immediately by two other cars loaded with journalists. Fortunately, too, they didn't know the cul-de-sacs of Sheffield council estates like I did. So it wasn't too difficult to lose them.

But there was no way I was leaving the family alone in the house and they were adamant they were not going to be driven out of it by any ambush, siege or hunt. 'Tell us the story and we will leave,' the raiders yelled at the closed door. The story of what? I don't know what the papers were to print tomorrow, or what they would accuse me of. How could I defend myself if I didn't know what I was charged with?

It was a long, long day and eventually the siege lasted until Monday afternoon. Clive Betts, the Sheffield whip, managed to push his way through to my front door and give me a number to telephone the Labour Press Office and Chief Whip Ann Taylor. I told them what I had told my family. They too said to say nothing.

Later I managed to contact Arthur Davidson and also Ian Burton, who rang the *News of the World* and suggested they tread carefully. The *News of the World* reporter at the door asked me to open it, which I warily did, to see as expected a photographer taking my picture on private property (against the Press Complaints Commission's rules but no doubt 'in the public interest'), but because of Ian Burton's intervention, the following day's front-page smash didn't give my name, but referred to 'a senior Labour MP'.

However, the *Mail on Sunday* had no such qualms. They simply took a chance and let their front page spread the headlines of 'Massage Parlour Mystery' and 'Veteran Labour Party MP Joe Ashton was last night embroiled in a mystery over a police raid on a massage parlour . . .' and from then on the 'news' was in the public domain as it is called and anybody or everybody could jump on a horse and join the hunt for the fox. The headlines from then on shrieked and roared like whizzbang firecrackers on Millennium night. Any and every combination of the words MP, massage, Thai, illegal immigrants, police, raid, sixty-five-year-old son of toil, resign, lies, etc., etc., is irresistible to all news editors, feature writers, columnists, leader writers, cartoonists and readers.

When it comes to selling newspapers those words are pure gold.

As for the fox in the hole and his family there is nothing they can do but lie low, suffer and take the blows. We couldn't even get to the porch to take in the Mother's Day flowers our Lucy had ordered. If the fox comes out of his hole to defend himself nobody will listen to his pleas of innocence or his request for a fair trial. Trials by newspapers last just one day, as they did in medieval times, and any defence will be instantly ridiculed, hammered and laughed at on the page opposite, to provide yet another day's headlines and scorn, to bring even more publicity and grief.

On the other hand, if the victim doesn't say anything, then the story must be true because he 'never denied it'. I had never said one word to the papers yet in big headlines they were screaming that I had given a false name to the police. How did they know? Who had told them that? The leak could only have originated from a police source, even if it wasn't the police who actually told the press.

By Monday morning the hounds and tally-ho were barking mad and slavering at fever-pitch. Naturally the huntsmen hadn't stopped at our house, but were scouring Northampton too for any other angle or interview. We were still locked in although our Lucy bravely went to work as usual, with the cameramen outside taking pictures of her driving away and saying she was my wife. Lucy's good colleagues at the *Barnsley Chronicle* had cut out and deleted every mention of our nightmare from the morning papers to help ease her pain and distress. These people were journalists who were deeply sympathetic because they knew full well how merciless a flogging from the national tabloids could be.

To be fair, the long-suffering, patient journalists and photographers on our doorstep did not break any Press Complaint Commission rules either. They had not trespassed or caused any personal problems and were as fed up as we were. These journalists are not the ones at the top who demand sex, sex, sex in every

336

story. Newspapers are an industry with fifty trained reporters chasing every job. The media studies courses at universities churn out thousands of newcomers every year, and if they don't do the dirty work which tabloid editors demand, they will be out on the street in a week and scratching for freelance money on doorsteps.

The editors themselves are no different to football managers. Highly paid and totally vulnerable to instant dismissal if the circulation figures drop in the same way as a football club drops points. And who suffers from this frantic slaughter of famous foxes by trained hounds? Everybody except those who own the medium and take the profit, the pleasure and the power.

By Monday afternoon Arthur Davidson and Ian Burton agreed we had to make a statement to counteract the fantasy stories. This was not going to be a one-day, tee hee, what a lark, pants down, yah boo, jibe and jeer wonder.

I wasn't just a veteran MP. I had been a Fleet Street award-winning columnist for many years in the Eighties. Although I had never gone in for the vindictive personal spite that some specialists churn out simply by picking up the front page to see who is on it, then retching out any combination of 500 words of bile, sick and poison. We politicians hold them in contempt. Politicians have to have the guts to joust face to face with our opponents in an arena, or on TV thinking on our feet, and taking the blows as well as dishing them out. We can't hide behind a word processor and a multi-million-pound organization. Which is maybe why so many newspaper writers are so poor on television and are rarely asked to appear. The stand I had taken over the years in Parliament against the abuses of the press barons, campaigning for restraint on their overwhelming one-sided attacks on politicians, had annoyed the media masters at very high levels. Now was the time for their revenge. It was going to be hard, fast, painful and long.

Ian and Arthur advised me on drawing up a printed statement to put the facts right and I gave it to the guardians on the gate who snatched it and left. It said the reports and the story in the press could only have originated from one source, the Northamptonshire Police. Only they and I and my two legal advisers know what happened between the police and myself that day.

I said in the statement that I did not give inaccurate particulars of my name and address and the reports were misleading. I did not partake in any, or pay for any, sexual services either. And I was considering with my solicitors the implications of the publication of unauthorized police information to the media, and whether there was a case for an investigation by the Police Complaints Authority or the Data Protection Officer. Which caused an instant response and furious uproar from the Northamptonshire Police. The Chief Constable went on TV to say that any staff who had been involved in leaking information to the media about the raid would be dealt with in the strongest possible way. All the police had done was to confirm that only one man was present when officers executed their warrant, he was not committing any offence, and he had declined to assist the police as a witness, which he was perfectly entitled to do.

Robin Corbett, the MP for Erdington, Birmingham, a lifelong friend and journalist, immediately raised the matter in Parliament that Monday afternoon. In questions to the Home Secretary Robin protested angrily about the way in which the information was leaked three months after the event and about the hounding and harassment of innocent citizens whose names had been revealed through 'malevolence'.

I drove down to Parliament that Monday evening to apologize to a very sympathetic Chief Whip, Ann Taylor, and the two MPs for Northampton, Sally Keeble and Tony Clark, for all the embarrassment, and was overwhelmed by the very large number of MPs from all parties who went out of their way to shake my hand and offer condolences to me and my family (and even offers of hideaway cottages or *gîtes* to disappear to for a couple of weeks). Cabinet ministers Clare Short, Mo Mowlam, Jack Straw,

David Blunkett, Gordon Brown, Robin Cook, Margaret Beckett, Frank Dobson, David Clarke, and literally an army of back-bench MPs, offered their support and sympathy. Bruce Grocott, MP for Telford, Tony Blair's Parliamentary Private Secretary, confidant and minder, and a former TV presenter, was a true friend in need too. It was all deeply touching. Many of them had suffered their own lash of unfair ridicule and hatred. None more so than John Prescott, Peter Mandelson and Geoffrey Robinson.

Jack Ashley, a life-long friend and a saintly man (now a lord) was very supportive too. Jack and I shared an office for many years and would joke that for every thousand votes he gained for me with his similar sounding name, I lost five hundred for him with the stunts I pulled and scrapes I landed in. In my Attercliffe school days I grew up with several deaf children and learnt how to communicate with them. Jack was the only deaf MP in parliament (he lost his hearing in an operation after he became an MP) and could easily read all he needed to know in Hansard and the papers. But as a former BBC producer he sadly missed all the insider gossip, rude jokes, heckling and backstabbing plots, which are the whispered fabric of politics, which I readily translated for him. Joyfully, Jack regained his hearing after a new operation a couple of years ago and nobody deserved it more. His campaigns for the disabled were, and still are, legendary.

Dozens of journalists, too, in and out of the House, especially from the broadsheet serious newspapers and radio and television, profusely apologized for the 'shitty end' of the profession in which they had to live.

The old saying that it is in times like these that you find out who your friends are is absolutely true. Maggie found the same response back home from her personal friends, our neighbours, Party members, constituents, long-lost acquaintances and a large number of Tory voters all the way to the local chip shop, pub, newsagent, garage, postman and our fiercely protective relatives.

We have a strong family and roots running deep which is all that's needed in a crisis. Letters flooded in from everywhere and the number from the usual bile-peddlers, weirdos and psychopaths didn't even reach double figures.

But none of the support was of any concern to the *Sun*. On Wednesday morning, the day after the Northants Police statement, the paper printed a three-inch headline screaming 'LIAR' on the front page, over my full-length figure picture. As usual, the fox was not going to be allowed to have a defence.

There was only one thing to do and that was to come out of the hole altogether and face the press in Parliament for questions from the Lobby journalists there. Which I did. I told a crowded committee room the full story, admitting that I had knocked six months off my age, which is a 'crime' that half the country must have committed at one stage in their life, especially if they were a pensioner and still working. I typed and handed out a statement giving all the full details so that nobody could get it wrong. But, for the jibe and jeer gang back on the tabloid news desk, it was a total waste of time.

The serious broadsheets printed my defiant defence but the *Sun* ignored it completely and didn't print a word. Other tabloids jeered and ridiculed the true facts and printed the usual close-up of a left nostril picture which they love to take of politicians with a few sneering captions, but at least it looked as if the playground mob might be getting tired of sport especially as the war and conflict in Serbia and Kosovo began to appear on the front pages instead. As a former tabloid writer myself, I should have known better.

The words that 'I did not partake in any sexual services' had a Bill Clinton ring to it, and Monica Lewinsky was over here that very day to promote her book. So surely our torment could be prolonged a lot longer, like the President's had.

To prove that I was a liar and they were not, the *News of the*

World found the girl who had been in the room with me when the police broke down the door and printed a picture of her and pages of interviews with the staff the following Sunday. They still ran the headline 'He Gave a False Name to Cops', even though I had proved I hadn't, and then quotes from the girl and her boyfriend, saying in all seriousness that the raid had been a blessing in disguise because her soul was now at ease, and as a devout Buddhist she was much happier to be back in Thailand.

The torment was beginning to put a racking strain of sleepless nights and loss of appetite on my family which was obviously going to have a long-term effect. We are very well known in South Yorkshire and it's no joke being stared at and noticing the public whispers. The stress and strain was beginning to tell on all of us by now and the wise old words that it is not stress which destroys people, it is distress, became very apparent.

I was away in Parliament but Maggie was often in the house on her own chasing off the bell-ringing hacks at eleven at night. When she insisted that the same *Sun* reporter who had bluffed his way into our house left the doorstep immediately, he then printed in the paper that she had 'abused him'. It is devastating for any wife to find out that her husband has been caught in a police raid in compromising circumstances, but even more traumatic to learn it from the front pages of national newspapers. Seasoned public performers such as Dawn French and Liz Hurley, well used to the spotlight, found it severely painful and distressing when Lenny Henry and Hugh Grant were trapped and hunted after a press tip-off. For a wife who had never sought the limelight in the forty years of our marriage it was searingly harsh.

Many times she was asked to speak about the ordeal both to broadsheet newspapers and to television producers who were genuinely sympathetic and our personal friends. We know they would have given the story an accurate and understanding airing. But we also knew that sitting watching the interview would be some freelance ready to take a few words out of context to 'put some spin on it' and make yet another day's story of taunting, sarcastic scorn to prolong the one-sided 'trial'.

Maggie and Lucy's loyalty and courage were heartwarming. Even when the *Sun* rang Lucy's boss after the crisis with an allegation that Maggie and I had split up. The hounds chased us for a week until finally one Sunday they arrived at our house at lunch-time to find the Labour Party having a happy and enjoyable family party and our forty-year marriage as rock-solid as ever.

I realized that although I was guilty of nothing I couldn't stay on as a Director of Sheffield Wednesday. A job loved and cherished for nine years. There would always be some yobbo in the crowd near the Directors' Box who would hurl abuse at me if the team were losing and cause embarrassment to the other directors and their wives. David Richards, the club Chairman, pleaded with me not to quit. So did Roy Hattersley, Arthur Davidson and Ken Bates, the Chairman of Chelsea. But my generation of politicians still hold some personal pride and hon-our in not letting down the team. So I resigned. It was public support like this from our loyal friends which kept us rock-solid and determined to sit it out.

If the old Fleet Street story that everything is a nine-day wonder was true, then after eight days including two Sundays, the legs on the story should have been worn out. But no. The following Saturday at eight-thirty in the morning, two weeks after the siege, yet another pair of hardmen turned up on my front doorstep, one with a camera, to tell me that I had announced I was quitting Parliament for a by-election! It was total rubbish, I told them. I had indicated to my agent, Sally Jackson, and several senior councillors a year earlier that I wouldn't be fighting the next election because of my age. There's no news in that, I added. They produced some ID when I asked, to show they were from the *Mail on Sunday*, and I got the impression one of them was wired for sound. Their request to take a picture on my front steps was adamantly refused. Another guy was posted to sit in a car all that day to stake out our house, as though we were drug peddlers or wanted criminals who might escape or run for help.

It was another night of anxiety for me, Maggie and Lucy, knowing that about nine o'clock the phone would ring incessantly for two or three hours with every news outlet from dozens of newspapers, radio stations, TV programmes, freelance agencies, etc., etc., insisting on a response to something I hadn't even seen or read and all desperate to meet a deadline and satisfy a demanding editor and producer.

How can any accused person defend themselves in circumstances such as that? If an experienced MP and journalist can't do it, what chance does a member of the public have? And what could now be a bigger story than the war in Kosovo where whole towns were being bombed, hundreds of refugees raped, thousands of war victims sleeping in the cold rain, desperate for food and safety, Government statements in Parliament every day, and television newsreels dominated by hours of heart-rending stories of turmoil and Serbian terror?

Believe it not, the bigger story was me. The *Mail on Sunday*, for the third weekend in a row, devoted the whole of its front page, not to Kosovo like all the other papers did, but to the headline 'Sex shame MP offers to resign'. Like the blitzkrieg in Kosovo, our house had been savagely strafed too.

I hadn't offerd to resign. But they needed a new angle to spread the story after their reporters had travelled all the way to a remote village in southern Thailand to interview the girl yet again and take photographs of her. And what did she say? 'I never offered him sex, and he never asked. I am so sorry for Mr Joe. I want people to know he did not do anything wrong.' Her friend said she had been offered a huge amount of money to say she had sex with Mr Ashton but she wouldn't tell a lie. The Thai girl went on to say she was back where her heart was in Thailand with her granny, and that everybody was chasing her but she didn't want to be famous, not for what happened on that day.

There was still another story waiting to come out after all the columnists' wisecracks had become stale and repetitive. Cabinet minister Stephen Byers had yet to issue his verdict on Rupert Murdoch's attempt to buy Manchester United. When he did, then without a doubt the Chairman of the Parliamentary Football Group in the Commons and Lords (me) was going to be inundated by the media for a reaction to the announcement. Especially as it was timed for Friday, 9 April during the Easter recess when Parliament was not sitting.

Once again it was a no-win situation. Except that this time the fox had a few days to think it out. We did what we should have done from day one. First change the telephone number of our house, which by now was known to everybody everywhere. British Telecom can and will change it in about two hours if a customer is suffering harassment, and the relief was sheer bliss. Then we left for an Easter hideaway and listened to the car radio as it was announced that Stephen Byers had blocked the Murdoch take-over. Millions were wiped off the Manchester United share price that day and BSkyB's value went down too.

Was there any connection between the hounding and my position as Chairman of the 150 football-loving politicians demanding the inquiry from the Monopolies Commission?

Nobody will ever know. Nobody will ever be able to prove, and I certainly can't, that I was bounty hunted or that it was simply a coincidence of six months' upheaval right through the football industry to 'sod's law' in Northampton. It's probably just a good read, that's all.

And just to show how fair-minded our Parliamentary Football Group was we vigorously defended Mr Murdoch's BSkyB's involvement in television football a few weeks later, when the

Government's Office of Fair Trading hauled the Premier League and BSkyB existing contract before the Restrictive Practices Court and claimed it was illegal.

I gave evidence to the court along with Kenneth Clarke MP, former Tory Government Chancellor and Home Secretary, and we helped to convince the judge that if the Government office insisted that each club had to negotiate its own individual contract, instead of the League doing it as a package, it would be chaos, with the rich becoming richer and dozens of small clubs going out of business. We stressed strongly how the BSkyB money had helped to rebuild Britain's ancient football stadiums after the Hillsborough disaster and how its TV coverage had revitalized the game and uplifted the attendances. We, and BSkyB and the Premier League, won the court decision. Which unfortunately cost the British taxpayer an estimated £19 million for the legal costs. But it did preserve the status quo of Mr Murdoch's major stake in football.

Arthur Davidson, a leading expert in libel, said that on a scale of one to ten in misdemeanours and misbehaviours mine would rank about 0.5. Yet every accusation, innuendo, jeer, jibe and crude joke, stretching from sarcastic mockery to despicable contempt and outright lies, had been heaped on me with more column inches in a month than all the criminals in court put together.

Was there any apology anywhere? Apology? Has anybody ever heard or read of a politician getting an apology from the press? Ask John Prescott. Or Robin Cook or Mandelson or John Major or even Prince Charles. Newspaper editors and proprietors or dogs never apologize to the lamp-posts. None of them is big enough.

They are big enough, however, to be able to fight any libel action with resources of millions of pounds to hire an army of the best lawyers, worldwide investigators and QCs to outspend any back-bench MP who would have to risk his house, his pension and all his savings to afford even one week in court. Never mind a two-year struggle to get there.

Some of those starting libel actions, such as William Roache (Ken Barlow in *Coronation Street*), have had to declare themselves bankrupt after losing everything through the technicalities of a libel action, which meant that though they were awarded damages they had to pay all the costs. Even when footballer Bruce Grobbelar won £85,000 from the *Sun* he had to risk paying costs of £400,000 if he had lost. Odds of five to one against are a great deterrent. Any sensible politician (not Jonathan Aitken or Neil Hamilton) knows that unless the plaintiff has the sort of cash that Elton John or the Queen possesses, then a libel action is not worth all the fresh public heartache in court, or financial risk, to wipe out yesterday's arse paper.

And what about the police? There can be no doubt at all that my name and details found their way from a police computer to the newspapers. The facts simply could not have originated from anywhere else. And therefore the Data Protection Act which covers all computers containing personal information about living individuals had been broken.

But by which person? Who had passed my name on? It doesn't take a wise man to know that the immediate response to any official Data Registrar's inquiry would be – not me, guv, I had nuffin to do wiv it. The tip-off would have been verbal and therefore untraceable to any single person.

The Data Protection Act of 1998, brought in by directive 95/46 of those good old humanitarians of the much maligned European Community, has safeguards to protect the use and processing of sensitive personal data and restricts its use where the outcome can have a significant effect on the individual. It can even cover computerized newspapers.

I asked the expert civil servants in Parliament who had drafted the legislation whether I had a case and they were fairly certain that I had. The law had been broken. What's more, if an individual suffers 'damage' because personal data held by a registered data user (such as the police) is disclosed without authority by the bureau or one of its employees, or access to obtain it gained without authority, then compensation can be claimed in court. But for some daft reason 'damage' includes financial loss and physical injury but not 'distress'. If only distress has been suffered, no compensation is payable. The law was drawn up to protect companies and organizations. As usual there was no recompense for the ordinary guy in the street.

Protesting to the Data Protection Registrar would mean a whole lot of written evidence, weary repetition, time-consuming bureaucracy, with the police having all their lawyers lined up against my complaint, and nothing at the end of it but perhaps an apology.

What about a complaint to the Police Complaints Authority? Forget that too. An inquiry by the Home Office Select Committee in December 1997 showed that out of 10,243 cases investigated that year only 251 policemen were disciplined or found guilty of criminal charges. Another 1,018 were simply 'admonished', often after being suspended on full pay for up to a year.

The Select Committee was scathing about the 'excessive protection' for police officers under investigation, who could take early retirement on sickness grounds and refuse to attend hearings because of the stress induced by the inquiry. They were always represented by their own trade union lawyers, and action can only be taken if it is proved that an officer has broken the police discipline code. The burden of proof has to be made on a criminal 'beyond a reasonable doubt' basis instead of simply on a 'balance of probabilities' as in all other civil cases. At the end of another long, weary saga of investigation, examination, report submissions, questions, cross-examinations and dialogue, the complaint would quite likely end up with nothing being proved and case dismissed, much to the cheers and chortles of the tabloid editors.

Why didn't I even complain to the mighty Press Complaints Commission? Those High Poo Bahs who so solemnly pronounce on the newspaper industry's dubious activities. A jury which consists of seven editors (including those of the *News of the World* and the *Daily Mail*), three Lords, a Bishop, a Dame, a Sir, a Professor, a surgeon, and a representative from the private schools. Pick me up off the floor when I have stopped laughing.

With nobody on it to represent Joe Soap victims and the catch-all get-out of the good old 'public interest' on any inquiry into privacy and harassment, or payment for stories, what justice would there be from that lot?

If the Complaints Commission do demand the utmost punishment, it is simply a mere apology. Even then the guilty editor is never named or shamed, and just carries on sticking up two fingers regardless. A press victim can't get justice. And that's the end of it. There isn't an MP who has been in Parliament for any length of time who hasn't received constituents' complaints about the police tipping off the press on private personal stories. Even those involving road accidents of children, rape victims, suicides, breathalysers, arson or burglaries, long before the relatives of the victims have been informed, and without any care or concern as to the effect the shocking news might have on the family.

Those at the top who run the police force (not the bobbies themselves) and their public relations departments will always look after the police interest first and the public interest second. So where does that leave Joe Soap public? Nowhere. There ain't no such thing as media justice. Certainly not for free, because there is no legal aid either.

Way back in 1948 after a war to bring everlasting 'individual freedom', the politicians of Britain, along with other major countries, signed the Universal Declaration of Human Rights. Article 12 states: 'No one shall be subjected to arbitrary interference with his privacy, family, home or correspondence, nor to attacks on his honour and reputation.' Article 8 of the European Convention on Human Rights said pretty much the same thing in the Fifties, and so did Article 17 of the United Nations on Civil Rights in 1966. One day the politicians will get round to implementing it and rule that the freedom of the individual is just as important as the freedom of the press.

But don't keep your fingers crossed. It will take a very brave politician to do it.

Sixteen

LAST OF THE SUMMER LABOUR

IT was Bill Clinton who showed New Labour how to crack it. Ever since the war, government in Britain and the USA had been a see-saw. All any party tried to do was to get 51 per cent of the voters on its side, and tip the rest. The parties even carved up the boring issues between them. Labour would take the Health Service, housing and schools, and the Tories tax cuts, law and order and defence. Unless one side or the other made a hash of it, and fell off the plank, their turn on top would come.

Arkansas Bill simply straddled the see-saw plank to become all things to all men. Or more importantly women, who live longer and carry more votes. He simply pinched the best bits from his opponents on the other side, ditched the unpopular bits on his own, and won in a landslide.

Tony Blair, also adored by women, did exactly the same.

Astonishingly, there would be no tax increases under Labour, the unions and Town Hall loony left would stay shackled, and Blair would be tough on crime and tough on the causes of crime.

What's more, he courted the press, and set up the best 'rebuttal unit' ever seen in politics. For years Tory leaders had got away with telling lies that previous Labour Governments had cut nurses' pay, or pensioners' heating allowances, etc. Blair and Mandelson used the best of modern technology to challenge the media allegations instantly with proof that we had not. Lies about Old Labour were stopped dead before they reached the studio.

Over thirty-two years I have sat just a few feet away from six different Prime Ministers and nine Leaders of the Opposition of all parties. Without any quibble of a doubt at all, Tony Blair is light-years ahead of them all both in politics and government.

Blair's landslide was a British political upheaval which ended a century of government by combat. Previous Prime Ministers in Downing Street never had any option but to run the place like the fire brigade, fighting crisis after crisis and hoping to survive until Monday. Tony Blair, supported on all sides, could now make long-term plans, certain that he could carry them out.

Peace and harmony rule the land. Even on the back benches of Parliament. And in all the nine Parliaments I have been in, it is the most boring, bland, uncontroversial, sycophantic, tedious, yawn-making assembly ever housed under the roof of Westminster.

All the average British voter asks for is a decent house, a regular job, two weeks by the sea, a good local school, a nice hospital, five hours of daily television, and they are totally content.

The trouble is that once they have got it, they don't bother to turn out and vote. Or get angry enough to join political parties to try to change anything. The status quo reigns, and if only a quarter of the punters turn out for local or European elections, the party activists have done a good job.

In the House of Commons, apart from the Wednesday hulla-baloo ritual of Prime Minister's Question Time, the pictures of the deserted benches are worth a thousand words of Hansard. The bars, tea rooms and other plotting sheds are taking a third less cash than they did in the last Parliament, and the whole building now has the calm, measured ambience of old cathedral cloisters, or a cobwebbed university.

There is no more dissent. No more rows about apartheid, the

Cold War, poll tax, union-bashing, or nuclear weapons. There aren't even any loonies. No enemies of the people, and consequently no fire, passion or demos, even about student grants. It is the unity of the graveyard, and the number of Labour MPs educated at public school is now far higher than those who were once manual workers.

So it was not surprising that my old union, the Engineers, announced it was putting a million pounds into a fund to help genuine workers to get to Westminster, to balance the sixty-one Labour MPs who went to Oxford or Cambridge, and the sixty-seven who attended public schools, including Eton and Winchester.

A policy quickly condemned by Mr Mandelson, who was reported as having said: 'It would be a disaster if we ended up with some tidy quota system of blue-collared working-class northern dirty-overalled people. Merit is the most important word here.' He would not dare say that about dirty-overalled blacks, or women, only northerners, who vote for him in thousands in Hartlepool. Actually, to be fair to Peter, it is not true that he once called mushy peas 'avocado mousse', although he has never denied it. That gag originated from an American TV researcher who accompanied Arthur Scargill during the miners' strike and hated fish and chips, but just loved the 'guacamole dip'.

In 1992 there were sixty women in the Commons. Following Tony Blair's landslide the number nearly doubled to 119, and New Labour has 108 of them. The impact of the new women in Parliament has, however, been social rather than radical. Most of them stood in seats which were marginal. A lot of the women never expected to win, but were putting down a benchmark for a future career. Instead, the astonished winners were plunged into a Westminster of Blair Babes, photo-calls, soundbites and power dressing.

The old green benches had never looked nicer, or more colourful. They even smelled sweeter too. What's more, the women insisted on civilized behaviour. One new woman MP seriously suggested that heckling in the Chamber should be outlawed, and the clapping of speeches introduced instead, because women did not have loud voices, and heckling was not fair to them.

Others smartly took the career opportunity to have a young-ster as part of their Parliamentary contract, and why not? In any marginal seat, there are more votes in taking your kid to the local playgroup than there ever are in sounding off about the Maas-tricht Treaty to an empty House.

Having to work with so many women is a very strange feeling for the Old Compo Brigade. We have not known anything like it since we were in infants' school. After that, we lived through single-sex schools, the shop-floor, national service, football, poli-tics, the Miners' Institute, all of which were labelled 'His' and 'Hers'. All this new harmony is unsettling. After thirty years of daily Parliamentary punch-ups, it has become 'Blessed are the peacemakers for they shall inherit the majorities'. We brawlers miss the daily fix of macho adrenaline.

Sometimes I feel it all needs livening up with a 'Captain Webb Magic Lantern' just like Compo had in the *Last of the Summer Wine* and like we had in infants' school. Very few of the viewers ever knew what was in Compo's matchbox when he slowly slid it open to shock Nora Batty and make her chase him down the street with her brush.

Captain Matthew Webb was the very first Channel swimmer back in 1875, and on the front of the box was a picture of him standing erect, arms folded, in his wet, clinging Victorian woollen costume. He was a fine figure of a man, with a great 'lunchbox' as it is called today. Cheeky lads would frighten little girls by slowly sliding it open to reveal another picture of Captain Webb inside the box, but this time displaying one solitary red match-head proudly sticking out. George Pellow went even further one day. He anchored a wriggling, fishing maggot with two little balls of chewing gum to the lunchbox and Miss Teacher confiscated it. She went all red, and had to sit down.

I don't know what would happen today to any MP daft enough to do this in Parliament, but it might liven things up a bit. Even the new blokes are so deferential, cautious and wary. I sometimes think they must drive their cars with the handbrake on, and a condom on the end, just to make sure.

Twenty-five years younger than me, they are all Thatcher's children who were traumatized by rocketing unemployment and nil job prospects in the early Eighties, and like all that generation daren't say boo to a boss, never mind go on strike and miss a month off the mortgage. As for the whips, despite the massive majority the gangers are worse than ever. If Labour's majority falls below 200 it is total panic. They think they will all be made redundant.

Every new MP now has to pay for and carry a pager on their belt (about the size of a matchbox) to tell them when a vote is due and not to skive off (as if they would). Dennis Skinner and I refused to have one. We old sea dogs don't need a leash. We can sniff the wind and tell our masters when the other side are bluffing.

The biggest campaign we old-timers have managed so far is to protest that we only get steak and kidney pie once a month, instead of twice a week. It is the best steak and kidney pie in London. Instead, we have to make do with a menu full of wine-bar rubbish such as *bic fen*, samphire, *taboulleh*, *sabayon*, *penne cotta*, *paillard*, mascarpone and *framboise sabayon*. We have not been allowed any oxtail stew since the Mad Mullahs, never mind the mad cows. No wonder all the young women in the cafeteria are so thin, and have to smoke to kill the hunger pains.

Ah well, the Old Contemptibles after the war never got much gravy either. And neither will that unsung, beleaguered garrison of Labour MPs who held the ranks of the Labour Party together through the terrible dark times of eighteen years of Tory government, twelve of which were a nightmare for Labour.

Loyalist MPs like Andrew Bennett, Dale Campbell Savours, Dennis Canavan, Tom Cox, Lol Cunliffe, Gwyneth Dunwoody, Terry Davis, Tam Dalyell, Kevin Macnamara, John McWilliam, Robin Corbett, Ernie Ross, Bob Sheldon, Peter Snape, Roger Stott, Austin Mitchell, David Winnick and several other good Labour men and women, were all veterans and survivors who soldiered on from the full eighteen years of one Labour Government to the next without any medals, rewards, official limelight position, or glory when victory finally came.

From 1980 to 1992 these honest, decent Labour MPs were surrounded and besieged on all four sides. By the Tories on the right, the Scargill unions and Livingstone loonies on the left, the treacherous back-stabbing SDP to the rear, and practically the whole of the media kicking us in the goolies at the front.

This small, battered battalion of Labour MPs loyally fought all the hopeless elections, reselections, campaigns, constituency plots, all-night sittings and all-day trench bombardments, and today have nothing to show for it.

Without that dogged defence, there would not be any Labour Party left for New Labour to rebuild on. And when the victory did come, many of the battle-scarred comrades were tossed on one side, and the new Government posts went to the Conference assassins of the Eighties instead. The latest officer generation in the chauffeur-driven ministerial cars should always remember it was today's Old Labour's Contemptibles playing their mouth organs in the street, and the hundreds of other fallen comrades at the ballot box too, who kept the regiment together.

Basically, it seems that what we fought for is now just running the status quo, and running it on whichever flavour of the month the voters will buy. The problem is that the status quo never stands still. Sooner or later Parliament has to be about power, not public relations. Politics is no fun any more. Not even on TV. The crusty old cobs who used to tell it in words that Albert Steptoe, Alf Garnett, Victor Meldrew or Spike Milligan would use, are not allowed on the box because the politically correct thought-police will not allow it. Politics should be about feelings, about people and passion, not profit and public relations, but now it is not.

When the Sheffield canal was built in 1819 the power lay with those who owned the land and controlled the food supply. Then it moved on to those who controlled the energy of coal, oil, steam and electricity for the industrial revolution, which spawned the unions and the Labour Party too. Now it is information technology, computers, internets and websites, with Mr Murdoch and his friends far out in front of any government. Soon, if governments do not band together to control the greatest power of all, currency, including the euro, these people will run the world. And who will control the status quo then? Labour? The voters? Or Media Moguls Worldwide Stupendous Ideas Inc.?

When my future grandkids say, 'Tell us what other battles you lost, Grandad,' I shall have to reply, 'Well I once took on Cardinal Hume, and the Catholic Church, and lost that one too.'

After your great-grannie Nellie took seven years to wither away and die from Parkinson's disease, I brought in a Doctor Assisted Dying Bill to allow any terminally ill patient to have the right to die at her own request. When she chooses, and not if and when God or the doctor chooses for her. It is another human rights issue. It would only apply to those 300,000 people who are terminally ill at any one time. All the requests would have to be registered with the Coroner, with the agreement of a hospital consultant. An opinion poll showed that 80 per cent of the British public approved of having this choice for themselves.

But Cardinal Hume told every Catholic church in the country

to threaten their MP with hell-fire and no votes if they supported it. So we lost by 223 to 89.

Old Maloney would have been proud of me.

But I also won a couple. One by asking a question at a Home Office Select Committee about a little boy who had been sodomized by his stepfather, currently serving six years. Who has put in a claim for criminal injuries for him, I asked. There was a deadly silence, because nobody had. Neither had any other Town Hall put in claims for their kids in care. Inside a year, hundreds of youngsters were getting the cash, and also help and advice, on suing the care homes and churches which had supposedly been looking after them.

Then there was the 'Ashton Amendment', as it was called. A huge majority of MPs, including me, were in favour of lowering the age of consent to sixteen for gay boys. However, the Utting Report, based on the Esther Rantzen TV programme, *That's Life*, proved that literally thousands of both young boys and girls in care were being sexually abused every year, and ending up on the streets, homeless.

So I laid down an amendment saying that the age of consent, in a situation 'where any adult was in a position of trust or authority' over a sixteen-year-old, should be eighteen, not sixteen, to stop the adult abusing his power. Lo and behold, after a rare rebellion in the Commons, where the Government's majority fell from 200 to 40 inside ten minutes, the Government accepted it, and went on to set up a very stringent paedophile register.

All a Parliamentary foot soldier can ever do is chip away at a block of marble with a hammer and chisel, hoping that in twenty years a statute will emerge. Even then, son, remember that the bad will always drive out the good. And me and Bill Clinton will only be remembered for one thing.

Maggie and I don't live among the steelworks or the slums any more. They have all been pulled down. Including several thousand houses which Roy Hattersley and I set up plans to demolish. We live on the hills of leafy Ranmoor on what was Sheffield's Hampstead of the 1890s. A designer nob hill for the Victorian steel barons where the clean air from the moors blew first, and where the landscape gardeners planted today's mighty oaks, chestnuts, conifers, copper beeches and laurels. It's not too good for the working class because now the area is a cosmopolitan, university students' bedsitter, old folks' home, social care centre, parish hall, late-night shopping, wine bar museum piece.

And I fervently hope the Little Joe steamroller, which has chased me so often, has finally run out of push, because I have.

Sometimes I still walk the canal.

On the May Day Bank Holiday in 1999, I walked the towpath. It was beautiful. The fish were biting in water which was once more oil and effluent than liquid, and half a mile away in the distance lies Meadowhall, the biggest hypermarket in Europe, standing on the site of a former steel mill, with its own Supertram to pour in its 80,000 Saturday visitors. It was England's Green and Pleasant Land. Jerusalem had arrived in Attercliffe, I could almost hear a heavenly brass band playing it.

In the distance was a huge warehouse with three teenagers running across its roof carrying a carpet they had pinched. 'Has nobody got a mobile phone to ring the police?' I asked the elderly anglers. Mobile phone? Mobile phone? The old guys laughed. Where has tha been all these years, Joe?

It was still Full Monty Sheffield.

Before I die I cannot make up my mind whether to be buried near the ghosts of the empty steelworks of Sheffield, or the derelict pit slagheaps of my Bassetlaw constituency. No doubt they will put up a headstone which will read, 'Here lies the body of Joe Ashton. He was an MP, and an honest man'. To which some wag will say, 'Bloody hell. The Council must be getting hard up. They are having to bury two blokes in one grave now.'

BIBLIOGRAPHY

T<small>HE</small> author would like to acknowledge the following books which were particularly helpful in verifying dates, times and places, and also the unfailing courtesy, often amusement and curiosity of the staff in the House of Commons Library, in locating Hansards and committee reports showing where the true facts are buried.

Adams, Jad, *Tony Benn, A Biography*, Macmillan, 1992

Benn, Tony, *The Tony Benn Diaries 1969–1990*, Century Hutchison

Carvel, John, *Turn Again Livingstone*, Profile Books, 1999

Fitzwalter, Raymond and Taylor, David, *Web of Corruption*, Granada Publishing, 1981

Harris, Robert, *The Making of Neil Kinnock*, Faber and Faber, 1984

Heffernan, Richard and Marqusee, Mike, *Defeat from the Jaws of Victory*, Verso, 1992

Hollingsworth, Mark, *MPs for Hire – Secret World of Political Lobbying*, Bloomsbury, 1991

Parris, Matthew, *Great Parliamentary Scandal*, Robson Books, 1995

Routledge, Paul, *Scargill*, HarperCollins, 1993

Shawcross, William, *Murdoch*, Chatto & Windus, 1992

Tomkinson, Martin and Gillard, Michael, *Nothing to Declare. The Political Corruption of John Poulson*, John Calder, 1980

INDEX

INDEX